Fired, Downsized, or Laid Off

ALAN L. SKLOVER, ESQ.

Fired,
Downsized,
or Laid Off

WHAT YOUR
EMPLOYER
DOESN'T WANT
YOU TO KNOW
ABOUT HOW
TO FIGHT BACK

AN OWL BOOK

HENRY HOLT AND COMPANY · NEW YORK

Henry Holt and Company, LLC
Publishers since 1866
115 West 18th Street
New York, New York 10011

Henry Holt® is a registered trademark of
Henry Holt and Company, LLC.

Library of Congress Cataloging-in-Publication Data

Sklover, Alan L.
Fired, downsized, or laid off : what your employer doesn't want you
to know about how to fight back / Alan L. Sklover.—1st owl ed.
p.   cm.
"An owl book."
Includes index.
ISBN 0-8050-6084-7 (pbk. : acid-free paper)
1. Lawyers—Dismissal of—United States.   2. Law—
Vocational guidance—United States.   I. Title.
KF297.S446   2000
340'.023'73—dc21   99-10389
                                                    CIP

Henry Holt books are available for special promotions
and premiums. For details contact: Director, Special Markets.

First Edition 2000

Designed by Victoria Hartman

Printed in the United States of America

10 9 8 7 6 5 4 3 2 1

To my son, Sam,

the sparkle in my life

Contents

viii | Contents

VII. If Negotiations Fail

VIII. Post-Negotiation Concerns

Acknowledgments

> Do not forget little kindnesses and do not remember
> small faults.
>
> —Chinese proverb

The efforts, support, and inspiration of many others have made this book possible.

My "right hand" throughout this process has been my personal assistant, Sanja Hruskar, whose constant good cheer, support, and insight have been immeasurable.

My office staff—Judy Schwartz and Julie Rivera—have, in turn, supported Sanja, and me, with the patience of saints. My good partners, Andy Himmel and Allyn Shepard, served as informal sounding boards for my ideas, and the fruits of their suggestions must be acknowledged.

My agent, Laurie Harper, of the Sebastian Agency in San Francisco, helped mold the idea of this book as an artist would, and her introduction to the world of publishing has been an education for me.

And last, but surely not least, I acknowledge and give thanks to Amelia L. Sheldon, my editor at Henry Holt and Company, for her interest, her intense work, her good cheer, and her simultaneous attention to detail, perspective, and message.

Acknowledged, as well, are my many clients, from Brazil to Brooklyn, from Tokyo to Tenafly, and from Abu Dhabi to Arizona, who have entrusted me with the care of their careers in their severance negotiations.

Fired,
Downsized,
or Laid Off

Introduction:
It's No Secret:
The Workplace Is Now a Negotiating Place,
Like Never Before

> A journey of a thousand miles must begin with a
> single step.
>
> —Lao-tzu

In the course of advising and representing many executive, managerial, and professional employees facing job loss over the past fifteen or so years, I have discovered firsthand a number of secrets of the trade. I have seen which general approaches and specific practices seem to work best for my clients, repeatedly and dramatically. In this book I want to share what I have gleaned from hundreds of negotiated employment transitions: the information, insight, and understanding you need to successfully negotiate your own severance package or buy-out proposal.

That such a book is needed in the first place is testament to a fundamental change that has taken place between employer and employee over the past ten years. How, when, and why we work for others has been completely redefined during that time. Just a decade or so ago, most of us worked for one employer. So long as you showed up, didn't engage in any serious misconduct, and performed your assigned tasks, you could fairly safely presume your job would be your job until retirement. Everyone felt relatively safe and understood the main rule: that seniority equaled security. However, since the convulsive downsizings of the late 1980s and the early 1990s, most of us have realized there is just no more general sense of "job security." It makes no difference whether times are good or bad economically; no one feels very safe in their jobs now, and no one seems very clear on what the rules are or, indeed, if there are any rules anymore.

This societywide change has altered many of our attitudes about the employment relation. Lifelong employment with one employer was previously considered an indication of personal stability, and even strong character. In stark contrast, today many view such an employment pattern as a sign of passivity and indicative, perhaps, of a lack of motivation as well as limited experience. Likewise, loyalty to one employer was formerly viewed positively, whereas today it is snickered at.

Even our words associated with the workplace have changed. Who ever heard of "downsizing" before 1985? It's interesting to note that the automatic spellchecker on my state-of-the-art word processor knows what "seniority" is, but most of my clients under the age of forty don't. At the same time, my spellchecker does not recognize the word "outplacement," but everyone these days is, unfortunately, quite familiar with the term. Perhaps most telling—indeed, chilling—of all is the near-universal replacement of the phrase "Personnel Department" with "Human Resources." Yes, like it or not, you are now a resource, a human-type resource. A business has natural resources, financial resources, even mechanical resources. You are a human resource. And, like every other resource of a business, you are to be:

- acquired as inexpensively as possible;
- maintained in good working order;
- utilized efficiently and effectively;
- eliminated with as little cost and disturbance as possible when no longer needed.

Yes, welcome to the world of employment relations in the late 1990s and beyond. In this new world, when you're not needed, you're not wanted, and you will likely be either "downsized," or perhaps "outsourced," even "severed," or still worse, "terminated." Ouch.

To survive and thrive in today's work environment, with its new rules and ways, you have to be as smart, as agile, and as tough as you can be. I want to help you be as resourceful and resilient as possible in the process of leaving your employment.

As an employee you are probably used to negotiating when you are being hired for a new job, and perhaps even doing a little negotiating when you ask for your annual raise. Increasingly, this is just not enough. To further your goals and protect your security, you need to negotiate every day, about every aspect of your employment, including your termination. In, up, and out: negotiation is now continual, and this probably won't change soon. When I use the word "negotiating," I don't just mean sitting down across from the boss's desk, haggling, and meeting halfway on job responsibility, salary, and bonuses. Instead, I use this word to describe a process similar to "negotiating" a raft down a rapidly moving river, full of large rocks, deadly whirlpools, and poisonous snakes. It's constant, it's intense, and it's a matter of survival. Liken a day in your job to a day in that boat. You move through your tasks with energies and instincts that are sometimes focused on your boss, sometimes on your skills, and sometimes on your goals. Some of you may also turn to prayer. Viewed this way, negotiation is more an ongoing process than a singular event.

Severance negotiating is a crucial juncture in the journey through a job. It is a time of transition, often an involuntary transition, from a known situation to a completely unknown one, which is, of course, anxiety-provoking. While you will most likely turn your thoughts, fears, and concerns on the past, they need to be refocused on the future, in much the same way that the rapids and rocks ahead of the raft are more important to think about than the rapids and rocks you just passed. That's why severance is now frequently negotiated at the time one takes a new job, and why a good part of negotiating is done with the next, rather than the last, position in mind.

Many of my clients ask this question: "In these severance negotiations, what's my leverage?" Three separate and distinct societal shifts in employment relations give employees unprecedented and commonly underappreciated leverage in their workplace negotiations today. First, the period of corporate downsizings in the mid-1980s and early 1990s was soon followed by a dramatic increase in the number and power of employee rights and protections from employer abuses, including illegal discrimination, workplace harassment, pension fund abuse, loss of insurance coverage, unfair termination, and others. These rights and protections are guaranteed through new laws passed by Congress, and the courts' interpretations of such laws, so that employees have much greater negotiating leverage than they've ever had before in their workplace negotiations.

The second societal shift that gives employees newfound leverage is the increased extent employers will go to avoid risks. Not only has a new industry emerged to help employers manage employees without fear of costly litigation, called "employee relation consulting," but a brand-new branch of the insurance industry—known as employment practice liability insurance—has developed. Yes, employers are now buying insurance policies to protect them from employee lawsuits arising out of their abuse of their employees. Employers know full well that mistakes they make in their treatment of employees can now prove quite costly. As a result, employer's are now more willing to negotiate to achieve fairness than ever before. They do this to avoid the alternative: facing a jury composed mostly, if not entirely, of disgruntled and abused employees, friends of disgruntled and abused employees, and family of disgruntled and abused employees.

The third societal shift that gives employees great leverage in their workplace negotiations is the general perception that employees are the most important part of any business. Among the panoply of business resources, the "human resource" is the most scarce, valuable, and irreplaceable. Senior management understands this crucial insight, about their workers and about themselves, too: treat your workers fairly, with some sense of dignity, and it will be to your benefit in the long run. If you need certain people to stay and build your business and profits, show them that fairness and reason govern all employment relations, even the end of those relations.

This book is conceived, designed, and tailored to provide you with the new tools you need as an employee who might face the need to negotiate severance. It is intended to meet the needs of those in relative crisis—those who either suspect or know that employment termination lies directly ahead. The lessons I've learned—and the "severance secrets" I've assembled in the hundreds of severance negotiations I have overseen—I have set down here for you.

Taken together, parts I and II, entitled " 'Getting a Grip' on What Lies Ahead of You" and " 'A Warm-Up': What Do We Mean by Severance 'Negotiating,' " represent the first half of the material I cover in initial consultations with executives from Abu Dhabi to Tokyo, from Boston to Burbank. They are meant to help you understand the severance process, and your most productive role in that process, and are necessary precursors for your successful severance negotiations.

Part III, "Preparation 'Pointers' for Your Severance Negotiating," provides the most important insights into the negotiation process itself. You will need to know what these points are and how to use them. While most people picture two or more people talking back and forth when they envision "negotiation," I'd rather you picture your employer as your "negotiating partner," and imagine the things you believe make him or her happy, sad, proud, or fearful. That's the empathetic way really effective negotiating starts.

Need an employment attorney? Maybe, and maybe not. Chapter 10, "Is Legal Representation Necessary for You? Perhaps Not," and chapter 11, "Seven Suggestions for Working Most Productively with Your Severance Attorney," give helpful pointers on how to make the hiring decision, how to find the right attorney, how to pay him or her, and how best to work with your attorney should you decide you need one.

The next four sections present the practical information you'll need for each step of the severance negotiation: "Who, When, and How to Ask" (part IV), "What to Ask For" (part V), "What Your Employer Will Ask of You and How to Respond to Each Request" (part VI), and "If Negotiations Fail" (part VII).

Part VIII, "Post-Negotiation Concerns," gives practical guidance on such matters as 401(k) rollovers, whether you can apply for unemployment insurance benefits, and whether severance payments are taxable. Following negotiations, my office staff spends considerable time with almost all of my clients on these nonnegotiating, nonlegal, yet crucial, continuing concerns.

The appendix provides sample letters and agreements for your use. These documents will be very helpful especially if you decide to do your negotiations without an attorney.

This book is an outgrowth of the concern I feel for all of my clients who must face the severance dilemma. It is my effort to empower you to deal with your own facts and circumstances with new understanding, skill, and confidence. Use this book as you would a map to unfamiliar territory you must travel through. It gives you the lay of the land, the location of most of the danger points, and a few tricks on how to deal with obstacles you might encounter. Some foreknowledge, some understanding of local ways, some hints, as well, of how others have found their way may help you survive and thrive in your own severance experience. While not all circumstances you will encounter in your own travels are described here, the information, insight, and understanding you find in these pages should enable you to deal with them successfully.

—Alan L. Sklover

PART **I**

"Getting a Grip" on What Lies Ahead of You

1

The Three "Big Secrets"
of Severance Negotiating

> The louder he talked of his honor, the faster we counted
> our spoons.
>
> —Ralph Waldo Emerson

I've participated in many, many negotiations of severance and buyout packages, in all sorts of companies, on behalf of all sorts of employees. There is a truth about all of these severance negotiations that the employer wishes the employee didn't know: that the employee can have a significant role in determining their outcome.

We all have some idea of the process of negotiating, for we've all done our share of haggling over, say, the price of a house or a used car. The seller starts high, the buyer starts low, and they try to meet somewhere in the middle. Most negotiations happen this way. However, in severance negotiating, there is an imbalance in the relationship between the two parties. It is the employer who usually holds the upper hand, and most employees continue their submissive role in employment-related negotiations. In addition, in severance, the employment relationship is coming to an end at the initiation of the employer. This further accentuates the employer's controlling position. The sense that the power is inherently on one side is the number one impediment to fruitful severance negotiating. There are three essential secrets of severance negotiating you need to know to address this imbalance.

Secret 1: You Can Survive Severance Negotiations and Continue to Pursue a Thriving Career

Many people shy away from the very notion of engaging in severance negotiating because they fear it will result in the death of their career. That's simply not the case.

It is truly survivable. Indeed, "thrivable." While I can never provide absolute guarantees of anything, you need to know that you can approach your employer (even after being advised of your termination) and ask for treatment different than you've been afforded so far, without fear of a threat to your career. Rest assured, as long as your request is reasonable, you ask for it nicely, and provide a good reason or sensible rationale for why you should receive it, there really should be no downside to speaking up.

Most of my clients get through their severance negotiating not only with their careers intact but often with greater severance pay and benefits than they had initially thought possible. They also emerge from the process with a new understanding of and appreciation for the employment relation. In fact, one client of mine who has now been through two severance negotiations—the first when his company decided it would disband his operating unit, the second when the new start-up venture he was hired to run was closed down after initial disappointing sales efforts—sometimes jokes that he makes more money in severance negotiating than he does when working.

Secret 2: Severance Is Truly Negotiable

Although the employer and employee negotiate on a playing field that is far from level—one tilted to a large degree in favor of the employer—the terms they are discussing are, in fact, much more negotiable than many believe.

Severance negotiation appears to be a tougher challenge than, say, the negotiation of a house sale. Aside from the fact that the two parties in a house sale are equal, neither the buyer nor the seller is usually in desperate straits. Some are more highly motivated than others, whether they want to avoid foreclosure or perhaps need to take up residence before the new school year begins. But even in the case of a truly desperate seller or buyer, there usually is more than one possible house to buy, and more than one possible buyer out there, as well. So there are alternatives available in the event of a failed negotiation in these situations. On the other hand, in severance negotiations there are only two possible parties: only one possible "seller" and one possible "buyer." If either one walks away from the negotiating table and fails to return, there's simply no deal for either one. It is this reality that often makes the negotiating parties in severance negotiations, especially the terminated executive, that much more hesitant to rock the boat, for fear of drowning.

Also, your employer's Human Resources personnel will frequently present severance offers as if they were firm, "written in stone," in an attempt to convince you that negotiations won't be permitted. They hope you will believe such statements as "That's it; take it or leave it—there's no room to move." Severance negotiating, done well, can almost always get around such bluffing.

This point is well illustrated every time a large company announces a significant downsizing and tells two different stories to two different audiences. To Wall Street, it announces a large write-off to cover the costs of the downsizing, which represents a pool of money it predicts will be sufficient to cover the cost of severance it plans to pay out to employees. There is always extra money in that pool, to cover any unexpected contingencies. If not, later, additional write-offs would need to be announced, and these would disappoint analysts and investors alike who were told the initial write-offs were sufficient. If, on the other hand, the downsizers don't spend all that money on severance, they will have unexpected profits in the next quarter or next year, to the delight of management, analysts, and investors. To the terminated employees, Human Resources staff tells a far different story: "We have no flexibility." Between these two stories—one to the outside world and one to the employees—lies the negotiating room, and it is significant. Smaller, nonpublic companies have the same room for maneuvering, in their own fashion. You must bear in mind that HR has a job to do: obtain your peaceful, orderly, nonlitigating departure at a reasonable price. HR is as determined to close this transaction as you are, and as concerned that it will flare up into adversary relations as you are.

That's the second secret of severance negotiating: you hold far more cards than you realize. Severance is highly negotiable.

Secret 3: Severance Is Highly Customizable

Unlike most negotiations you may have experienced before, this one can be as creative as you make it. In a house purchase, as part of the deal you may get the seller to throw in the backyard swing set and repair the leaky kitchen sink. But you'll never get her to have your car repaired. In severance, on the other hand, I've arranged for things that might well startle you, including the payment of the employee's salary after his death, continuing on throughout his wife's life, reimbursement of his legal fees, fees for the rewriting of his will, and a retroactive raise, as well. That's severance negotiating at its most customized and creative.

This approach to negotiating severance has actually changed the way some employers make their initial offers, particularly to downsized executives. I am seeing more and more companies offer a menu of severance benefits, with an aggregate value for each executive. From this menu each executive can select the most appropriate, beneficial, sensible items in view of his or her individual circumstances, needs, and concerns.

The third secret of negotiating severance is that your negotiations can and should be customized to reflect your individual circumstances. With perseverance and prudence, you should be successful in obtaining the severance package that suits you best.

With these three essential secrets of severance negotiating in mind, you are ready to start preparing for your severance negotiating.

2

The Three Major Challenges You Face

> The biggest tragedy in America is not the waste of natural resources, though this is tragic. The biggest tragedy is the waste of human resources.
>
> —Oliver Wendell Holmes

Every week I talk to two to eight new clients, either in my office or over the telephone. Some of my clients come from such exotic places as Brazil, Abu Dhabi, London, and Tokyo; others hail from the more common Des Moines, Palo Alto, Miami, and New York. These initial consultations are my opportunity to delve into the particular facts and circumstances of each person's predicament, and to give some preliminary advice. Following my interviews, without exception, every one of my clients asks the very same question: "What should I do now?" And I always give the same answer, regardless of their particular facts and circumstances, and regardless of their locale, their title, or their income. That answer is the essence of this chapter.

I tell each client: You have three distinct, urgent, and fundamental tasks before you. Each task is critical, and necessary for your survival and success in dealing with your job loss:

1. You must deal in some effective way with the stress you are experiencing. You are experiencing stress even if you are not aware of it.

2. You must consider your next career move, whether it is to continue in your present field and in a similar role, or to return to school, or retire, or open your own business, or pursue another goal.

3. You must take a proactive role in negotiating your severance.

That's it. You must focus on just these three simple things. Sure, I'm being facetious when I say "these three simple things," because they are, perhaps, the three most overwhelming problems in your life right now. And I know that. But to begin to carve up your overwhelming burdens into "three simple things" is to begin to make your tasks a lot more manageable. Creating a To-Do List is the first step you should take in any action plan. It is your first step toward gaining control over a process that is now controlling you, and hurting you, and your loved ones.

Fundamental Task 1:
Find a Way to Deal with Your Stress

You may not be aware of it, but it is extremely likely that you are experiencing right now a high degree of personal stress. I'm not a psychologist, but I am experienced in dealing with people, like yourself, who are on the doorstep of involuntary unemployment. As such, you may very well be facing circumstances that you consider extremely unfair, and see little or no way of exerting your control or influence over them. You're facing loss of livelihood, loss of professional esteem, loss of influence and power, and loss of daily purpose, for reasons that may have little or nothing to do with your own performance on the job. In fact, many of my clients come to me because they feel they are being let go precisely because they were so effective and successful that they seemed to represent a threat to their superiors.

The stress you are experiencing is not "just" emotional or psychological, but physical as well. Over and above the rage, sadness, confusion, and fear reported to me by so many of my clients, I hear, too, about the physical manifestations of stress. Men usually mention having problems with their backs and their stomachs. Women commonly talk about their significant hair loss, and note they are seeing far more than the usual hair or two in the shower drain. Both male and female clients frequently tell me they are having problems sleeping, eating, and relating to their loved ones. Often, I have seen that stress—both emotional and physical—become strong enough to affect the spouses and life partners of terminated executives.

Given the debilitating effects of stress, the very first task before you is to find your own unique way or ways to counteract and address your own stress. Nothing else is more important, because, quite simply, nothing else of significance is likely to be accomplished while you are stressed out—not your preparations for severance negotiations, not your participation in severance negotiations, and not your move toward your next job or career path. Nothing can be accomplished until you address your stress.

While I can tell you what your most important task is right now—dealing with stress—I can't tell you how to do it. Everyone has, or must find, their own way. It may be walking, playing with kids or pets, perhaps prayer or meditation, bowling, or sailing. Whatever you find helps—do it! So long as it's not a harmful activity like drinking more alcohol or smoking more cigarettes, DO IT. And do it A LOT. If your usual exercise walk is two miles, try six or even eight miles. If your usual Bible reading or meditating time is a half hour each day, try three full hours or four.

My advice to each client, and to you, is simple, and direct, and unmistakably clear: your first and most important task is to determine how you will counteract the inevitable stress of job loss, and to start doing it, and to continue doing it, for the foreseeable future. Once you've done that, Fundamental Task 1 is accomplished. You've started. From here on out, it just gets easier.

Fundamental Task 2:
Decide What to Do with "The Rest of Your Life"

Fundamental Task 2 is to give very serious consideration to your next big life step. For you, this may be simple because you want nothing more than to get back into a similar position, if not a better one, in the same field, and continue on with the most interesting, challenging, and rewarding work you can imagine. If, on the other hand, you are considering a career transition, Fundamental Task 2 is more daunting. At the very least, you should begin to think about how you enjoy your life and what in it you'd like to change. Request feedback from your spouse, good friends, and your adult children. You might even consider talking over coffee with a qualified career counselor. Outplacement counseling often provides services in this area. In fact, if you are considering a change, you may consider requesting in your severance package the provision of outplacement counseling by a company that meets your approval.

In discussing severance negotiating, I always tell my clients, "Your future is more important than your past." While it is important to address the wrongs done to you, your recent work history should serve primarily as a backdrop in negotiating, and your focus must be on your future. For example, if you are going to leave the corporate world to establish a chain of bagel shops, surely you do not need outplacement assistance. And your need for a good "departure statement" or job reference would not likely be very high on your negotiating list. Instead, continued salary, paid in a lump sum that you'll use to bankroll your new business, would be of greater benefit to you. If you plan to return to school to brush up on the latest software in your field, you might be best served by an educational allowance, which I've often found to be available for the asking. If you are considering going into your own consulting business, it may be of great value to you to have your employer as your first client. In these examples, and others, you can see how crucial it is that your future goals be your focus, and they should guide your severance negotiations. I have found that many of the "noncash" components of severance packages, which you can request with future plans in mind, seem to be more easily provided in negotiations than straight cash. (These choices are reviewed in detail in later chapters.)

Effective action is always goal-oriented. Choose your goals before beginning your actions. Once you've begun giving serious thought to your own future life goals, Fundamental Task 2 is being accomplished, and you can turn your attention to Fundamental Task 3: severance negotiation.

Fundamental Task 3:
Negotiate the Terms of Your Severance Package

Here's where this book comes in. I believe you have come to the best source for detailed and in-depth analysis of "What to Ask For," "How to Ask for It," and "What Your Employer Will Ask of You." For me, this is the easy part. For you, proceeding on to the rest of this book, and to your own severance negotiation, with careful and planned and proactive steps, is the surest sign that your burdens will become manageable, that you are beginning to have influence in this process, and that you may even take control of it, all to your benefit. Read on.

PART II

A "Warm-Up": What Do We Mean by Severance "Negotiating"?

Upcoming Dynamics:
Negotiation Is a Process, Not an Event

> It's a rare person who doesn't get discouraged. Whether
> it happens to us or to an associate we're trying to cheer
> up, the answer centers around one word: perseverance.
>
> —anonymous

Before we get down to the details of negotiating your severance or buyout proposal, you need to get comfortable with the negotiating process, and how it works in the context of employment termination. Severance negotiation is the process of preparing for and going through that journey, from initial receipt of a termination notice to final resolution of all transition issues—on topics ranging from continued payments of your salary to reimbursement of your legal fees. Negotiation is a process, not a particular event. You might consider negotiation a planned series of interconnected events, which you have prepared for, set goals for, and each of which should provide you at least some of what you seek.

A. Analogy: Riding the Rapids

I present the idea of negotiation as making your way down a rapidly moving river. Consider that analogy as you read this book and enter into your own severance negotiating process. It's going from one place to another. It is not a situation where the winner takes all and the loser takes nothing, or at least should not be. Nor is it "teaching a lesson" or being taught one. It is not getting even or being either dominated or predominant. Instead, it is a process of doing your best to achieve your best. The analogy used here—of riding the rapids—is a good one, because it portrays some of the attributes of the ride, and of your upcoming experience, quite well.

B. Unpredictability

Expect the unexpected, and the expected, as well, and you're bound to have no surprises. Nothing can be guaranteed to happen in your upcoming negotiation. I continually emphasize planning, being proactive, being bold, and being positive in spirit. Using those tools will help you keep this process nonadversarial and moving along, while avoiding common pitfalls and proceeding toward the resolution you want. Nonetheless, don't expect everything to happen as you'd like. That's one of the few things I can guarantee won't happen.

C. Go with the Flow

For most of us, being somewhat out of control is frightening, and we actively fight the notion that some Human Resources representative has too much control over us. Tensions like these are exacerbated in cases where the Human Resources representative used to take directives from the terminated executive. Almost every company assigns one or two people, either from Human Resources or from the general counsel's office, to run the negotiation. While many of my efforts, described later, are intended to take the initiative in the process, I always caution against directly confronting these people and questioning their own authority. In most such direct confrontations, company representatives will receive significant support from higher-ups. Instead, suggest a form of "principled" negotiation, coupled with a kind of "smart negotiating," which I discuss later in significant detail and depth. Openly and directly challenging authority is not wise. Don't try to control the river.

D. At the Same Time, Steer the Boat, or It Will Steer You

Going with the flow does not mean you are without influence. You've got two good oars, as well as your own body movement, at your disposal. You can steer your own boat and deftly defy the overwhelming power of the river if you practice your negotiating well.

Even when I am negotiating for a lower-level employee, with a very large employer, and without any significant leverage I'm aware of, I proceed as if that difference in size was not there, and often find I do have significant leverage. There's just no substitute for giving the appearance of confidence, which is one of the oars that is always in our boat.

E. Paddling Upstream Is Still Forward Movement

One particular aspect of negotiating that I find particularly difficult for my clients to place into perspective is that not everything goes smoothly or directly to your desired goal. Sometimes you have to paddle up a section of the river to avoid a particularly dangerous section of rapids.

Negotiations by their very nature require some give and take, some movement forward and some back, both progress and disappointment. Take the good and the not-so-good, and keep moving forward with each stroke. Recognize every push forward and appreciate it as a victory. Accept each push backward and consider it a challenge to overcome, reverse, find a way around. Two strokes forward less one stroke backward equals progress. Bear that in mind.

F. Respond to Obstacles, Don't Worry About Them

As you encounter each and every obstacle in your own negotiation, remember that you can do one of two things: either sit and worry about the obstacle, or respond to it as a challenge to be overcome. Sure, there might be innumerable, particular ways to react to each of the myriad obstacles that might arise, but my experience over years and years of engaging in negotiating is that worrying and responding are the two general choices offered to employees facing possible termination.

Using the negotiating techniques and approaches presented in this book, you can overcome whatever degree of dread, anxiety, worry, or inertia you may feel when facing your own situation. None of these negative emotions will help you overcome an obstacle to, for example, gaining more severance payments, or a better "departure statement," or longer extension of crucial benefit coverage. Rational, reasoned, focused response will. Keep that in mind.

G. Refocus, Reevaluate, Respond

The process of negotiation requires that you maintain a posture of ready-response, not a posture of constant demand. At each turn of events, at each point of discussion, be ready to refocus your vision, and your negotiating partner's, and to respond with your goals in mind.

Your Focus:
Motivation and Perceived Interests

> A person usually has two reasons for doing something: a
> good reason and the real reason.
>
> —John Pierpont Morgan

We're all familiar with the general notion of "negotiation." The word generally conjures up an image of two or more people, usually sitting across from each other, over a tabletop, talking, arguing, or even pounding the table, until one side or the other generally prevails. Indeed, that really is what many negotiations look like, that is, the "outward manifestations" of negotiations. But what is really going on inside that negotiation—inside the people, and between them—is motivations, and that is the focus of this chapter.

The reason for concentrating on motivation is to help you get to the root of what *should* happen in the negotiation. Your maintained focus on motivation will get you through your own confusion, paralysis, and anxiety, and the manipulative efforts of others, as nothing else will. Focus your thoughts and efforts on the motivation of your counterpart. If you know the real dynamic, which is motivation based on perceived interests, you'll concentrate on the real issues and recognize real progress. You will be far less likely to be befuddled or frustrated by other, essentially meaningless things.

A. Motivation: With Understanding Comes Control
MOTIVATION: *a force leading to behavior directed toward the satisfaction of a need*

Recently I supervised a negotiation between a client and the client's employer, a top-tier Wall Street securities firm, over a very political severance. I was initially hired on an unseen or "ghost" basis. Due to the approaching retirement of a department head, friends of the new department head wanted our client out. It didn't matter that she had worked at the company for nineteen years and had just been named "Employee of the Year"!

As is usually the case, an initial severance offer was made to my client, she responded with a severance counteroffer, and the negotiating began in earnest. After I began to participate openly we had three or four telephone calls and two meetings with her employers. The employer's legal staff drew one draft of a severance package agreement. At that point the employer's negotiator—a senior member of the general counsel's staff—was getting very testy.

From my own vantage point, things were proceeding very well. The employer was now offering two years' salary, which was different from its initial position: that never in the company's history had it given severance pay of more than nine months. The employer was also offering three other items—out of our original list of six.

Nonetheless, to my surprise, my client was upset. "This is *so* confusing . . . everything we ask for they refuse, and even what they offer, they take away. I'm getting ready to explode!" There was such a flurry of activity, the client lost sight of her path and failed to appreciate the significant progress we had made together. She had simply no perspective on the process; she had gotten lost within it. I have seen this happen to many people in similar situations.

When I reminded my client of her significant progress, and how her negotiations had in fact proceeded according to plan, she calmed down, resumed her good efforts, and felt far better throughout the rest of the process.

But what is the necessary focus of negotiation? In a nutshell, it is motivation. Providing whatever spark, push, encouragement, or energy it takes to get your "negotiating partner" to agree to give or do or say what you want him or her to. *It's that simple. Your first focus at all times should be your negotiating counterpart, and that individual's perceived needs and desires, not yourself or your needs or your desires. Nothing else is more important or effective.*

The purpose of the entire process of negotiation is to motivate your counterpart.

B. What Buttons Are Available?

> I like players to be married and in debt. That's the way
> you motivate them.
>
> —Ernie Banks (baseball coach)

To motivate another person to say or do or give something, you need to know, first, what makes that person say or do or give things, in general. Is your negotiating partner, for example:

- a person with a great personal *need for acceptance and approval*?
- *under strict orders* to give no more than $X?
- actually free to give you $100, but *seeking to make himself look good* by getting you to accept $10?
- feeling *unappreciated* by his bosses, and therefore resentful?
- totally *uncomfortable with confrontation*?
- *fearful of losing her job* if she lets you walk out the door to work for a competitor?
- *unsure of what she is doing,* and looking to you for direction and limits?
- a *sucker for a compliment*?
- an *egomaniac* who is happier to talk about how great he is than focus on negotiations?
- a *control freak* who loses sight of the bigger goals in order to micromanage every step of the talks?
- seemingly more *concerned with dating you* than with negotiating with you?
- *secretly planning his own buyout or severance package* proposal, and *taking tips from you*?

If you can get some sense, some feel, or some insight into what can appease your negotiating partner, you can provide that motivation. Locate the buttons and press. Bear in mind that there is a carrot approach to getting things said, done, or given, and there is a flip side, or stick approach, as well. It is my steadfast belief that the carrot approach—luring someone into compliance—is very underutilized, and although it's more subtle than the stick approach, it is much more powerful in its application.

Case History: In one direct negotiation with a major lending institution represented by a large law firm, the head of the law firm's employment law group negotiated with my client and me as if she had all the cards in the deck. Nothing seemed to get her to budge, on any issue. Not an appeal to reason or fairness or anything else. In fact, she was not only a senior member of her firm but president of a federal bar committee, which made her a major player among lawyers and judges. In our talks she was consistently dismissive and abusive. She ranted, raved, threatened. As our negotiations rolled on, I tried everything but could not seem to motivate her.

Then she made one error, which cost her the war. Because I had the temerity not to give her my comments in one neat memo (as she no doubt required of her assistants) within a period of one day, she let loose a diatribe which ended with a comment she apparently thought would frighten me: "Mr. Smith [the CEO] wants to present this severance deal for your client to the board of directors at their annual meeting in October, just three weeks away. This is very important to him. I'm warning you, Sklover, if he doesn't get what he wants, before that board meeting, there will be hell to pay." I said to myself, "Who will have hell to pay?"

It was wonderful! She had just told me *exactly what motivated* her: giving her client what her client wanted. *And* I'd been told how I could control that. She had revealed to me in one sentence how to motivate her to give me what I wanted. Since the involuntary termination and severance arrangement was not what my client wanted, but was very much what her client, the employer, wanted before the upcoming board meeting, I could motivate her to bargain by doing nothing, except watching the clock and stalling.

The situation was actually quite comical. I started to stall: not returning calls; leaving messages late at night; taking other steps that would use up precious time. As *her* deadline approached, *her* client became first annoyed, then angry, and then even threatened to fire *her* law firm. Sure enough, she became more reasonable as *her* deadline approached. The cards were all in my hand, and *she had given them to me.* I never threatened; I only lured. Her tone became civilized. Frustrated, but human. Little by little I gave her what she wanted and needed, which was resolution on issues, but only if and when I first got what I wanted, which was the items on my client's negotiation wish list. In fact, we got almost everything we'd initially asked for. And even some things we'd never even asked for. We did come to an agreement before the board meeting as well.

To discover what makes your negotiating partner tick, or perhaps shudder, try different tactics in your conversations. Consider sending up a trial balloon of sorts regarding your preference for litigation. Or tell your negotiating partner you have knowledge of earlier severance negotiations involving the company. See if sharing stories about your children seems to make him or her more receptive to your concerns about the high cost of private school tuition. You will get a good sense of a person's concerns, and this is what you need in order to prevail. Also, remember the old saying: "You know what frightens your enemy by observing what he uses to try to frighten you."

> To provide motivation, consider what your counterpart cares about most, and place that very thing in jeopardy; alternatively, suggest strong support for your negotiating counterpart's most urgent needs and desires.

C. "Reverse Motivation": What Are Your Own Buttons to Avoid?

Negotiation is always easiest for the party who cares least.
— anonymous

Again, I stress: focus your thoughts and energies on *motivating your negotiating counterpart* to *want* to give you what you desire, by the stick or carrot approach.

> Don't flag your concerns.

But what about your counterpart's efforts to discourage your efforts, to press your own buttons, or to get you to accede to his or her wishes? First, hide your buttons. Or, better yet, disconnect your buttons. That is, while this process is about negotiating for money and other benefits, it is also about your motivating the other party to agree to give them to you. Personal attacks, hurt feelings, and side issues should be recognized, but not given the focus of your attention. Management's claims of your incompetence or poor performance or even suggestions and innuendo about your character are mere ploys to change the issue. Ignore them.

In one severance negotiation I conducted for a computer engineering specialist at a world-famous retailing company, the opposing counsel continually raised seemingly irrelevant issues and unnecessary obstacles that challenged our very ability to remain in the room. The opposing counsel was obviously trying to press buttons. At one point, I was renamed "that sleazebag." My client was called, with increasing regularity, the "incompetent one." My client, a dignified, gentle man who'd lost his job after severe racial animosity had been exhibited toward him, was beginning to lose his cool.

I recognized the employer's lawyer was attempting to confuse us with anger, create false issues, destroy our focus. Our strategy: simply ignore these tactics, except to request, to ask politely, that they be halted. When we asked whether this verbal treatment was given to all people in my client's position, or only to those of his race, the name-calling ceased. We sent the message that the issue would not be lost or confused, and suggested that this very conduct would be shown to be a racial tactic. Discrimination was at the heart of our case, and our counterpart's conduct was, itself, to be evidence. Well, that seemed to finally motivate a change in our counterpart's behavior, because it related *to her own interests*. Our button was not pushed; hers was. Our conduct remained the same; hers improved. The motivation for settlement developed, and we soon settled. And quite successfully, at that.

It's essential to be prepared, as well, to give up points where and when you can do so without great effect. You must bear in mind that this is a mutual game of motivation, and just as it is unreasonable to expect to lose nothing in the process, you cannot plan on winning every point, either. In fact, you can and should presume that your negotiating counterpart is very aware of, and quite adept at, this dynamic. You should presume she is a very good negotiator and has spent considerable time and energy deciding what she can do—by way of threat or inducement, by offering up what you want, and by withdrawing those offers—to motivate your acceptance of the company's preferred resolution.

Case History: I was retained to represent a garment industry saleswoman in a severance matter that arose in the context of sexual harassment. Before she hired me, and upon her initially confronting her harasser with a firm demand that the conduct in question be stopped, my client had been offered a set severance figure by the company CEO, who was himself the harasser. She was then told she would have to sign a severance agreement, part of which required strict confidentiality about the incidents in question. She then insisted upon a larger severance figure, to which the CEO agreed.

The next day, by Federal Express, a proposed severance agreement arrived, which my client brought to her first meeting with me. For a variety of reasons, the client and I decided to request a higher severance figure. That request was made in a letter to the company.

The response was most interesting, and a first for me: I received a letter from an attorney who advised in no uncertain terms that he represented the CEO, not the company. He conveyed the message that if the company's original offer was not accepted, the CEO would have it withdrawn, completely. This letter, which was outside the loop of the employee-employer communications, achieved the intended motivation: my client chose to accept the offer originally made, and not to risk its possible withdrawal. My client and I didn't get exactly what we had hoped to, but did walk away with an offer that she could live with. She did not hold out for everything when she faced the risk of getting nothing. You may face similar decisions in your negotiation. You may not get all you want.

Now, let's take one last look at the keys for getting as much as you can in your negotiations and then move on to your rights and the law. You may want to jot these points down and keep them handy when you are negotiating:

1. The purpose of the entire process is to motivate your negotiating counterpart to give you what you want.

2. To motivate your counterpart, consider his perception of his own interests—what he cares about most—and place that very thing into jeopardy (the "stick"); alternatively, provide support for what he believes he needs most (the "carrot").

3. Don't flag your own concerns, and ignore smoke screens and side issues, to frustrate "reverse motivation."

5

What About Legalities?:
Severance and the Law

> Someone has tabulated that we have 35 million laws on
> the books to enforce the Ten Commandments.
>
> —Bert Masterson

Does the law give me a right to severance pay or any certain severance benefits, when I'm terminated?" That question is posed to me by
a new client almost every day. The answer is "No." A more appropriate
question would be the following: "Are there any ways that the law
would support my request for a severance or buyout package, or a
better one than I'm being offered?" The answer to that question unde-
niably is "Yes."

There is, in actuality, no law on the books of any state entitled
"Right to Severance." Nor is there at this time any distinct body of
law recognized as severance law. To my knowledge, there is no text-
book or guidebook on the subject. If anything, severance law is an
amalgam of many aspects of different areas of the law—contract law,
negligence law, employment law, antidiscrimination law, labor law,
pension law, and the like—relevant and applicable to the situation of
employee termination.

Before long, severance law will become a newly recognized body of
law. It is currently in the process of being made by those very few attorneys who specialize in the area. That is, the law of severance is what we
are making it. Almost never can we point to a particular law on the
books or decision of a judge or high court to support our arguments
underlying claims for severance payment and benefits. Instead, we
point to many different laws and cases, and principles of fundamental
fairness, as well, and argue that they are applicable. It is a very creative

process. It is interesting, and exhilarating as well. Increasingly, our arguments for severance pay, and for increased severance benefits, are winning at the negotiation table, winning in the courts, and winning in the larger, less formal court of public opinion.

The essential legal basis of support for severance packages is this: if you've been promised continued employment and that promise is now being broken, or if you've been promised certain severance benefits, and that promise is now being broken, you have a clear, direct right to a severance package. That does not mean, though, that you will get what you deserve without having to fight for it. If unsuccessful at the bargaining table, you may have to go to court—first, to prove you have that right to a severance package, and second, to enforce that right— before you can collect what is due you.

If, like most people, you haven't received a promise of a certain period of employment, or a promise of severance benefits if your employment ends, you may still have valid, valuable, enforceable rights to receive a severance package, or other legal claims against your employer, for which you may receive severance payment and benefits in a trade for your agreement to waive those other rights and claims. Almost as a rule these days, companies are willing to give severance packages for the very simple reason that they want departing employees to release them from any legal obligations they may have to them. While you don't need to become an instant employment attorney to help yourself negotiate your severance package, your familiarity with the basics of severance law can only help you help yourself. Here are some of its tenets you may find useful to know.

A. "At-Will" Employment:
No Right to Employment or Severance

Historically, the law in most states and localities generally allowed employers and employees to end their working relationships whenever either party wanted to do so. This is commonly called the "at-will" doctrine of employment law, and it is seen as a basic form of freedom. Actually, the constitutional prohibition against forced labor, or slavery, is at the root of the "at-will" doctrine. It is also a cornerstone of our notion of a free and unfettered economic system, in which people can buy and sell goods and their own services as they wish.

In some states, particularly those in the eastern parts of the United

States, the "at-will" doctrine is applied strictly, with very few recognized exceptions. In other parts of the United States, particularly the states of the West Coast, it is considered to have so many exceptions that it is often considered practically inoperative. For our purposes, we'll assume that this doctrine applies everywhere, at least to some degree. And it is to be understood, as well, that the at-will employment doctrine applies to all aspects of employment relations, including employment itself, notice of termination of employment, and severance packages at the end of employment.

However, the number and extent of the exceptions to "at-will" seem to increase daily. This development stems from societal demands for a new form of "job security" in response to the growing insecurity experienced by so many in the workplace. Most important, these exceptions to the at-will doctrine of law are the direct legal bases—or arguments in favor—of severance payments, and increased severance benefits as well.

B. "At-Will" Exception 1: Express Agreements

The first exception to the "at-will" doctrine is that it doesn't apply where the parties (employer and employee) have agreed it will not apply. The agreement between employer and employee to guarantee a certain period of employment, or to require a certain kind of termination notice, or to provide certain severance benefits, or any number of other things, may be set forth in a variety of ways: in a formal, written employment agreement, in an informal employment memo, in a welcome-aboard letter to a recent hire, in an employee handbook/policy manual, or even in a conversation. These "express (or expressed) contract" exceptions differ in many ways, especially in our ability to prove or enforce them, but they remain a fundamental part of the law of severance.

Express agreements are literally just that: a shared or mutual understanding (that is, agreement) that has been communicated in writing, in speaking, by electronic means, or even by radio signals. It is truly surprising to many of my clients that we can piece together many detailed terms of their employment agreements by gathering such diverse sources as memos, e-mail, witness affidavits, newspaper stories, payroll records, and, in one case, even a birthday card notation.

To the extent that we can weave the pieces of evidence we may have into a fabric representing a cohesive agreement, we can use that agreement to justify a request for a severance package, and to insist upon the enforcement of its provisions. Consider, for example, the case of a client named Martha, a pediatrician, who worked for a large medical professional corporation owned by several doctors. Verbally, she was promised a 5 percent raise every six months. This promise was honored for eighteen months, but not after. With the help of her pay stubs and the professional corporation's bookkeeper, before whom the promise was verbally repeated, we successfully presented and enforced a claim for back wages—and future increases—based upon this oral contract amendment.

C. "At-Will" Exception 2: Implied Agreements

The second exception to the "at-will" doctrine, that is, our second legal basis for claiming a right to employment or a right to a severance package, is that, under certain circumstances, the law will recognize an "implied" agreement to provide employment, compensation, or severance benefit, even if the parties (employer and employee) did not expressly—that is, in written or spoken words—agree to one. The best examples of implied agreements are those from our everyday experience: the case of a man going into a barbershop and getting a haircut without ever *expressly* agreeing beforehand to pay for it, or a woman going into a restaurant and having a meal without first *expressly* agreeing to pay for it. In both cases the law implies—and will enforce—the customers' respective obligations to pay for the haircut and food, even though neither agreed, expressly, to pay before receiving the service (haircut) or goods (food). In one case I handled, an employee quit a good job and moved his family to a different state to take a new position, only to be advised two weeks into the job that the employer decided he was no longer needed. I argued that the parties had obviously intended a longer tenure, and that the employer should therefore be required to provide substantial severance and re-relocation benefits, sufficient to right the wrong. The basis of my argument was an implied agreement: that any employee, or employer, would reasonably expect such assistance if the job was only to last two weeks. The settlement agreed to for the employee, on advice of the employer's experienced counsel, was quite considerable.

D. "At-Will" Exception 3: Statutory (Written) Law

A third, and rapidly expanding, exception to the "at-will" doctrine is statutory law: the laws passed by local city councils, state legislatures, and the U.S. Congress. Increasingly responding to public sentiments of concern about employee abuse, these legislative bodies have limited the the reasons for which employees can be terminated and the loss of benefits that may come about from such an end to employment. These statute-based claims to continued employment, lengthy notice before termination, severance monies and benefits upon termination, are our third basis for severance negotiating.

To use some current examples: An employer cannot fire an employee based upon his or her race, ethnic origin, age, sex, physical handicap, or religion, among other bases. Nor is an employer permitted to terminate an employee for joining a union or hiring an attorney or approaching the age at which pension benefits are vested. In addition, certain large companies are not allowed to close large facilities, such as factories or offices, unless the affected employees are given sixty days' notice. These laws, and the cases that interpret them, represent the area of greatest recent expansion of the right to employment, and the right to severance payments and benefits, and represent, as well, clear and severe limitations on the "at-will" doctrine. With these, an employment safety net of sorts has been created to protect otherwise vulnerable employees when their employment ends.

E. "At-Will" Exception 4: Wrongful Termination;
Growing Case Law (Judges' Opinions)

A fourth exception to the "at-will" doctrine is the growing body of case law (the opinions of judges, which are read, interpreted, and followed by other judges) that has served to limit the instances of legally permitted unfairness, bad faith, and wrongful conduct in employment relations. For example, as societal attitudes have changed, the law will no longer stand by if an employee is fired for refusing to engage in sexual relations with his or her boss. Likewise, the law will no longer tolerate a firing based upon an employer's unheeded demand that an employee not take the maternity leave to which she is entitled. In one case I handled, an employer lured away a key employee from his competition and had required the employee to take with him certain customer-related, confidential information. The employer promised him he would receive in return greater compensation and long-term job security. After the new employer took hold of the valuable information and the employee had worked for only one week on the new job, the new employer reneged on his promise of greater compensation, taunting the employee with "If you're not happy, go back to your old job." This theft of valuable trade secrets was wrong; both employer and employee were at fault. Still, the growing case law would hold the new, unscrupulous employer liable for his conduct here. I found this intolerable and presented my view to the employer. Eventually, the employer came to see the error of his ways and made appropriate amends.

F. "At-Will" Exception 5: Termination Buffers

With an increasing frequency and broadened scope, we are witnessing attempts by both Congress and state legislatures to legislate continuing employer obligations to employees during, or even after, employment termination. Therefore, the ability of employers to sever employment relations—and terminate all obligations to employees in crucial areas of their lives with little or no notice—is being curtailed to a greater extent all the time.

The most commonly known "termination buffer" is the federal COBRA statute (Consolidated Omnibus Budget Reconciliation Act of 1985). It requires most employers to continue to allow terminated employees to remain on the company's health insurance program for eighteen months postemployment, at the employees' expense. Another exception is the federal ERISA law (which stands for Employee Retirement Income Security Act). This law affords terminated employees many rights and protections regarding the safeguarding, distribution, and transfer of pension monies upon termination. Recently, reacting to the terrible loss of pension vesting rights suffered by many terminated employees, and the continuing difficulty in reaching "vested" status due to increasingly short-term employment, many in Congress have proposed allowing employees the right to continued participation in pension programs even after termination, or to transfer pension rights and entitlements from one employer to the next. Free transferability of pension rights would represent tremendous assistance to both the financial security and sense of independence of all American employees.

These termination buffers being enacted into law represent yet another sharp departure from the essence of the "at-will" employment doctrine and help us in our severance efforts immeasurably.

Using "At-Will" Exceptions to Support Your Position

When clients initially come to see me, I go over with them, several times, all the facts of their hiring, their employment, and their termination, to determine which area or areas of the five "at-will" exceptions noted above are applicable to their situation and thus may form one or more of the legal bases for my arguments in support of their severance requests.

The facts and circumstances of each and every person's termination are unique. No one should ever presume that one or more of the legal bases for a strong severance argument are not applicable to them. To the contrary, I find almost every prospective client that comes to me has at least one good legal basis to support a defensible argument for severance benefits to ease his or her employment transition. From these legal bases, I then craft a negotiating strategy, and a litigating strategy in the unusual case where I cannot achieve a just settlement by negotiation.

Generally, employment is terminable by both employers and employees whenever it is their will to do so; no one is legally entitled to continued employment, or to receive severance benefits in lieu of employment, *unless*:

1. The employer and employee agreed to a certain, specified period of employment, or a specified period or type of termination notice, or severance benefits in event of termination. Or:

2. The employer agreed to continued employment, or termination notice, or severance benefits. Or:

3. The employer has or may have terminated employment due to illegal discrimination or in violation of another applicable law. Or:

4. The employer has engaged in some other conduct that has harmed the employee, for which the employer would be legally responsible. Or:

5. The circumstances of termination are just so unfair, unjust, or mean-spirited such that severance is called for. Or:

6. Certain benefits and aspects of employment relations, which we term "termination buffers," may be required by law to continue.

In following chapters we'll revisit the most widely applicable legal arguments available to support your claim to severance benefits. For now, your understanding of the sources of these arguments, and their general meaning, are sufficient to move forward.

6

Your Own Job-Loss Context:
Often a Negotiation Predictor

> Today, loving change, tumult, even chaos is a prerequisite for survival, let alone success.
> —Thomas J. Peters (noted business author)

Severance is a unique part of the overall process by which employee and employer part company. This parting of the ways can be brought about for innumerable reasons, among them:

- downsizing
- restructuring
- outsourcing
- merger or acquisition
- voluntary departure
- discriminatory events or harassment
- performance and compensation disputes
- company or office politics
- abusive, harassing, or violent behavior by supervisors
- personality differences
- allegations of misconduct

A. Context as Pretext

As the saying goes, "Looks can be deceiving." Many times a client has remarked to me, "I really can't believe *this* is happening." Quite often I have responded, "It may not be." No, I am not suggesting that my client may be delusional, but merely suggesting that the client may be incorrect in accepting what is said as truth. The real truth is that those in power will often manufacture a bonus dispute or performance issue as a pretext for getting rid of someone they wish to dismiss.

As an illustration, a year-end bonus expected to be at least $100,000 turns out to be only $1,000. While poor performance is the reason given, the real reason may be illegal discrimination, retaliation for the spurning of sexual advances, political, or just personal reasons that are not illegal or even surprising. It is difficult, at times impossible, to determine a person's true motivation with certainty. But we all have witnessed situations in our lives in which cover stories are being substituted for the truth. That can happen on the job as well.

B. Context as Category

When clients facing possible termination and severance come to me, I spend a considerable amount of time with them trying to figure out what their company and their direct supervisor have been doing recently. I also often speak with a client's coworkers, order business-information reports on their employers, and, at times, even hire investigators to satisfy my search for the facts. Finding out as much as I can helps me place each termination into a legal framework I can recognize from experience. Once I have done this, I can form the negotiation strategy and tactics for my client's case.

While this is usually not necessary in the case of a mass termination due to broad-scale downsizing, often called a reduction in force, or RIF, it is necessary in many other situations. Even in downsizings and restructurings, the choice made regarding who goes or who stays may be worth exploring. Perhaps my client, let go during a large downsizing program, was chosen to be one of those downsized because: (a) she is approaching retirement; (b) her salary and benefits are higher than those given to younger workers; (c) she is of a certain ethnicity, national origin, religion, or race; (d) she has lost her mentor/ protector in the restructuring. Sometimes these factors are the real reason, placing a particular case in two or more severance categories. Once I form an opinion on what was the employer's motivation for terminating my client, I can predict with some accuracy the events likely to follow.

C. Context as Predictor

While the essential dynamic of the severance transaction remains the same in most cases, the context can change, altering the specific way each case unfolds. Depending upon the context, I expect to encounter the following:

- There is an atmosphere of overall negotiability.
- Both employer and client are willing to consider continuing consultancies.
- The client has the opportunity to be considered for other positions within the company.
- I have sufficient time and opportunity to strategize on behalf of the client.
- The employer is concerned about attendant publicity and desires confidentiality.
- The employer runs the risk of retaliation or lawsuit.
- There is an adversarial tone to our discussions.
- The employer is willing to provide reimbursement for legal expenses.
- The employer is flexible in responding to my requested modifications.

While these generalizations do not hold true for all severance cases, they are certainly applicable to most, to varying degrees. You may see certain aspects of your daily working experience illustrated in these pages, and may come to see a little more clearly what you are likely to experience as your severance process unfolds.

Let's now look at each of the more common contexts in which severance arises and the aspects of the severance experience that generally follow from each.

1. Downsizing, Restructuring, and Outsourcing

Large-scale employee-level reductions—the ones we read about in the newspaper involving thousands, or perhaps tens of thousands, of simultaneous layoffs—are the most visible incidents of employee severance. They occur frequently and involve companies in every segment of the business world.

In large-scale reductions the severance packages, usually termed employee "buyouts," tend to be well considered and carefully prepared. The appearance of the presented termination/severance notice suggests that the terms are firm and cannot be negotiated. This is often not the case. Many such reductions in force (RIF's) are submitted to employees only after the employers have made sure it complies with strategic objectives, state and federal laws regulating treatment of employees and pensions, as well as their specific cost-reduction targets. My friends in Human Resources departments tell me that the appearance of uniformity is intended to suggest inflexibility in benefits.

Negotiations in these matters generally involve the full range of benefits to be provided, not just the amount of compensation. For example, in these packages, it is not unusual to see a schedule such as this one:

> 1–2 years of service: 3 weeks of salary
> 2–6 years of service: 5 weeks of salary
> 6–10 years of service: 12 weeks of salary

These formulas are not generally negotiable. The primary exception is in cases where the next anniversary of service (such as the sixth anniversary in the above scenario) falls very shortly after the termination date. What is more commonly negotiable in large-scale terminations is the specific mix of menu items included in the package. For example, I have several times successfully requested an extension of outplacement assistance in place of continuation of unneeded medical or dental coverage. That is, negotiation is more commonly available on the scope of items in the package, not the financial compensation.

In downsizing, restructuring, and outsourcing, I often see educational and training moneys as well as relocation benefits available for the asking. Alternate employment with the company may be available to an employee facing severance in these circumstances to a greater extent than in any others. In one recent downsizing of staff following merger of two banks, senior executives were provided virtually unlimited opportunity to gain new skills to assist them in reemployment, while compensation levels were not negotiated at all.

In these circumstances, the company's decisions regarding who goes or who stays is essentially strategic, not personal. For this reason, there are relatively few claims of discriminatory motivations here. Still, statistics sometimes do prove an overall effect (not intent) of discrimination, since some employers seek to trim their payroll of more expensive employees, who are usually older, before trimming younger ones. Thus legal recourse is sometimes available. I have brought successful claims in large-scale downsizings most commonly in two scenarios: (1) where younger, lower-paid employees were given the jobs previously held by more experienced, higher-paid employees, and (2) where downsizings affected primarily those who were about to fully vest in pension programs.

2. Performance and Compensation Disputes

Performance and compensation disputes represent the opposite end of the spectrum from downsizings and restructurings: they are not large-scale in nature but tend to focus on the individual. In performance disputes, it is the employer who is claiming that the employee has not upheld his or her end of the bargain, while in compensation disputes, it is the employee who feels that way about the employer.

The basis for most serious workplace issues regarding performance and compensation is breach of contract. As noted above, performance issues generally involve employer claims that the employee is not performing to a necessary standard, while compensation issues generally involve employee claims of inadequate compensation. At the heart of almost all such claims are "issues of understanding": Are performance standards clearly laid out? Is performance being evaluated fairly and consistently? Was the compensation level expressly promised or suggested or implied? Is a formula being miscalculated? These issues involve the actual or mistaken understanding between the two parties.

Where good faith and good sense prevail, employers and employees can resolve many of these issues by compromise or a mediation effort. Where requisite good faith does not exist, or where compromise and mediation fail, or where one or both parties has concluded that a parting of the ways is necessary, severance terms, alone, become the issue. The backdrop of severance negotiation in these contexts is generally the strength of the employee's case of unfair performance evaluation or breach of contract, and the perception by the employer of its potential lawsuit risk.

In these cases severance is not the subject of initial negotiations, but the outcome of them. Only then does severance become the distinct transaction we negotiate. Indeed, just raising the notion of departure by means of a negotiated severance package sometimes eases the pressure in these cases. A severance negotiation in this context is often a source of relief for both parties involved and can be easier than most negotiations.

In these cases the level of severance compensation is often highly negotiable. For an employee with five years on the job at one company, two weeks' salary may be the best and final offer made, while at another company of the same industry, similar size, and same geographic area, an employee with five years on the job may get one full year of salary continuation. It is the particular facts in dispute, and the ability and artfulness of the negotiator, that can lead to leverage and bigger packages in these negotiations.

Many employers are well aware that performance and compensation promises are not clearly defined, and that, therefore, loss in litigation or arbitration is a very real risk. A second risk is what we call the stampede effect, that is, the rush of other employees to cash in on a successful severance precedent set by one employee. For many employers both risks are strong, so once negotiations commence in this context they usually go quickly and smoothly.

While I strive to avoid court, pursuing instead negotiation-based resolution, it is a fact that more often in this context than in most others the initiation of litigation becomes necessary to address the employee's grievance. That is, the employer either offers no form of settlement or offers one that is insufficient and unacceptable. Both of these circumstances leave no alternative for the employee but to seek redress in the courts.

However, I often see the exception to this rule in companies that offer internal grievance processes, which are truly independent and fair, and those permitting or requiring one of the types of alternative dispute resolution, commonly called ADR. When the process of ADR is a fair one, and important legal rights are preserved, I encourage my clients to pursue ADR. Through its use everyone usually can avoid going to court.

3. Discrimination and Harassment Complaints
Many of us read about complaints of workplace discrimination—on the basis of race, gender, age, disability, and so forth—and believe that most of these cases proceed to a trial, often resulting in a large mone-

tary award. The truth is most of these claims with a factual basis are settled with a severance package.

The most common course of events in these matters is as follows: An employee will complain to his or her supervisor (or to the company Human Resources department) that a certain act, multiple acts, or a continuing course of conduct is motivated by illegal discrimination. Next, the supervisor will either ignore the complaint, respond to the complaint in a fashion that seems to the employee as not in good faith, or will react in a retaliatory manner by assigning the employee disfavored jobs to do, denying promotion, or by being humiliating, deprecating, or hostile. Then the employee will report the original act or acts and the company's failure to respond in a sufficient or appropriate manner to the U.S. Equal Employment Opportunity Commission and/or to the local or state civil rights, human rights, or equal rights agency. Most often, the company will then respond to an inquiry by the rights agencies' request for its side of the story by denying the discriminatory act or conduct or intent, and will informally isolate the complaining employee from the alleged victimizer, in the hope that the issue will pass.

If the employer-company believes the complaint poses a significant risk of bad publicity, money judgment by a jury, or damage to morale or career of a favored supervisor, it will then suggest to the employee that all can be resolved by way of settlement. If the matter proceeds in this fashion, the settlement will entail resignation of the employee, formulation of a severance package, and mutual releases of claims. The negotiation in now one of severance.

It is my experience that the primary issue in the minds of the employer's negotiation team is risk limitation. The team looks at the degree to which a given complaint poses risk to the company's public image, the morale of its employees, and the careers of favored executives. There is also the risk of having to pay out a substantial sum in a jury verdict. The infamous Texaco race discrimination settlement of 1996, involving a complicated settlement totaling approximately $175 million, shows how costly such settlements can be. It is relevant to note here that the primary focus of inquiry in most of these matters is not the initial discriminatory act itself but the company's response to it being reported.

In no other severance context is strict confidentiality regarding both the fact of settlement and the terms of settlement so important to the employer. The employer will insist that this restriction be adhered to both during discussions and after settlement. Many settlement agreements even require repayment of all settlement monies to the employer if the employee involved in the dispute discloses any information at all.

In no other severance context do federal, state, and local agencies take such an active and central role in the resolution process. These agencies' participation gives added impetus to settlement, because most of the agencies have their own investigative, enforcement, and hearing staff that can supplement the relatively meager resources available to employees and their attorneys. These agencies also have their own penalty processes, which are far less manipulable and open to delay than are the usual court-centered litigation processes.

In these severance negotiations, one of the most powerful tools I can use is corroboration of the employer's reported discriminatory acts, or statistics about practices over time, which can only be made available by other employees. A crucial affidavit from an ex-employee can be the essential ingredient to a successful outcome. It is for this reason that I sometimes employ independent investigators to assist in locating and interviewing potentially corroborative witnesses. One affidavit can literally ensure the success of such a case.

Most commonly these negotiations concern one thing: monetary award. There are usually such hostile and hurt feelings on both sides that items frequently discussed in other severance contexts are unusual here. The money should be sufficient to cover the employee for loss, including pension vesting, salary differential, as well as the significant pain and humiliation he or she has experienced. Increasingly, though, I am seeing a second focus in such cases, which I applaud: negotiations concerning an agreement by management to take substantive steps designed to prevent, weed out, and punish future discriminatory conduct, practices, or patterns.

Though many find it surprising, the law generally applicable to cases of sexual harassment is an outgrowth of the law of discrimination based on sex or, to use the word I prefer, "gender." In short, the treatment of an individual within the workplace environment based upon that person's gender—whether it provokes hostility or desire—is deemed wrong in the law. Said another way, it is equally illegal to hire or fire someone who is wrong or right for the job on the basis of that person's attractiveness to you. This is a relatively new development. People who are younger than forty-five or so may find it hard to believe, but until fairly recently, all help-wanted ads in newspapers were entitled either "Help-Wanted-Male" or "Help-Wanted-Female."

Many may also find it surprising to learn that an employer is not generally liable for the sexual harassment of one employee by another, unless it has been previously reported and insufficient corrective measures were undertaken. It is the employer's reaction, not generally the coworker's original actions, that are the focus of the law here. Of course, if the company CEO or owner is the harasser, it may be difficult or impossible to go over his or her head to seek relief.

There are two basic grounds holding an employer responsible for behavior that is considered sexual harassment. The first is a "quid pro quo," which is Latin for "this for that." In other words, it is classic sexual harassment for an employer to say, "Do this, and I will promote you," or, "If you don't do that, I will fire you." Quid pro quo cases of sexual harassment are the most direct, clear cases to identify and prove.

The second general type of employer liability for sexual harassment is under the doctrine of "hostile environment." Employers who are aware that the working environment is permeated with sexual taunting, continual catcalls, or perhaps the granting or denial of resources or promotions based upon sexual taunting and the like are deemed liable because once aware of such behavior, they are responsible to put an end to it.

Each of the characteristics of severance negotiations, described above, that are commonly seen in discrimination complaints are equally applicable to those arising from complaints of sexual harassment.

4. Voluntary Severance

In my legal practice over the last few years, I have increasingly witnessed a phenomenon that I call "voluntary severance"—to use an oxymoron. I define "voluntary severance" as employment termination, initiated entirely by the employee, that includes significant benefits and/or compensation to that employee provided by the employer.

Voluntary severance is seemingly an outgrowth of the early days of large-scale downsizings in the mid 1980s. Such downsizings were preceded by offers of an employer to "buy out" employee job positions, with the notion, expressed or implied, that if sufficient numbers failed to take advantage of voluntary "buyouts," involuntary layoffs with little or even no compensation would follow. This created something of a calculated gamble on the terms of an individual's termination. Offers of employment buyouts continue to this day. But of late I've helped an increasing number of employees leave their positions, entirely of their own accord, with a certain package of salary, bonus, outplacement assistance, and/or other benefits normally granted only to those terminated involuntarily.

The most common motivation of those seeking voluntary severance is a desire to leave the corporate environment, which has been their home for their entire working lives, and enter a self-employment phase or, alternatively, assume a less demanding role, perhaps in a trade association, nonprofit organization, or teaching capacity. Because employees considering this step typically have been in the corporate world many years, they have acquired significant savings, pension rights, and professional relationships, which, taken together, allow them to consider such a transition. In many cases, employees in this situation are looking toward retirement or semiretirement.

The second most common motivation of those seeking voluntary severance is the desire to remove themselves from what they see as an unsatisfactory spot in the company hierarchy. To leave an apparently losing situation without rancor and indignity, yet with significant compensation and additional benefits, some look to voluntary severance.

On the most senior level, it is not unheard of to have a new CEO come to the office of an existing senior executive officer, with a severance package in mind. The new CEO suggests that the other leave that office with a "golden handshake" worth, perhaps, millions of dollars, which often consists of stock option grants and so may not even cost the company anything on its balance sheet.

Of all the severance negotiations I have been involved in, voluntary severance negotiations are the most nonadversarial. Indeed, they are quite often congenial. The reason for this is that a voluntary parting of an employee is frequently viewed as serving the interests of those in authority. If a political battle is being waged in the workplace, the departure of an executive deemed to be on the other side is viewed as a victory for the ruling powers. And it often seems that the current power holders are happy to give such an executive a healthy severance package because this establishes a tradition of kind treatment—and every executive knows that he or she may be the next to depart. My preferred view of most severance matters as essentially business trans-actions is best illustrated by negotiations of voluntary severance, because both sides usually leave the matter feeling something positive has been accomplished.

I always advise my severance clients that their future is more impor-tant than their past. Because of this, all your severance negotiating should be formulated with your future goals and objectives in mind. Voluntary severance negotiations usually focus on four things:

- *Bridge to retirement.* This is, in essence, a recalculation of time served or time yet to be served, so that full retirement benefits can be granted. One example would be an arrangement whereby the employee continues working for three months, while being paid one-quarter salary for twelve months, to cross the necessary "bridge" to retirement at a certain length of employment, age, or both.
- *Pension accommodations.* These provide for the outright addition of years to an employee's age, or years of service, or both, to pro-duce a more attractive, and more immediately available, pension program.
- *Continuing consultancy.* With a continuing consultancy the em-ployee achieves his or her independence yet has a parachute of sorts to ease the landing to new ground. In one type of continuing consultancy, the terminated employee becomes a vendor to the employer. I worked on a case where the employer committed itself to purchase no less than 25 percent of certain, specified pro-motional items from a new company to be established by the sev-ered employee, provided quality, price, and delivery were each competitive.
- *Stock options.* These can take several forms: granting of new stock options; exchange of existing options for new, more attractive options; redrafting of the terms of existing options, regarding vesting dates, exercise dates, and/or strike price. So long as gener-ally accepted accounting standards for stock options remain as liberal and flexible as they now are, we expect this avenue of severance negotiation to become more and more common.

If you are looking toward voluntary severance, be sure you consider all of these alternatives in your negotiations.

5. Pure Politics

Corporate, office, and personal politics—being on the right or wrong side of those with power and influence—often plays a very large role in the termination of employment and in severance negotiations. These negotiations tend to proceed more smoothly in large corporations, especially publicly held ones, and less smoothly in smaller companies and privately held ones.

6. Whistle-Blowers

Those who decide that, for legal, moral, or other reasons, they must report wrongdoing by their employers to public authorities—law enforcement, regulatory, tax collecting, or others—are in many cases protected by local, state, and federal statutes from retaliatory firing. In some circumstances, these statutes even give the whistle-blower financial rewards. Efforts to maintain employer compliance with laws, regulations, and legal directives are to be praised, but should be undertaken with care. I strongly suggest you consult with an attorney before you initiate any whistle-blowing efforts.

Be aware, however, that an employee cannot tell an employer, "If you don't promote me or reward me, I will report you." Words similar to these probably constitute the crime of extortion and could even result in the employee's arrest and conviction. Severance negotiations on behalf of those contemplating, suggesting, or participating in whistle-blowing must be treated with the utmost of care, to prevent the actuality or appearance of illegal payoff to the employee.

Those with knowledge of wrongful conduct that deprives the federal government of monies—through fraud—are in the enviable position of being able to share in the proceeds collected.

7. Constructive Discharge

One of the few times severance is discussed after an employee has quit his or her job is in the circumstance called constructive discharge. This is the application of a recently developed legal doctrine that says: if an employer, supervisor, or coworker acts in a threatening, menacing, or hostile way toward you, and appropriate management has been told about it but has not responded sufficiently, you do not have to stay at the job until you are physically harmed. You can, in effect, consider yourself fired.

Severance negotiations in these cases center almost exclusively on two crucial issues: Can the offending events be proved? Were appropriate members of management made aware of them? If both are answered affirmatively, negotiations primarily concern compensation.

8. No Rabbi—No Group

An important aspect of the developing corporate models of many companies and firms is that the process of corporate restructuring has created, in place of one great, monolithic structure, a collection of interrelated groups, islands, fiefdoms, or profit centers. Almost every time I discuss this development with my clients, especially since the mid-1980s, they nod their heads in silent agreement. It is as if everyone must have a leader, mentor, or "rabbi" to whom they look for protection, and to whom they owe allegiance. While some may argue that this has always been an element of survival in the workplace, most would tend to agree its importance has never been greater, as ongoing change, reengineering, and downsizing have destroyed the notion of long-term job security.

In fact, this increasingly presents us with a new context for severance: having "no rabbi or group." That is, after discussions with my clients, investigation, and reflection, I came to conclude that many of them lost their jobs primarily because they had lost their protector. Even when an employee has maintained great value and productivity to the company as a whole, if no profit group sees him or her as contributing significant profit directly to the group, no profit group may be willing to accept the employee's compensation and benefits as an entry on its own balance sheet. Often this is expressed as a "prior-commitment withdrawn."

Severance negotiation in this context is unusually difficult, because Human Resources may have few, if any, profit groups willing to supply the severance monies requested. Still, a commitment made by a company official authorized to do so is a binding obligation of the company. A commitment is a company commitment, regardless of personalities present or now missing. My advice is generally to seek out the CEO or board chair, and to make this, again, into a company issue, to, in effect, put the ball back in management's court. Being a contractual matter, convincing the company that the commitment was, indeed made, will be your chief job. Seek and gather evidence.

9. Nonprofit Context

Official not-for-profit (until recently called charitable) organizations have, as their central premise, the notion that they are not operated in pursuit of private gain, but instead are devoted to enhancement of the public good. Because of this central premise, not-for-profit organizations are exempt from paying many of the taxes shouldered by other, profit-based organizations—such as income taxes, sales tax, and property taxes—and can offer tax deductions to contributors.

As a corollary to this basic premise, both federal and state laws prohibit these groups from operating as an official, qualified not-for-profit organization (commonly referred to as "501(c)(3) organizations," which is the relevant Internal Revenue Code section that sets forth the qualification procedures and requirements) for "private inurement." That is, most of the revenues of these organizations must be devoted to the enhancement of some one or more public goods or purposes. If a disproportionate degree of revenues are devoted to generous salaries, benefits, and perks for the organization's executives or board members, the issue of private inurement arises, and federal, state, and local laws may be considered violated as a result.

To determine whether an executive employee is paid so much that negative legal and tax consequences are likely to occur, including loss of tax-deductible status and even criminal prosecution, requires a multifactored approach. In cases involving this possible situation, the following questions are frequently raised:

- What proportion of total revenues are devoted to the public good? To private gain?
- Does the executive have effective control of the organization's board of trustees?
- How does the executive's compensation compare with that received by other not-for-profit executives? By other for-profit executives?
- What degrees of special experience, specialized skills or training are possessed by the executive?
- Are lavish perks provided, such as first-class travel, expensive meals, and vacations?

- Do members of the board of trustees receive remuneration? Lavish perks?
- Are members of the executive's family on the organization's payroll? The board?
- Are board members aware of all forms of compensation provided?
- Does the executive possess unique skills required by the organization?
- Does the board retain independent counsel to negotiate executive compensation?

When issues are raised regarding private inurement, it is usually in the context of complaint to public authorities, investigation or audit by public authorities, or board dissension. Executives contemplating severance from not-for-profit organizations, especially local ones, are encouraged to seek competent legal advice on this issue in particular.

10. "Quality Versus Politics"

This severance context is reported to me quite frequently—so frequently, in fact, that in my office we simply refer to it as QVP.

"QVP" stands for "Quality vs. Power," our shorthand description of the two basic orientations of employees, which often clash. Some are concerned primarily about the quality of their work, while others about obtaining control over, or credit for, the work of others. Whether it is the success of a new marketing campaign, the efficiency of a recently restructured distribution network, or the increase in the number of the bank's private clients, the quality-oriented seek continued improvement, and the power-oriented seek their own control and credit: who gets the credit, who gets the staff, whose client roster is assigned the new clients. Quite often, these disputes end up in termination of the quality-oriented employees; it is the power-oriented, the politicians of the workplace, who prevail.

Irrational as it may seem, it is often the employees most concerned about the quality of work and achievement, and insufficiently focused on credit and compensation for that achievement, who are denied the rewards they deserve. Conversely, quite often it is the employees who think about nothing but their appearance and politics who end up on the "long end of the stick" in terms of rewards. These battles over credit and reward, between the quality-oriented employees and the power-oriented employees, commonly end up with the quality-oriented employees' being asked to leave with a severance package.

It is this apparently inadequate power orientation that leads to many severance packages, initiated and motivated by—you guessed it—the fame/power/glory seekers themselves.

11. Allegations of Illegal Conduct

It is probably surprising to many, but very few clients come to me facing involuntary termination related to allegations of criminal activity or wrongdoing. Most people who face such allegations may be in no position or have no inclination to attempt negotiation, for negotiation requires leverage, and those who have committed wrongdoing usually seek only mercy.

Although those who know they have committed mistakes have little leverage to negotiate, I believe there is always a reason and a basis for negotiation. There is a better chance for successful negotiation when many in the company were involved in the criminal behavior, when others knew of its occurrence, or when the employee in question erred in this instance but has a past history of good service and commitment. I have also successfully negotiated on behalf of employees mistakenly charged with wrongdoing or irregularities. This severance context is perhaps one of the very most sensitive to negotiate, for it may affect the future well-being of the client far more than most.

12. "I Just Don't Know"

It is especially unnerving when a few of my clients come to me with no idea why they are being let go, and I am, likewise, unable to help them zero in on a good reason. In certain companies, a termination notice comes from Human Resources only, and in certain circumstances, the only explanation is that a decision has been reached. These circumstances are especially difficult for long-term employees. While negotiating severance in this context, I can only try to work from the view of the client's future needs and his or her past contributions on the job.

• • •

Every employment termination takes place for its own unique reasons, and in its own unique circumstances, as we have seen above. Still, the negotiation of severance in all contexts entails certain common experiences and requires certain common preparations, detailed in the next chapters.

7

Experience: Reflections, Observations, Suggestions on Negotiating

> If you win all your arguments, you'll end up with no friends.
> —anonymous

In this chapter, I take one last opportunity to share certain general observations about negotiation of severance I've made over the course of my work with hundreds of people in your situation. While severance negotiations are fundamentally no different from other negotiations, they do have some unique characteristics.

A. This Negotiation Is Essentially a Business Transaction, Not a Legal One

Throughout your reading of this book you may be struck by how much I emphasize the business side of negotiating severance issues and related disputes, and how little I stress the purely legal side of things. My purpose and reasoning are simple: I believe severance negotiating is essentially a business transaction to be resolved, if possible, in a businesslike manner. Attorneys can guide, assist, and perhaps lead it, but this is essentially a business matter, not a legal one.

While severance negotiations may arise from a problem, a voluntary departure, or a termination, they are still best viewed as a business transaction, and one should try to reach agreement in a businesslike fashion and strive to prevent future disputes, so that litigation does not become necessary. The avoidance of litigation is of mutual interest to employee and employer and should never be underemphasized. As an attorney, I am trained, experienced, and capable of analyzing the strengths of the parties as regards their chances of success in court. But as a legal counselor, I know that litigation is always best prevented. The severance negotiation does unfold in a legal context, utilizes a negotiated, legal separation agreement, and maintains a back-drop of litigation as an available dispute mechanism, but remains essentially a business transaction, with short-term and long-term career ramifications for the employee. It is these considerations—career ramifications—that you must keep uppermost in your mind throughout the negotiation process.

While those going through severance look for guidance on the legal issues and strengths of their case, overemphasis on the legal side is a mistake. It would be wrong for me to suggest that the legalities are not important, especially the assessment of relative strength of a litigation, but the focus of thoughts first and foremost must be the business transaction taking place.

B. Your Approach Must Reflect Your Circumstances

It's something of a hobby of mine to peruse books on the subject of negotiation. I find that most are far too mechanical and formulaic in their approach. Many suggest certain rules are applicable to every situation. It's the old cookbook approach. I don't believe in that at all. There are many general principles and observations to bear in mind, but each negotiation is unique and should be approached and treated as such. Your own negotiations must suit you, your own circumstances and needs. But there are some broad strategies that I have found to be successful in many negotiations and others that rarely work for me.

For example, as I later note, in severance negotiations, when compensation discussions about "dollars" are at a standstill, it is always wise to consider asking for benefits instead of dollars. This has proven to be a very effective and worthwhile approach for me and my clients. It's not a "rule," it won't work every time, but, wow, it's gotten a lot of benefits for my clients that I didn't expect to win. Dollars and certain things requested in negotiation—such as moving allowances, educational benefits, pension recalculations—are essentially interchangeable. That is, certain requested items that employers are often more prone to give up in negotiations are nothing more than dollars in a different form. Try this strategy in your own negotiations.

Likewise, my concept of the "three C's of a good employment relation" comes in very handy in severance negotiations. These are *clarity*, or asking for revisions to avoid future confusion; *commitment* in a fixed payout term; and *community* in elements of profit sharing.

These are but two of many general approaches that have been effective for me. As I've said, no approach will be applicable to every situation. It is just that my overall philosophy emphasizing respective interests, mutual concerns, and shared goals is best served by these methods. Other methods may be best for others.

I will say that one negotiating technique I have very little faith in is what we call in my office the "bomb-thrower" approach, which is most commonly manifested in outrageous, unrealistic demands accompanied by obvious and obnoxious threats of lawsuits, unfavorable publicity, and public dissemination of harmful allegations. This is practiced by those who think the strong always prevail and that what goes around never comes around.

A second approach I find without great value is the mechanical approach to negotiation, which presupposes that offers, counteroffers, suggestions, and responses can be charted beforehand, as in a chess game. One book I have in my collection actually provides a sort of program that dictates a negotiation response as if the game was one of checkers. I find the art of negotiation to be far too dynamic and quick changing to be predicted as these guides suggest.

Every company, every industry, and every city is a small world where, I believe, honesty, integrity, and courtesy leave a lasting trail of good Karma. In the short run, too, I believe that the carrot approach to achieving motivation is more effective and powerful than the more commonly threatened stick. Both of these negotiation philosophies I prefer tend to keep dealings more civil and as pleasant as possible while providing results. I can't say the same for those other methods.

C. Preparation and Proactivity Are Key

Due to the very nature and relationship of the parties in a severance negotiation—employee and employer—the need for preparation and proactivity on the part of you, the employee, is great. In severance negotiating, it is almost always true that the employee is smaller, weaker, more defensive, and feeling put out, rejected, and isolated as the less powerful party. These feelings are accentuated by other aspects of the negotiation. For example, the timetable and deadlines are usually set by the employer, the initial draft agreement is prepared by the employer or company attorneys, and meetings are usually held at the offices of the employer or company attorneys. In addition, law firms representing management tend to be large, while attorneys representing employees tend to be either from small firms or sole practitioners. As you can see, employers hold an unequal share of the power and also almost always have greater financial resources available than employees.

While it is important to be prepared and proactive in all negotiations, the factors noted above, and others, make it necessary for the balance of power to be evened out through a kind of "hyperpreparation" and "hyperproactivity" on the part of the employee and his or her attorney. Let me assure you that this can be done. I have frequently won arguments with attorneys for employers simply by taking advantage of their overblown belief in themselves, and their slow-moving decision-making ability due to their large size. I have done so by being the more prepared party and by being ready, willing, and able to make suggestions, proposals, and take the initiative in my negotiations with them. This "hyper–P & P" approach, as we sometimes refer to it in my office, is what's necessary to overcome the relative disadvantages of employees. In addition, intense preparation and proactivity tend to encourage the positive feelings and thoughts that, in themselves, are some of the most powerful and convincing negotiating tactics that I and my clients have at our disposal.

D. Short and Friendly Is Our Ideal

Quite often I am asked by my clients how long it should take to negotiate and come to the conclusion of their severance dispute or agreement. My answer is always the same: two to four weeks. If it takes any longer, it will probably not happen. Therefore once I take a client on, I am always pushing forward, forward, forward, headed toward successful conclusion.

I find negotiations move more quickly and smoothly when I establish and maintain the most cordial relations possible. Sometimes, however, personalities, the friction of the circumstances, and the stress of negotiation give the negotiations a most unfriendly tone. Even when an increase in negative emotions and exchanges occur, I know in my heart that just by tuning down any hostility in my own communications I can tune it down in all communications. Not only does this make the overall negotiations more pleasant, it enhances my credibility, develops a basis of trust, keeps up the necessary momentum, and, I'm confident, results in more gains for my client than adversarial relations would.

Case History: At the conclusion of one severance dispute-resolution negotiation for a client, an investment banker at a European securities firm, I prepared a memo of the points of resolution and submitted it to the employer's in-house counsel for his review and initials. This is a common practice of mine, intended to set down clearly our collective memory of the matters agreed upon, so that the final settlement papers are as free as possible of confusion. In this particular case, we had negotiated quickly, amicably, and fairly to a just conclusion. The discussions were always centered on the business points, and our concerns were addressed in a very professional fashion. Attention was devoted to substantive issues, and all parties felt well treated. Not only had a sense of mutual respect and trust developed, but a kind of friendship and admiration had grown between the negotiators as well.

When my office received the memorandum of resolution back from our negotiating counterparts, the amount of agreed severance compensation to be paid to my client was modified upward by $25,000, in handwriting, without explanation. That is, my client was apparently going to be paid some $25,000 more than we'd agreed to settle for. I was puzzled, to say the least. I kept looking for a mathematical error or perhaps some way in which I might have been misreading the document.

But soon I discovered the source of the modification: alongside the handwritten changes were the opposing counsel's initials, with the words "Received authorization for this today." It was a change I had requested but had been told would not be possible. So I had agreed to accept the lower figure. The upward modification was purely a negotiation gift. The employer had provided this out of simple generosity since we had already agreed upon a lower figure. In my fifteen or so years of negotiating, this was the most striking example illustrating that there is good reason to practice good negotiation after all.

• • •

These reflections, observations, and suggestions about severance negotiating are the result of my hundreds of experiences in this process. Not all are as grand and memorable as this last case history, but bear them in mind, and they will serve you well. As you will recall, I have mentioned that preparation is the most important element to severance success. To explore exactly how to do this in your case, let's move on to the following section.

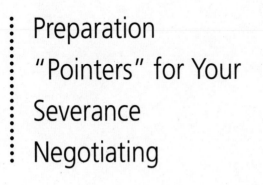

PART III

Preparation
"Pointers" for Your
Severance
Negotiating

8

Avoiding the Common Emotional Pitfalls

> My father worked for the same firm for twelve years.
> They fired him. They replaced him with a tiny gadget,
> this big. It does everything that my father did, only much
> better. The depressing thing is my mother ran out and
> bought one.
>
> —Woody Allen

In chapter 1, I presented the three secrets of negotiating your severance. In chapter 2 I stressed that your very first task is to find a way to manage your stress level, which can otherwise make you unhealthy in spirit and body. Now I would like you to consider your emotions, and especially those common emotional pitfalls that may defeat or derail your negotiating efforts.

Major transitions in life are stressful. And employment transitions are among the most stressful of all. So I tell every one of my clients going through employment transition that they should be aware of the negative feelings they will have and to take the most positive approach possible. I will suggest to you, as I do to them, that if you focus on and nurture your health, sanity, and close personal relationships, most likely the rest will work out for the best. I know for sure that if you fail to tend to these things, it never bodes well for the negotiation process or, more important, your next career step. Your stamina and self-confidence are crucial at this time. Do all you can to boost them. Here are some thoughts I share with my clients and that you might find helpful.

You Are Not a "Failure" in Life

Perhaps the first thing to remind yourself is that YOU ARE NOT TO BLAME; YOU DID NOT FAIL. YOU ARE NOT A FAILURE IN LIFE. Again and again, I hear my clients make the following statements:

- "I should have seen this coming."
- "If I had played my cards right, this would not have happened."
- "I could have done better, worked harder, perhaps been more aggressive."
- "Being fired is not the kind of thing that happens to people like me."
- "I've let my family down."

While these feelings are understandable, they are self-defeating. The last thing you need right now is to have one more problem to wrestle—your own bad attitude. Avoid these expressions of self-blame. Focus your thoughts, feelings, and efforts on positive matters, such as taking care of yourself, your family, and your future. To do so effectively, you will need every ounce of your former self-esteem. Look deep inside yourself and find your strongest reservoir of self-confidence. Make that your powerful negotiation companion. The very best executives have all been terminated, but they are the ones who are able to bounce back, stronger than ever. I tell myself, over and over, perseverance makes the difference, and I share this mantra with my clients. Ultimately, it is your resilience in life, not the absence of pitfalls and challenges, that will determine your success.

Resist the Urge for Revenge

One particularly strong emotion felt by many in your circumstances is the understandable urge for revenge, the desire to hurt those who have hurt you, your career, your self-image, and your family. In fact, it's not at all unusual for my clients to tell me that they want, above all, to teach their former employers a lesson. I always tell these clients that I cannot help them do that, and that perhaps they are not ready to negotiate at all. Negotiating requires goals that are antithetical to revenge seeking, and "teaching a lesson" is a code-phrase for revenge.

You *must* avoid this reaction, at all costs. Taking steps to hurt others is the worst possible action you can take. It might ruin your career and could be criminal as well. Although the feeling is understandable, any actions that stem from it are not. Revenge will never help you; remember that. It can only hurt you and those you care about.

You must remember the old adage, "The best revenge is living well." Yes, your future success will be your best revenge. Focus on that, and you'll benefit in career and spirit.

Avoid Isolation, Denial, and Paralysis

These are the three states of mind you want to watch out for, more than others. Paralysis is the most common. It is simply the act of not moving forward. If you find yourself without a game plan, or notice that you are not taking steps toward the activation or fulfillment of that game plan, you may be locked in paralysis. Get moving and keep moving. If you haven't developed a game plan or a To-Do List, that's the first step you can take to release yourself from an emotional freeze. If you're not a self-starter, ask friends or other supporters for help. Alone or with the help of others, set small goals. Establish daily, weekly, and monthly objectives. Keep moving toward these goals and keep a log of your accomplishments.

Don't isolate yourself now, even if your first instinct is to do so. Isolation at this time is definitely not helpful. If outplacement is provided to you, take advantage of all aspects offered, even seminars or counseling you're not interested in. You may be lucky to find someone either attending or teaching who is destined to be a new soulmate, buddy, or mentor during this process. If you don't have outplacement or you have exhausted it, join a job-search support group that meets regularly. These groups serve as a tremendous source of support and motivation for many who are between jobs.

At times I find clients to be in a state of denial about their finances, their grief, or their anger, or perhaps a combination of these and other problems. Don't be afraid to face facts squarely, accept your present circumstances for the time being, and take reasonable steps to address them. Ask close friends to tell you *exactly* how they see you and your situation, both the good and the bad. Don't be afraid of your facts, your circumstances, or your present difficulties. Embrace them.

You're much better off if you know yourself well right now. Honestly seeing your challenges as well as your goals will help you move ahead with greater benefits and fulfillment than if you hide from them.

Keep a Healthy Prospective:
"You Don't Have a Problem . . . Stewart Does"

My old friend Stewart, a single parent with two young children, is struggling with pancreatic cancer, a life-threatening illness with a particularly low rate of survival. You are facing job loss. Would you be interested in changing places with my dear friend? I would guess not. With all due respect, Stewart has a real problem; you do not. Don't despair. Keep the larger picture in mind and forge ahead.

Use Your Anger as Your Personal Rocket Fuel

I'm a true believer in the notion that we usually don't get over the more serious hurts in life, we just learn to cope with the residual pain. If you're angry, don't be ashamed of that. But don't let it eat away at you, either. Instead, use your anger to motivate, invigorate, stimulate, and elevate you to higher ground, positive thinking, planning, doing, and winning. Use your anger as rocket fuel for your new guided-missile career move. At a time like this, anger can be your best energy source if it is properly directed.

Treat Depression for What It Is: A Real Illness

If you find yourself without the energy, optimism, determination, or will to get up and face each day, or if you find yourself without the desire to see friends and loved ones, you may be suffering from clinical depression. Especially if you experience this for several weeks or months, consider getting professional help. Depression is an illness that requires treatment by a professional. Don't be afraid to seek the support you need to pull yourself out of it.

Visualize Your Future, Not Your Fears

As a committed devotee and daily practitioner of visualization, I can attest to its power. In simplest terms, visualization is nothing more than picturing yourself happy, successful, being loved, and all of the other things that you seek in life. Believe it or not, if you visualize such an existence, you are more likely to achieve it. On the other hand, if you constantly imagine yourself as a victim, without input or effect on your life, or as unlucky in all things, that, too, is more likely to take place.

Practice positive visualization on a daily basis. It's a discipline that, at the very least, can't hurt you, and, at the most, will truly change your life for the better. Imagining good things is a lot more fun than bad dreams. Give it a try.

A Few Suggestions for Getting Control of Your Emotions

Over time, I've gathered the following simple, practical tips for reining in your emotions and avoiding their potential pitfalls while you're under the stress of the severance process:

- Spouses and life partners are often the best source of support through this stressful time. Do all you can to protect this relationship. I always encourage my clients to involve spouses and life partners in severance matters in a sort of team effort. You may find the insight and added energy they can give you now is your strongest aide. At the same time, you must bear in mind that your loved ones may share much of your fear, anger, and bewilderment. So don't presume they will provide nothing but strength. Talk out what you are both feeling. Keep communications open.
- Exercise and additional rest and relaxation time seem to be the best antidotes to the physical stress of this process, as I have mentioned before. It's amazing how important they may be. Walking is free, easy, and available to all, everywhere, without cost. I urge you to take it up.
- If you are one of those who have experienced substance abuse problems in the past, I strongly suggest you maintain your usual methods of management or control and consider seeking addi-

tional sources of support at this time. The very last thing you need now is to resume old, bad, harmful habits. But times of additional stress are what can bring them on, as you know.

- Some nutritionists suggest that in times of stress it is best to maintain a diet that is full of fruits, vegetables, and light carbohydrates. Avoid foods heavy on fats, sweets, and caffeine.

- Former coworkers are usually not a good choice for sources of consolation or support now. First, your confidence in them often places them in an uncomfortable position. Second, communication with them is sometimes even viewed by employers as an effort to obtain confidential information. Ultimately, such communication usually proves disappointing. This is the time to confide and receive support from friends who have no connection with your former workplace.

- If you are not continuing to work in the office during severance negotiations, it is usually a good idea not to spend the day at home. Instead, I suggest that you maintain your usual commuting routine, and that you spend the day in the office of a friend, in an outplacement firm if such service is being provided, or even at the library. Spend your time locating future positions of employment or reassessing your career goals. This daily plan, I have found, helps clients stay focused on their future goals and retain their self-confidence. Whereas sitting at home watching TV can erode both your focus and self-worth.

- You may want to consult a therapist to help you sort out and resolve severely conflicting emotions, or seek a psychiatrist if you are struggling with depression. Even short-term treatment or counseling can often do wonders. Don't underestimate its worth.

- Some psychologists stress that it is especially important at this time to make extra efforts to pamper yourself. Have your hair cut. Get a massage. Buy a new pair of glasses. Perhaps get a shoe shine daily. Or even consider going to a tanning salon. Make yourself look and feel good, daily. This will only help you make a strong impression when you are searching for a new position and will help boost your self-confidence during this stressful time.

- Ask a good friend to be a special, regular sounding board during this process. Such an ongoing exercise will help you get out a lot of your frustration and anger and give you honest answers to the question, "How am I doing?"

- For those who find peace, refuge, consolation, and meaning in the process of religious worship, I recommend that you spend additional time in these activities. Many of my former clients tell me that prayer, meditation, and increased time spent in their religious community were helpful to them.

Emotions are an integral part of human life, and you should expect them to emerge from within with increased volatility around times of severance. Take all steps available to you to diminish the destructive elements of your emotional discharge, and to channel those emotions into the focused and determined energies you'll need to succeed in the severance process.

9

Consider Your Employer's Perspective

> There is only one boss: the customer. And he can fire
> everybody in the company, from the chairman on down,
> simply by spending his money somewhere else.
>
> —Sam Walton

There's an old saying that it is more important to know your adversaries well than it is to know your friends well. I believe this applies quite forcefully to severance negotiations. My observations about the ways employers and their Human Resources representatives view severance negotiations are frequently confirmed for me in one especially convincing way: After my negotiations with Human Resources executives on behalf of my clients, it is my good fortune to represent many of the same Human Resources executives in their own severance negotiations. Each of them that I work with on both sides of the negotiating table tells me that there are many different ways to negotiate severance with management, but the approach presented in this book is simply the most effective. Why? Because it focuses more on smart negotiating, rather than on pleas for mercy and outright threats. And so they choose it for their own severance process and come to me for counsel and representation.

Knowing your audience, your customers, your clients, your adversaries, and your negotiating partners is the key to your success in your efforts, whatever they may be. Knowing your targets is what negotiations are all about. See the world from their perspective, and you'll see your way to success. Let's take a look at how I see employers viewing severance time and again.

A. A Mere Task to Be Accomplished;
a File to Be Closed

Though this is clearly a major event in your life—one that almost consumes you right now and will dwell in your consciousness for a long time to come—you must bear in mind that your severance is initially viewed by corporate HR as nothing more than a task to be accomplished, a file to be closed. The HR staff do not see this as an item of major importance, but one of many tasks on their everyday To-Do Lists. It's a cold thought, but a truth, nonetheless. This is especially true in cases of mass downsizings.

It is not my intent to suggest that your severance matter is not important. To the contrary, it is so important that it is absolutely necessary that you understand and appreciate the actual mind-set of your negotiating partner, whether in corporate Human Resources or on the legal staff. Your understanding of the other person's point of view is essential for good negotiating.

How does this translate to value to you? One of your primary—though unspoken—objectives in your severance negotiations will be to elevate the importance of your case in relation to other matters of concern to your negotiating partner. Indeed, you would do well to elevate your own negotiations, and their peaceful, successful conclusion, to perhaps the most important thing in the life and mind of your adversary. In later chapters we'll discuss when and how to do this. For now, bear in mind only how important an objective this is, and that you need to think long and hard about how to accomplish it in your specific case.

B. A Business Transaction; "It's Nothing Personal"

It is also important to bear in mind that from the employer's viewpoint (and this is meant to include the view of the employers' Human Resources and legal staff as well), the severance process is primarily a business transaction, in which your removal is sought, preferably at minimal cost. That is how your negotiating partner views your severance negotiation, even if he or she has been your golf buddy, your lunchmate, and your office neighbor for thirty years.

There are three important points to remember in your discussions with your negotiating partner. First, never expect this individual to feel your feelings. Don't be shocked, disappointed, dismayed, or angry when your assigned negotiator seems not to appreciate how urgent and important this matter is to you, your family, and your lives. If you let any of these emotions take hold of you, you will be a less effective negotiator. Second, don't believe it if your assigned negotiating partner takes the opposite approach and claims to know, appreciate, and take to heart your difficulties and circumstances. False empathy is a very real, powerful, and destabilizing tactic in these negotiations. Human Resources negotiators are taught this tactic and practice it quite often. Don't fall prey to it. Third, understand that your negotiating partner knows what he or she is doing: this *is* a business transaction. Your employer is involved in many business decisions each day. Your severance is just another one.

Two more points to remember: (1) The greatest breakthroughs in severance negotiating start when the more natural roles begin reversing—when the employer's negotiators start taking these negotiations personally, and the terminated executive starts treating them as a business transaction. (2) In the business transaction of severance, the employer is buying closure, that is, your permanent agreement not to sue, bring claim, expose, compete, or otherwise pose some risk. The essential issue is your price for such an agreement. As the seller, you set that price. In doing so, don't be any less cold, tough, or realistic than you would in any other business decision you might make.

C. Risk Avoidance by Management

Since the large-scale downsizings of the late 1980s have evolved into the strategic rightsizing and selective cleansing of the 1990s and beyond, senior management is more and more sensitive to the decreasing job security they, themselves, experience daily. As these executives find their own jobs as insecure as all others, I have seen a definite refocus of their own perspectives on and attitudes toward each severance matter. As a result of growing insecurity, their primary focus is now one of risk avoidance. Management efforts are increasingly directed toward achieving an orderly process of termination and severance, while avoiding the many losses posed to them in the event that the employee: (1) decides to sue (I discuss the legal bases of lawsuits in later chapters); (2) threatens to disclose strategic plans, past errors that have been "rug-swept," or other confidential information, including the details of this severance package; and (3) competes with the company, possibly luring away important customers, personnel, or other crucial business resources.

In any discussion of corporate risk, it is always necessary to bear in mind the ultimate rule of survival: first and foremost, watch out for yourself. That is exactly what each member of senior management does. The more your efforts call into question, and place into jeopardy, the many and varied interests of the company, the more leverage you have to reach a satisfactory severance from your employer.

D. Fear of Losing Face and Setting Precedent

What you need to consider is that your negotiating partner knows that he or she is being judged—from management's point of view—on the success of these negotiations. Don't needlessly embarrass, intimidate, or demean your negotiating partner, especially if negotiations are going well. If you have achieved most of what you need to, and have taken advantage of the other party's concern for risk avoidance, don't further his or her humiliation or exposure, for it may come back to haunt you.

• • •

Although there is an exception to every generalization I've made in this chapter, you should always understand and take advantage of the prevailing odds. You may likely represent only a file; but do all you can to make it your employer's most important file. Your employer's assigned negotiators don't consider your case a personal matter; when it becomes personal, they'll be highly motivated to work with you. They'll avoid risk, especially to themselves; you might even want to ratchet up their own risk factors. Like all people, they'll always seek to save face.

Now that we've considered your employer's stance in negotiations, let's move on to your own perspective and look at the topic of hiring a severance attorney.

10

Is Legal Representation
Necessary for You? Perhaps Not

Two farmers each claimed to own a certain cow. While
one pulled on its head, and the other pulled on its tail,
the cow was milked by a lawyer.

—Jewish parable

A. Do I Need an Attorney?

Quite often I am asked whether it is really necessary for an executive
to be represented by legal counsel in negotiating severance. In fact, I
believe many more people ponder this question by themselves but are
too polite to ask it of me and my colleagues. It is a very important question. My answer is simple: legal representation is never necessary,
unless court papers or appearances are imminent. Otherwise, legal
representation may be of varying value, depending on the issues, facts,
and circumstances you think you'll face, as well as your own strengths
and weaknesses. But legal representation is not essential, and in many
instances it can even be inadvisable. Let's take a look at this question
more closely.

Direct Discussions Are Best
First and foremost, don't forget that the ideal basis for discussion and
resolution of employment issues is through frank, open discussion
between employers and employees. This direct approach provides the
greatest chance for the best resolution for everyone involved. In the
context of new employment, this approach provides a unique opportunity for building a solid employee-employer relationship. However, at
the time of severance, the notion of building a good relationship has

frequently given way to one of crisis management. And while executive recruiters are often utilized effectively in new-employment negotiation, they should be considered either neutral or on management's side in all discussions you have with them. Never depend on them to resolve severance issues. Remember that employers pay recruiters and so have much more control over them than you do.

One thing no one else can do for you as effectively as you can do for yourself is call in personal favors that you've earned over the years. Many times I have seen a client fail to consider this an appropriate time to do so or feel uncomfortable doing so, only to have a friend later say that he was disappointed that he was not asked to help. An attorney cannot be expected to know the many favors and courtesies you've extended over the years, and to call them in for you. Have some personal, discreet, direct discussions with those who you feel could help you now.

I cannot overemphasize the potential value of direct severance discussions. Because such discussions can be difficult, they are often not attempted or not attempted with sufficient effort and will. But they should never be dismissed or discouraged without serious consideration of their potential advantages. If you are interested in direct, face-to-face severance discussions without an attorney, see chapter 14 for a list of ten severance secrets to bear in mind as you enter into direct negotiations with your employer.

Knowledge of the the Law
(Often Expressed as "Do I Have a Good Case?")

You can ask an experienced employment attorney, "Do I have a good case?" and expect to receive a pretty clear answer. This is the one significant, and undeniable, advantage of using an attorney to help you.

While it has never happened to me, I hope one day to have a client ask me, "Does my employer have a good case against me?" It would be refreshing because employees being terminated usually don't consider the reverse possibility: that they have done (or are planning) something that provides legal ammunition, if not artillery, to the employer to fire them. Examples would include offering to bring a confidential customer list to a new, competing employer or sabotaging a software system in anger. One client foolishly e-mailed to every employee of the company a list of bonuses received by each employee the previous year. A good, experienced employment attorney will ask you questions to properly and completely explore all possibilities under the law for you, both positive and negative.

Advantages/Disadvantages of Hiring an Attorney

Still, many people are uncomfortable with negotiations, especially negotiations with people whom they consider friends, about such a touchy subject as severance. For these people, the decision whether to use an attorney requires a careful, balanced consideration of the various pros and cons. One advantage of having legal representation in severance negotiation is that the attorney often acts as a buffer, to absorb or deflect any friction and antagonisms that may arise from time to time between the parties themselves. It is widely known that diplomacy has a greater chance of success if practiced by noncombatants. And the attorney falls into this category.

Another important advantage of having an employment attorney by your side who is experienced in these matters is that she or he has been through these discussions many times, knows what to ask for, what's really important and worth fighting for, and can also suggest alternative requests which may get you what you want through a strategy that you'd never come up with alone. For example, in one negotiation, I managed to get additional compensation for a client simply by calling it "post-termination consultation fees." In this way, a good attorney can carry forward a severance negotiation to successful completion with his or her knowledge of the terms and the law. Human Resource personnel know how to negotiate severance agreements for the employer. The employee needs to know the common deal points, the dynamics, and the standards of negotiating severance, to level the playing field. If you do not feel confident learning and using this information on your own in negotiation, you might want to strongly consider hiring an attorney.

In one negotiation, management would not budge on issues of severance compensation. My client wished to use the monies primarily to complete her MBA. When we asked for educational assistance instead of compensation, we were given all we asked for. Go figure.

On the other hand, it is sometimes the attorneys themselves who exacerbate tensions, who enlarge the gulf between the parties, either unintentionally by the nature of their personalities or far worse, intentionally, to increase their own hourly billings. I recently asked a good trial attorney to assist me with a dispute in arbitration. When he was told who the employer was, he responded, "We've got a problem. They always use [a certain law firm], and that law firm always bills $50,000 in fees before they talk settlement seriously." Fortunately, many law firms are better intentioned. Still, you should be aware of the fact that many attorneys will intentionally avoid settlement to serve their own selfish interests. To guard against hiring such an attorney, try to find a lawyer through referrals of people you trust.

I often say, "Businesspeople make business deals; attorneys make arguments." What I mean by this is that businesspeople generally have a greater understanding of and appreciation for the bargaining process and the need for both sides to come out ahead after business negotiations. It is my view that far too many attorneys, on the other hand, seek only to prevail. The legal system is essentially adversarial in nature. In light of this, I try never to speak primarily in terms of "battle"; but instead, concentrate on efforts to reconcile competing interests. When hiring counsel, listen to how the attorney talks about your case. If he or she is too adversarial for your taste, keep looking. You want reasonable representation and settlement, not a drawn-out battle.

Also, even when an attorney is soft-spoken and entirely reasonable in requests, some employers' attitudes seem to instantly harden at the sight of an attorney. Some people are just viscerally upset by the mere notion of lawyers.

Nevertheless, a good attorney will be able to anticipate possible future problems in severance negotiations—and will continually work his or her skills to set the terms of your agreement to avoid these potential problems. In this respect a lawyer is like a doctor who encourages preventive health care. Those who function in this way in both professions are often underappreciated because of their very success in avoiding problems before they are even raised or noticed by their clients.

Severance negotiations are sometimes conducted in "ghost fashion," where the attorney is not engaged in direct communications of any kind with the employer, and the employer often does not even know of the attorney's existence. One reason for this is to "let business-people discuss business." It is my experience that, in all probability, employers will immediately call in their own attorneys (either in-house staff or outside firms) as soon as I get involved; invariably, then, little gets accomplished while the attorneys "lock horns." Another reason for "ghost representation" is that sometimes my clients achieve unexpectedly good results simply in exchange for their agreement not to bring me into negotiations.

The one time using a lawyer in severance negotiations is always advisable is when, either as an alternative to negotiations or to gain leverage in negotiations, it appears necessary to initiate legal proceedings or a formal administrative complaint of some kind. (See the chapters 34 to 37 in part VII, "If Negotiations Fail.") When you believe you may be going against other lawyers in a legal or quasi-legal proceeding, hearing, or case, having someone knowledgeable and experienced on your side, to stand up for you, is always a good idea.

Costs and Terms of Legal Representation
Another obvious disadvantage to utilizing attorneys in severance negotiation is the cost of their services. Some attorneys work on an hourly basis; some work on a contingent, percentage-of-award basis; some work on a fixed-fee basis. Certain attorneys will work on any basis you choose. No matter what the fee structure, though, the involvement of attorneys is a significant expense and not to be taken lightly. Indeed, you can almost count on the fact that your legal fees will be far more than you originally estimated.

Likewise, retaining legal counsel is a separate and unique business relationship which, in and of itself, you must negotiate with care. Never retain an attorney without a clear and easily understood written agreement. Later in this chapter, I'll review tips on hiring and paying your employment attorney.

A question frequently asked about attorneys is, "Can I ask my employer to pay my legal bills?" For the answer to that question, read chapter 17, "The Ten Next Most Valuable Requests."

Limited or Partial Legal Representation
You must keep in mind that the decision whether to utilize an attorney in your severance situation need not be an all-or-nothing choice. Many of my clients retain me only to counsel, and oversee their own efforts. Others retain me just to provide counsel and to review documents to be signed. In fact, I set one fixed fee for "consultations only," one fixed fee for "consultations and document review," and one fixed fee for "full service—consultations, document review, and negotiations." Most

people are not comfortable with the negotiation process, but if you are, and feel you could negotiate well for yourself, feel free to suggest to your attorney a "partial representation" such as one of these or some other combination of service.

Group Legal Representation

In certain circumstances—including company downsizing and large-scale reduction in employment benefit levels—I have represented groups of people seeking to negotiate the same or similar issues with a single employer. Such an arrangement poses a risk of confusion of goals and requires careful attention to address all possible conflicts of interest, but it may significantly reduce overall legal fees and gain additional group-related leverage. That is, management may be willing to make certain concessions if, by those concessions, it obtains full severance agreements from many employees. Despite the potential drawbacks, you should consider group representation if you and other employees are facing a large layoff.

B. Locating the Right Attorney

> It is better to be a mouse in a cat's mouth than a man in a
> lawyer's hands.
>
> —Spanish proverb

I made the point earlier that it may not be necessary for you to hire an attorney to negotiate your severance. In fact, the very purpose of this book is to enable you to act on your own behalf with the information, understanding, and confidence that you need to do it well. The trick is knowing when you will be best served acting on your own and when you have a real need for an attorney.

That said, I would recommend you use a good employment attorney in any severance negotiation (1) to oversee your own efforts, (2) to assist you in any way that you (and perhaps the attorney) believe necessary, and (3) to step in with the necessary legal knowledge and experience in the event that serious problems occur. At the same time, I wholeheartedly recommend you do all of the preparation, negotiation, and confirmation you can, with the guidance and information in this book. This is unquestionably the ideal balance to be reached, if possible.

So how do you find the employment attorney that you can work best with, in your locale? There are lots of them out there, and three good ways to find them:

Ask for Recommendations

This is the number one way to locate a good attorney (or a provider of any service, for that matter). Among your peers whom you respect and admire, there are no doubt many who have found an employment attorney who represents people in your field, at your level, with sensibilities similar to your own. That's the best place to start. While there's no guarantee that you'll "click" with the attorney they "click" with, this is a good place to start.

Call Specialized Referral Services

Your local bar association or lawyers' guild should maintain a referral service that gives out names of members who are knowledgeable and experienced in employment law and in the negotiation of severance matters. Be sure to ask if the organization has a "labor and employment committee" or some similar group.

Bear in mind that some employment attorneys serve only the interests of management (actually, the vast majority), while others serve both employers and employees, and a smaller number represent only employees, as I do. My preference is the last of these three categories, but I would not hesitate to use an employment attorney who knows both sides of the arguments, so long as he or she has never represented your employer before and has no immediate plans to do so.

Web Sites and Published Books and Articles

Those who are the best at their chosen field of work are usually those who enjoy their work and are engaged in activities related to it. Scour the Web, your local bookstore, as well as business and trade magazines for articles written by attorneys who are heavily involved in severance and employment negotiating, and who show it through the presentation of their ideas on the subject in the various media. One fellow I have come to know well, who is an expert on the litigation of ERISA issues, I first met after cutting out a newspaper article he wrote on the subject. He knows his stuff, and knowing him is an asset to me.

Interview Your Candidates

Regardless of how you've come across your candidate for representation, request a short meeting, preferably face-to-face, to talk about how he or she would approach your case, how he or she sees the role of an attorney in severance negotiation, and whether he or she encourages your active input into the process. While many of my clients can appear to want only someone to stand up for them, I know that those clients who are the most satisfied with my work are those who work with me on their severance efforts. It's crucial that you have a sense of the person you're interviewing and whether the two of you may comfortably work together during a very stressful period of your life.

For anything more than a short meeting, you should be prepared to pay the attorney a consultation fee of a few hundred dollars or so. Ask about fees beforehand, so that there are no surprises for either party. If you do not think a candidate is the right attorney for you, don't hesitate to interview someone else. While time may be short, and the expense great for a few good ideas, I still recommend interviewing attorney candidates until you find one you feel comfortable with.

C. Legal Fees and Payment Options

> Don't put it in my ear, but in my hand.
> —Russian proverb

Once you've found a good employment attorney you feel you'll work well with, your next question will undoubtedly be, "How much will his or her help cost me?" That is a very relevant inquiry, all the more so when you are facing the possibility of losing your job and the salary that goes with it.

Hourly Charges

Most lawyers charge for their services on an hourly basis, as this is the way attorneys have traditionally charged.

Hourly fees are generally calculated in either six- or fifteen-minute increments. Hourly rates vary greatly from locale to locale, and between firms as well. The range is from approximately $175 per hour in smaller cities, or for the least experienced attorneys in larger cities, up to perhaps $450 per hour for partners in the largest firms in the largest cities. My firm, being both small but very experienced in severance, charges hourly rates from $275 to $400. In addition to the hourly fees, you are financially responsible for all expenses and disbursements incurred on your behalf.

Most firms require an initial "up front" retainer, against which they then bill for their services and, in effect, pay themselves each month. While retainers commonly range from $1,000 to $5,000, they are usually negotiable.

Although hourly billing arrangements can become quite expensive over time, there are some things you can do to keep your legal costs under control:

- Consider asking your prospective attorney if he or she would be willing to lower the hourly rate or lower it after the billing reaches a certain level.
- Ask your attorney to give you a dollar figure at which he or she would "cap" your charges, so that fees don't exceed your ability to pay.
- Suggest the option of paying over time, say, $500 per month.
- Request to be notified when the billing gets to certain agreed levels, say, each increment of $1,000.
- Make sure your arrangement includes the generation of a very specific, monthly statement. Ask to see what a typical bill looks like. Is it easily understandable?
- Look for ways in which you can carry the burden yourself and thus lower the charges to you. For example, you could contact your company's benefits manager to request a copy of all benefit plans, and you could review those plans, too, in order to keep your legal expenses down. Make sure your prospective attorney is comfortable with actions like these.

See chapter 11 for more concrete "Suggestions for Working Most Productively with Your Severance Attorney."

Contingency Payments

Like most employment attorneys, I find that many of my prospective clients ask about the possibility of paying for my services on a contingency basis, which means I get nothing if my efforts yield no results, but a percentage of the rewards if my efforts prove successful. I always entertain these requests and consider them very seriously.

If you and your attorney are contemplating working on a contingency basis, bear the following points in mind:

- Consider whether you will be comfortable if your lawyer makes $50,000 of your severance money after only working, say, five hours.
- Do not apply the contingency percentage fee to the initial severance offer, if any, but only to that increase your attorney's efforts helped bring about.
- My contingency fee is 33⅓ percent. Other lawyers may use higher or lower percentages.
- You may find it hard to assign a dollar figure to the concessions won by your attorney. How would you value the employer's removal of a covenant not to compete? Or a positive "departure statement"?
- There may be some "mechanics of payment" problems as well. How would you pay your attorney a percentage of an increased pension, not to start paying out for five years, but then paying you an additional $53.49 monthly thereafter for the rest of your and your spouse's lives?
- Most of all, do not forget about your favorite relative, Uncle Sam. Percentage payments are almost always a percentage of the gross (that is, pretaxed) result. Since severance moneys are taxable, the net (that is, after-taxed) result may look like your attorney is getting more than you are. Example: $100 result; yielding $66.67 to you, $33.33 to the counselor. But the after-withholding payout from the employer will be $100, less perhaps $38 taxes; yielding $62 to be split only $28.67 to you, $33.33 to your attorney.

"Fixed" or "Flat" Fees

Some firms, including my own, also permit clients to choose a "fixed" or "flat" fee arrangement, under which you pay one certain, preagreed fee for a certain level of service, no matter how much or how little effort is required. I am a big fan of such arrangements, for they provide the client with a limitation on his or her "cost-risk." They also give the client the freedom to discuss and question as much as may be needed without having to worry about the clock and the charges.

In return for granting a fixed-fee option, I require my clients to prepay the entire fee, which gives me freedom from "collection risk"; I also put an upper limit on the time frame during which the services are provided, which is usually three months. Otherwise, the matter will never be over. These fixed-fee arrangements are becoming more and more popular with my own clients.

Get It in Writing

No matter what fee arrangement you and your attorney may agree to, make sure it is in writing, that it is clear, and that it is signed. Remember, now, you're dealing with a lawyer! No, it's not the lawyer per se that you have to be careful about. It's misunderstandings, faded memories, and changed circumstances. As good fences make good neighbors, good agreements make good business relations. Clarity is the first requirement of a successful relation, in business or otherwise.

• • •

A primary purpose of this book is to enable you to do all you can for yourself, and to make the best decision possible about hiring an attorney. I hope when you are done reading it, you will feel confident in whichever choice you make.

Use of an attorney to help in severance negotiation may be advisable or advantageous, but it is never absolutely necessary. No matter what decision you make here, the important thing for you to keep uppermost in your mind is that you are in charge. You must be as self-directed as possible in this process to gain the most advantage in your dispute with your employer, as well as in your relationship with your attorney at a reasonable cost. Remember that a severance negotiation is an important process, for it may have significant, long-term effects on your career and happiness. If you hire an attorney, seek one with severance experience, one who is both dedicated to your concerns and focused first and foremost on your welfare. Consider this issue seriously.

11

Seven Suggestions for Working Most Productively with Your Severance Attorney

> Don't think there are no crocodiles because the water is calm.
>
> —Malayan proverb

A. Looking "Forward"

If you're going to work with an attorney to resolve your severance concern, it's just plain old common sense that you would be best served if you and your attorney worked together. You and your concerns must be the most important thing on your attorney's mind while he or she is talking to you or working on your behalf. Your problems are, in fact, your attorney's problems. Unnecessary difficulties, unnecessary time wasted, and unnecessary expense are to be avoided. After looking at the range of attorney fees in the previous chapter, I'm sure you will agree that productivity is your friend.

Here are seven suggestions for working productively with your employment attorney:

1. Be Honest. Be open, truthful, and frank with your attorney about every single facet of your severance problem, and about everything that might conceivably come up in discussions, negotiations, or even, heaven forbid, depositions. If you used to date the secretary who is now married to the CEO, let your attorney know. If you have secretly taken home and hidden copies of cost reports that evidence your superior's travel reimbursement for his fishing trips, let your attorney know. Above all, don't lie, mislead, or hold back any sort of evidence that might conceivably be used against you.

2. Don't Be Afraid to Say, "I Don't Understand." Even the best of attorneys sometimes forget that their clients don't understand legal jargon, legal theory, or "whattheyjustsaidsodarnfast." It really is your responsibility to tell your lawyer what you don't understand, so that he or she can try to explain it in another way. Don't be embarrassed to ask that your lawyer explain the reasoning just one more time, even if it's the fourth time.

3. Prepare for Meetings and Prearranged Telephone Conferences. A great deal of time, and therefore legal expense, is wasted when people—and that includes lawyers—are not prepared for meetings and telephone conferences. If you are going to discuss papers, have those papers in front of you. If you have not had time to review the papers sent to you for review, say so and end the phone call, instead of pretending you know what the attorney is talking about or, worse, having him wait while you look over a four-page memo. Likewise, don't sit idly back while your attorney does any one of these things, to you. Time is precious, and expensive, and discipline in such matters is your and your attorney's mutual obligation.

4. Make Appointments for Telephone Conferences. Like many of my fellow attorneys, I can be extremely difficult to get ahold of. It is perhaps my greatest failing as an attorney. There are days when I come back to the office from court at 2:00 P.M., and there are no fewer than twenty-five messages, all marked "extremely urgent." How can you make your case stand out from the rest?

Perhaps the best way I've been able to improve this aspect of my professional service is to have my staff ask all clients if they would like to set a time for a "telephone appointment" and to establish a list of items to be discussed. In this day of tight time constraints on all of us, setting aside a particular time for a particular person is a very valuable tool.

5. Keep Discussions of Your Anger to a Minimum. Like divorce lawyers, employment lawyers who represent terminated employees hear a lot about the anger their clients feel toward the people who have mistreated them. While the feelings may surely be justified, and their expression often provides some relief, keep the discussion of your anger to a minimum, because it diminishes the opportunity and resources available to your lawyer to do something about the cause of the anger in the first place.

6. Use E-mail and Faxes to Communicate. For those of us in busy practices, it is very helpful to receive a short communication from a client with a comment about a point we discussed, a question about an upcoming event, or even a note about something of significance that has transpired at the client's office. In like fashion, I can then answer the question, ask for more information, or ask the client for his or her thoughts, all at our mutual convenience. E-mail, especially, has become a very favorite tool of mine, particularly for communicating with clients on different continents and in different time zones.

7. Listen a Lot, but Make the Final Decision. If there's one kind of client I feel badly for, and at times badly toward, it's the client who never seems to have the time to listen. While I don't need the audience, I cannot perform my function unless there is two-way communication. I can't ask effective questions. I can't give effective advice. And I most assuredly can't counsel the client on what to do, how to do it, and when to do it if he or she is not listening.

If you remember to listen as well as talk, you'll get more for your money. In this context you are the boss, and you will ultimately make all the decisions of importance. That is your right—indeed, your responsibility. Listen to advice and then decide if you want to follow it. But you need to listen first, and listen intently.

•   •   •

Every one of the seven suggestions I've offered here aims to make the lawyer-client relationship a productive one, and each relates to an aspect of the communication process. How to get the other's attention, how to communicate efficiently, how to gain the most out of that communicating time, energy, and opportunity.

My clients' feedback has confirmed for me that you will profit greatly by a good working relationship with your severance counsel, should you retain one. You will need to work at making that relationship a strong one, but you will not regret the effort.

12

What Lies Ahead:
A Preview of the Severance Process

> *A former executive of a company which had been taken over in a corporate merger gave this description of what had happened to his company's executive personnel:*
>
> We got the mushroom treatment. Right after acquisition, we were left in the dark. Then, they covered us with manure. Then they cultivated us. After that they let us stew awhile. Finally, they canned us.
>
> —Isadore Barmash

Employees who have recently received either warning or actual notice that employment termination is in their future are in some degree of shock or anxiety, and with good reason. Most want very much to get a good picture of what they are likely to experience in that process. That is in large part what this book is all about.

My law firm is among the few law firms in the United States with years of experience in handling severance issues exclusively from the employee's perspective. Over these years my colleagues and I have developed successful strategies for dealing with management representatives. In turn, our dealings with these individuals have affected the way they approach the process, too. Over time I have observed predictable patterns of behavior by management facing severance proceedings.

While every severance matter I handle presents me with a singular set of facts and circumstances, and every employee and employer are themselves unique, I find the experience of almost every severance client can be compartmentalized into five general stages:

1. Notice of Termination (Inkling, Warning, or Formal Notice)
2. Identification/Clarification of Offered Severance Package, If Any
3. Assembling Facts, Assessing End Goals, Choosing Strategy
4. Negotiation: Maximizing the Package
5. Confirmation and Termination: Receipt, Waiver, and Release

If you have received warning or word of your impending employment termination, you're likely to experience these five stages. Let's take a closer look at each one.

Stage 1: Notice of Termination

Notice of impending or immediate job loss is usually directed toward one individual: one employee is asked to report to his or her superior, the Human Resources department, or the CEO, and is given notice of termination. Or it can affect a group of people at once: there is a public announcement of downsizing, restructuring, workforce reduction, or dissolution of an entire department or division. This is commonly referred to as reduction in force, or RIF.

While essentially the termination was an "event," many clients tell me they saw the end coming, heard rumors, or perceived its necessity long before the actual event. These early warnings are, to my mind, part of the notification process. Often, they are management's informal way of announcing its intentions.

Receipt of termination notice or notice of intended termination is the beginning of the process of negotiation. There is only one point to remember at this time: *sign nothing*. No matter how tempting it may be to move on, no matter how attractive terms of an agreement look to you, it's critical that you sign nothing.

The severance documents given to employees to sign are commonly called "Separation Agreement and Release," "Severance, Waiver, and Release Agreement," or words to that effect. I will discuss these documents in later chapters, in depth, as well as what your response should be when they're presented to you. You will feel some pressures—internal and external—to sign whatever is given to you to sign. Don't do it.

Emotions at this time frequently run high. Rationality, even among the most rational of us, is bound to be at a low point. It may be tempting to sign whatever is in front of you to get this unpleasant process over with now. Don't sign anything until you've had time to clear your head, speak to those who are important to you, and, perhaps, consult an attorney.

The law recognizes this predicament and, because of it, the laws of most states and several federal laws that give employees rights in this process offer two safeguards: a period of time (usually twenty-one days, sometimes up to forty-five days) for you to consider the severance and release offer, and a second period (usually seven days) for you to reconsider the papers even after you've signed them.

The reasons not to sign are simple: At the very least, you should understand the implications of what you're signing, both negative and positive. At the very most, since severance is negotiable, you may be giving up important, valuable, legal and financial rights by signing now. Your employer may even increase a financial settlement offer if you don't sign right away. Just don't sign now.

Stage 2: Identification/Clarification of Offered Severance Package, If Any

Upon receiving termination notice, you will probably receive some word, whether verbally or in writing, of the severance benefits your employer will provide you with, if any. The critical task before you is to identify and clarify the various elements of any package being offered. This is probably one of the most difficult and time-consuming tasks of the termination procedure; sometimes it lasts throughout the negotiation process.

As discussed in subsequent chapters, you may (and probably do) have more legal rights and negotiating leverage than you realize at this point. To take advantage of these rights, it is of utmost importance for you to determine: (1) what compensation, benefits, and/or items of value you are being offered; (2) what waivers, releases, and/or other infringements on your future freedom you are being asked to sign; (3) what negotiating you can do to increase your compensation, benefits, and items of value, and decrease your waivers, of releases, and infringements.

During this identification/clarification process, I assist my clients by reviewing with them the various forms of severance information disseminated by corporate Human Resources, interviewing my clients, preparing questions for them to submit to Human Resources, and, at times, talking to Human Resources representatives myself. Sometimes verbal promises or assurances are made, or memos are distributed, which are not embodied in the formal separation agreement a client of mine has received. I carefully gather and make note of them, but don't rely upon them, unless they are put into writing and then incorporated into the separation agreement before my client signs it.

Stage 3: Assembling Facts and Choosing End Goals

These two steps together comprise my basic preparation for upcoming negotiations. It is of considerable value for yourself, and for your attorney, should you retain one, that you assemble and consider all available and relevant facts about your work history and your employer.

Assessing end goals is perhaps more important than any other step in the severance negotiation process, for if your goals are not good ones, the negotiation is a pure waste of effort. In the end, you won't feel you have gotten what you need in order to move ahead. As noted earlier, I tell all my clients, "Your future is more important than your past." By this I mean that their efforts must be focused, first and foremost, upon their welfare in the future.

All of your negotiating goals should be determined by your future needs. For example, if you are determined to stay in the same industry, agreement on a positive reason for departure may be an important negotiating goal. However, if you are certain that you want to leave the industry and never return, choosing, for example, to open a franchise business instead, the reason for departure may not be important, but a lump-sum cash payout may be most valuable. As you can see from these different situations, you need to do some serious self-assessment before you can move forward to the next negotiation phase.

It may be difficult to address your life goals and perform critical self-assessment at what you feel to be a time of crisis, but it is essential for you—and your loved ones—that you do so anyway. Others can assist you as well, including spouse, attorney, therapist, and financial planner. I've said it before and I'll say it again: don't be afraid to ask for help.

Stage 4: Negotiation: Maximizing the Package

Negotiation of severance matters starts with a simple communication to your supervisor, corporate Human Resources, corporate general counsel's office, or whoever is responsible for your severance. It is a simple communication expressing that your package, as currently structured, is not acceptable but requires some limited clarifications and modifications.

By stating this simple fact, you enter the negotiation stage. This is the most difficult part of the process to describe, because each negotiation is unique. But I can say that your overall goals in the negotiation phase should be fourfold: (1) to broaden the scope of severance benefits provided by requesting benefits not offered, (2) to increase the amount of those benefits offered, (3) to secure eventual receipt of the severance benefits you and your employer finally agree upon; (4) to eliminate (or reduce) restrictions on your future activities.

As we've seen, negotiations are sometimes conducted in "ghost" fashion, which means an employee's attorney is not engaged in direct communications of any kind with the employer, and oftentimes the employer does not even know of his or her existence. It is my experience that, in all probability, employers will immediately call in their own attorneys (either in-house staff or outside firms) as soon as I get involved in a case. In some instances, my clients achieve unexpected positive results simply in exchange for their agreement not to bring me into negotiations.

The underlying rationale for severance is fundamental fairness. Just as my goal of negotiations is basic fairness, so too does my method of negotiating stress fairness. Each step of the way, I present what I believe to be arguments for fairness—taking into account the unique facts and circumstances of each client. Of course, my view of basic fairness may not coincide with the employer's view.

In negotiating, I also stress those aspects of the law that support my arguments. The basis of my argument—what we attorneys sometimes refer to as the "hook" on which our argument rests—may be a form of illegal discrimination, a breach of contract, or a combination of two or three legal bases at the same time. The particular bases, or hooks, are determined by the facts and circumstances before me. I discussed these legal basics in part II, "A 'Warm-Up': What Do We Mean by Severance 'Negotiating'?"

Negotiations often happen in two or three stages, in which the employer makes modifications to the severance package, all reluctantly, until it appears my client and I have reached our goal or obtained all that seems possible. A certain sensitivity in this regard is reached only after years of experience in these matters. Parts IV, V, and VI—titled, respectively, "Who, When, and How to Ask," "What to Ask For," and "What Your Employer Will Ask of You and How to Respond to Each Request"—describe in greater detail more of the ways in which I negotiate severance and you can too.

Stage 5: Confirmation and Termination: Receipt, Waiver, and Release

This last stage in the severance negotiation process is carefully reviewing the various documents involved to ensure that all agreed severance benefits are clearly set forth. You should also be sure, to the greatest extent possible, that these are secured against loss in all events and circumstances, while no unnecessary obligations or restrictions on your freedoms are inserted. In this stage the precise wording of papers is often the subject of considerable debate.

During this last stage in the severance process, you may very well be preoccupied with the transition from your old work life to your new job, career, or another activity. At this point, you are probably going to be quite eager to finalize this process and move on, to collect what is due you and sign whatever seems necessary. However, it is an important part of your job to remain steadfast in insisting that nothing be signed until you have received and secured every benefit and protection possible.

Over the two to four weeks generally needed to complete the termination process, each stage unfolds in its own unique fashion, depending on the facts, circumstances, and people involved. But so very much also depends on your attitude, the approach and the proactivity you bring to your severance negotiation process. You do in fact determine to a large degree the manner in which your negotiations will play themselves out. Let's now explore how you can come to the table prepared to get what you want.

13

Preparing Your Pre-Negotiation Checklist

Chance favors the prepared mind.

—Louis Pasteur

Almost every single day I speak to prospective clients who are going through some aspect of the severance process. Some have already received notice of termination. Some have only a vague suspicion that their job is insecure. Others have received word that their employers will be going through a downsizing, merger, or restructuring, but they are unsure if they will be one of those affected. Still others have received a formal separation notice, a proposed severance agreement or buyout proposal, and additional materials from Human Resources.

Since termination of your job is just slightly more fun than having your teeth pulled without anesthetic, many people ignore the signs and signals that may have tipped them off to the end of their current position, and go into denial. But remember, preparation is key, and it is an affirmative, proactive activity that also signals to yourself that you are not going to be a passive victim. Whether you saw the end coming or not, from now on, you are going to engage in negotiations with self-esteem and confidence, determined to make the bad news, no matter how bad, into something better than it initially appears to be.

No matter what you do in life—and that includes severance package discussions—your preparation is always a key determinant of your success. By following the steps discussed in this chapter, you will better prepare yourself and your negotiator, should you choose to hire one, for what lies ahead. Note that some items may be more or less applicable to your own particular circumstances. Concentrate on those that are important to your case and future plans.

These steps will be helpful to you in at least five ways:

1. They will start you on your path toward a resolution of your present dilemma. As such, they will help you transform the nervous, anxious, angry, and self-doubting energies you may have into energies that are useful and positive.

2. They will assist you in organizing and focusing your thoughts during a chaotic time in your life.

3. They will enable you to tap into the many sources of support you'll be needing to replace those you have lost as a result of losing your job.

4. They will allow you and your attorney, should you choose to hire one, to assess your strengths, your weaknesses, your target, your objectives, and your strategy—that is, your entire game plan for dealing with your job situation.

5. They will make your mind, and your arguments, that much sharper, more focused, and more powerful at the time of your negotiation.

The steps I recommend are the following:

- Prepare for the effects of severance on your *Personal Life*.
- Prepare for a possible *Career Transition*.
- Consider your *Legal Rights*.
- Prepare your *Severance Negotiations Checklist*.

Your consideration of these matters, jotting down notes, and sharing them with your attorney, if you hire one, will prove to be extremely helpful to you in your severance package negotiation efforts. They are necessary to identify and assess your strengths, your weaknesses, your target, your strategy, and your goals in your upcoming efforts. Taking these steps will begin your thinking in the right direction, start the actual process of negotiation preparation, and enhance your chances of success in your upcoming negotiations. We will now discuss each of them in turn.

A. Prepare for the Effects of Severance on Your Personal Life

You should not ignore matters of personal concern when you prepare for severance. Some, in fact, would consider them paramount.

1. Personal Property

In your workplace environment, plainly personal items are yours; if and when you leave, you will probably have no problem retrieving them. However, if you brought with you telephone numbers and addresses of business associates, resource manuals, or books relevant to your industry when you started this job, you should presume you'll have a problem taking these materials with you when you go. If possible, take them home with you piecemeal and discreetly. If you have been given little or no severance notice, and thus no opportunity to secure these items, make a list of them for future reference and in your negotiations request they be returned.

2. Personal Information

The flip side of the coin is that personal information on your office computer or in your office files, such as tax returns or divorce papers and wills, is no one else's business. You should delete, destroy, or take this information to a secure place, as is appropriate. Either photocopy or make computer disk copies of your personal rolodex and all other personal information in your office; then delete all personal information from your computer. While the employer has an interest in protecting "trade secrets," you have an interest in protecting your legal rights as well.

3. Review of Personal Finances

I recommend that those facing employment insecurity, whether or not related to severance:

- Submit all unreimbursed expense vouchers for prompt reimbursement.
- Pay down debts.
- Move financial resources to less volatile investments to avoid risk of capital loss.
- Avoid entering into investments that restrict liquidity or provide penalty for withdrawal, such as long-term certificates of deposit, annuity contracts, certain limited partnerships.
- Attempt to accumulate a readily available cash cushion of at least six months' gross salary.
- Consider joining organizations or societies that offer members

access to insurance plans not otherwise available to individuals, or offer them at lower prices than you'd receive elsewhere.

- Prepare a list of people who may provide financial support in times of difficulty, such as parents, in-laws, and close friends.

4. Tax Withholdings

Because you may enter into a period of tight cash flow, you should consult with your accountant or tax adviser about submitting a new W-4 form to your employer listing nine personal exemptions, so as to decrease your tax withholdings and thus increase your net take-home pay. This increase will come in handy during any period you may be unemployed, to help pay expenses as well as any related legal fees. If you experience no period of unemployment or no related expenses, you can always reverse this move.

5. Pension Information

You should contact your pension plan administrator to request an immediate printout of your pension plan rules and your pension fund assets. You may also consider requesting a meeting with the plan administrator or Human Resources director to review the process for borrowing from (or against) pension monies and to get answers to any questions you may have. It is important to know as much as you can about your pension plan and its fund at this point in time. Also, since you may be asked, as part of any severance arrangement, to sign a release of claims against your employer, knowing about your pension history can allay fears that you are waiving important rights in this area.

B. Prepare for a Possible Career Transition

Like it or not, severance for many people represents what is ultimately a career transition event. You should bear in mind that this may be a great time to reevaluate your life goals and an unexpected opportunity to make a career move that you have been longing to make. Also, your age, assets, perspective, family circumstances, and, perhaps, even your health status have all likely changed over time. If you have children and they are beyond college age and settled in their own lives, it may now be possible, for the very first time in decades, to try your hand at something new or even consider returning to school.

This type of preparation requires great clarity of mind and may be especially difficult while you're experiencing the stress of losing your job. Nonetheless, it is especially important now, because your negotiation goals should take into account where you'd like to be headed in your career.

Severance may involve a significant transition—job change, retirement, or self-employment. Therefore, you should start looking at your career options once you've received any form of severance notice or just simply have concerns about your job security:

1. Give serious thought to your life goals and direction. Include your spouse in these discussions. Might it be time for a change in direction?

2. Consider career counseling. You should think of such counseling not as a source of embarrassment or humiliation, but as a very positive way of reassessing your direction.

3. Start testing the job-replacement waters. Speak to trusted friends and colleagues about your industry or profession, and what "it's like out there right now." I would suggest you also speak, on a confidential basis, to one or two headhunters.

4. Update and redesign your résumé. Consider adding new skills, new accomplishments, new directions.

5. Determine whether any lists you may have of customers, clients, client prospects, referral sources, and the like can be utilized in your future plans. This information is especially tricky from a legal standpoint. While many employers would consider it their property, depending on your circumstances, it may not be. Consider, too, that your employer may not ask you to return such information. You may very well have developed your own rights to this information while on the job or even before. If so, prepare and safely store a complete list of such resources. I recommend you copy any referral information you have and keep it at home. If your employer makes a demand for it, you should, in all cases, review your rights and obligations in this regard with an attorney experienced in employment law.

6. Ascertain whether you have rights and/or obligations with respect to ideas, inventions, improvements, and other intellectual property you have conceived of, developed, or marketed during your tenure with your employer. Because such rights and obligations are also tricky

from a legal point of view, it's a good idea to prepare a summary or synopsis of all intellectual property for review by your legal counsel.

For more on these issues, see chapter 25, "Confidentiality, Proprietary Information, and Trade Secrets," and chapter 31, "Return of the Employer's 'Property.' "

C. Consider Your Legal Rights

It is almost undeniable that knowing your legal rights cannot hurt you, so I always recommend that those in or near severance circumstances speak with an experienced employment attorney to get a good notion of where and how the law applies to them and their particular situation. At the very least, everyone in these circumstances should be prepared to locate and retain an experienced employment attorney even though they may not end up following through with representation. Many employment attorneys offer an initial consultation session for a set fee to provide general advice and an opportunity to get acquainted. Chapter 10, "Is Legal Representation Necessary for You? Perhaps Not," chapter 11, "Seven Suggestions for Working Most Productively with Your Severance Attorney," and the "Ten Tips for Attorney-Assisted Negotiation" found in chapter 14 should prove helpful if you want to look more closely at this question.

D. Prepare Your Severance Negotiations Checklist

By attending to the items on the following checklist, you'll be well equipped to embark on your severance negotiations.

1. *Prepare a comprehensive description of the terms of your employment, as you understand them.* If you have a written employment contract, you should start with that. But even if you have a written employment contract, has it been modified? Sometimes contracts are written, but the parties then work out their own sensible, day-to-day adjustments to accommodate practical needs. Make a note of these adjustments as well. They can be added as contract amendments.

If you don't have a written employment agreement, as most people don't, jot down the common understandings you and your employer have always worked under: what is your title; your compensation; your pension program, if any; your vacation; your other benefits and perks; your required dispute resolution mechanism, if any; your entitlements to termination notice or severance, if any.

2. *Assemble all other papers that may evidence, indicate, or suggest the terms of your employment.* These may include your written employment contract, a new-hiring memorandum, a "welcome aboard" letter, the original newspaper advertisement for the position, recent pay stubs, personnel policy manuals or policy statements. You can only be a better negotiator than your counterpart if you have essential data like these at your fingertips to support your arguments.

3. *Prepare a list of all forms and amounts of your current compensation.* Salary, bonus, pension or 401(k) contribution, stock options, deferred compensation—all fall under the category of compensation. You need to know when bonuses are paid and how they are determined. As for stock options, find out when they are vested, and after vesting, when they are exercisable in your case.

4. *Prepare a list of all forms of employment-related benefits you receive or are eligible to receive.* These may include health insurance, life insurance, disability insurance, educational assistance, company car, company computer, purchasing discount, club membership, tuition assistance, matching gift programs, 401(k) contribution programs, travel preferences or allowances. Consider those benefits you take advantage of, as well as any that may have been offered or promised but were never provided or utilized. You may want to continue receiving certain benefits, such as a car or insurance; other benefits, such as a training allowance, you may be considering for the first time.

5. *Assemble all evidence of satisfactory employment performance.* Positive performance appraisals and annual reviews, honors, merit awards, promotions, new titles, new responsibilities, bonuses, salary increases, and notes of appreciation are all good evidence. Your negotiating partner—indeed, your own supervisor—may not know and providing this information may strengthen your argument that you are entitled to considerable severance benefits. Don't downplay this one. Be sure to include informal expressions, such as company newsletter articles, notes of appreciation, congratulation cards, and even e-mails that are positive in tone. Different companies have different policies about granting employees access to materials in their own Human Resource files. Go to Human Resources; ask to see and copy yours, especially performance reviews. Depending on your state laws, the HR staff may be able to refuse your request. But it can't hurt to ask.

6. Determine benefits of any type scheduled to accrue or vest in the upcoming months or years. These include stock options, 401(k) programs, pension adjustments, or participation in other deferred-compensation on deferred-benefit programs. Some programs permit, for example, free lifetime health coverage for those retiring at age fifty-five or older with twenty-five or more years of service. Other programs entitle employees to greater pension benefits if they satisfy "the rule of seventy-five or eighty-five," according to which age plus years of service equals one of these numbers. I suggest you carefully analyze any such "accommodations" to age and service, which can become an important severance-negotiating goal for you.

7. Prepare a separate, detailed schedule of all matters pertaining to stock options and their equivalents. Such a schedule should include, among other things: the number of shares optioned; the date(s) offered, granted, or to be granted; all exercise dates and methods; all strike prices, and current market prices applicable to each. Stock option grants may have conditions attached regarding granting, vesting, exercising, and transfer. If any exist in your case, be sure to note them. You may have to contact your benefits department or Human Resources to obtain this information.

It is in these matters that the most maneuverability exists with respect to severance compensation negotiations. One client of mine literally became a millionaire on the stock options she received at the time of severance alone. Pay close attention to these if you hold any.

8. Check into your insurance coverage. Do you or a member of your immediate family have a medical condition, physical ailment, or other disability or impairment that may be especially affected by the loss of your present insurance? Might such a problem make it difficult for you to replace current company-provided life, disability, or health insurance as a result of a preexisting conditions clause? Is any family member facing an upcoming treatment, surgery, or series of tests that may entail significant follow-up care and expense? Special accommodations, dispensations, or arrangements may be possible to arrange if you need them and, more important, if you request them specifically.

9. *Prepare a schedule of available liquid assets.* Consider seriously how long these will cover the financial needs of your family if you are not working. Is there an upcoming financial obligation that may affect your consideration of severance package offers, such as a child-care or education expense, parent-care expense, or debts coming due? Consider, as well, the other financial resources that may be available to you in a pinch, including pension or savings plan loans, parents and siblings, and available lines of credit or home equity accounts.

10. *Prepare a written statement if you believe you may have been the victim of discrimination, harassment, or other illegal treatment in the workplace.* Be sure to include when this mistreatment began, how it took place, and the names of any others who witnessed it or who were mistreated in the same manner. One especially important point to bear in mind when considering matters of discrimination and harassment claims: your employer may not be responsible for the actions of your coworkers or even your supervisor if senior management in the company was not made aware of the discriminatory actions or did not have good reason to be aware of it. Did you or others make complaints, or were the actions so obvious as to have resulted in putting senior management on notice?

11. *Determine whether there is some aspect of your particular field that would suggest a specific request in your severance package.* For example, those in the information-management technology field often consider a retraining allowance to be a critical negotiating objective. Likewise, registered representatives in the securities industry have a special concern regarding the information to be entered on their "U-5" termination notice filed with the National Association of Security Dealers upon their release. These matters may be of critical importance to you but beyond the scope of experience of your attorney. Be sure to mention them; otherwise they risk being overlooked.

12. *Consider asking for a copy of your personnel file.* If available, your personnel file may represent a veritable treasure of information and insight. Whether you have a legal right to see or have a copy of yours will vary from state to state, and will depend, as well, on your company's policy on the subject. You should consider submitting a request, preferably a written one, to the HR department head for a copy of yours.

13. *Look into your company's policies in negotiating severance packages.* In cases of large-scale reductions in force (RIF's), the word spreads pretty quickly among employees regarding the degree of flexibility being shown in severance matters. In cases of smaller-scale terminations and individual firings, you should ask around, especially among former employees, about the company's recent attitude toward negotiation. If people aren't willing to talk to you, that's a great sign that they have negotiated successfully but have agreed to strict confidentiality about it. If people have been unsuccessful in negotiating, they'll probably talk your ear off.

14. *Consider any pending or probable strategic developments at your company that might affect your negotiations.* These would include such possible events as merger, acquisition, spinoff, public offering or refinancing (especially an initial public offering), Employee Stock Ownership Plan (ESOP), or even bankruptcy. Also included would be an upcoming retirement for the CEO or board chairperson. If your employer is a public company, it could be especially beneficial to assemble annual reports to shareholders; these would be available from the investor relations department. Has the CEO or board chairperson recently appeared on business talk shows or been quoted by analysts or the press? If so, this could make a substantial difference in your employer's concerns about litigation or adverse publicity, and its ability to complete negotiations or honor its severance obligations to you.

15. *Gain insight into the psychology, or mind-set, of your company or its key players.* What, for example, may be on the mind of your company's CEO, your company's general counsel, or outside counsel? Is the Human Resources department manager a recent hire or perhaps rumored to be on her way out of the company? As discussed in later chapters, your choice of target for negotiations is a critical choice, and these matters may affect that choice.

16. *Share any skeletons in your employment closet with your attorney.* This topic is perhaps touchiest of all, but it is also usually the most important to share with your attorney or keep in mind yourself. If, perhaps, you have been surreptitiously dating a subordinate or have overextended your expense accounts, or even if you have "borrowed" funds without authority, this information will be revealed eventually in the course of adversarial relations in the negotiating process or in litigation.

17. *Create a clear career plan, goal, or destination that you'd like to pursue in the future.* Severance negotiations should be planned and carried out first and foremost with your future in mind, not your past. Consider seriously what you would like to do most with your life. This may prove to be a good time to review your basic values and reassess your life's goals.

18. *Think about contacting an executive search firm.* Do you have a working relationship with one or more of these firms? Recruiters can be of great assistance in assessing your market value, your personal skills that are most in demand, and whether your expectations about future employment are reasonable. This may be the right time to place yourself on the "radar screen" of those in a position to help you bounce back after severance.

19. *Write down your questions about the upcoming severance negotiations.* To the greatest extent possible, you should have a clear picture of the events likely to unfold in the severance process. After you've noted any questions you have, get answers through your own research or your lawyer.

• • •

The steps discussed in this chapter are the ones most likely to start you on the road toward successful negotiation. While they are preventive and preparatory in nature, they are truly proactive, that is, positive, forceful actions to take in resolving your severance problem to your optimal benefit.

PART IV

Who,
When,
and How
to Ask

14

The Ten Stages
of Severance Negotiation

Diplomacy is the art of saying "nice doggie" until you can
find a rock.

—Will Rogers

Before we proceed to the ten stages of severance negotiation, a short
review is in order regarding what this negotiation is all about. In its
essence, severance is a negotiated transaction, in which the employee
receives various forms and degrees of transition assistance and gives, in
return, his or her voluntary resignation, a release of all claims, a waiver
of all rights, and agrees to do so in confidence.

The negotiation of severance is the haggling over the price, if you
will. How much transition assistance? On what conditions? In what
time frame? With what measures of civility and self-esteem? And for
the employer, what limitations are on the release of claims? What
repercussions will there be if the employee tells the world how good he
did in negotiation? Will the employee agree, further, not to compete
with the employer for a year or two? There are so many possible permutations and deal points on each side. On behalf of the terminated
employee, I try to do my best, be my smartest, my most prepared and
focused, to do whatever I can to achieve a good, fair, reasonable resolution. That is what this negotiation is all about.

It's also important that you keep in mind the point of chapter 3:
negotiation is a process, not an event. In this process, each of the ten
stages is interrelated, intertwined, and interdependent with all others.
Of the ten stages presented in this chapter, *eight take place before the parties sit down at the negotiating table.*

With this chapter, we finally begin to discuss in more detail the actual stages of a severance negotiation. Some of these points will be familiar to you, because I have already raised them. Here I will revisit them briefly and put them into the larger context of the entire negotiation as it unfolds. In the next parts, "What to Ask For" and "What Your Employer Will Ask of You," I will address what are probably your most urgent questions.

These ten stages are in rough chronological order, but, more important, they are in a logical order designed to help you understand both the process as it usually unfolds and how to analyze it, so that we can, together, "manipulate" it for your best interests. The ten stages are:

1. Assembly of Data
2. Choice of "Target"
3. Recognition of Respective Interests
4. Establishing Negotiating Partners
5. Assessing Negotiation Leverage
6. Focus on Legal Theory
7. Choosing End Goals
8. Developing the Negotiation Strategy
9. Engagement
10. Confirmation

Note that each of these stages is an essential aspect of the process. And each has a relatively equal priority.

1. Assembly of Data

Negotiations entail motivating another person to take some action, convincing another person that it is preferable, wise, or perhaps in his or her best interests to give you what you want or at least some of what you want. I view my negotiation of each severance matter as telling a story—one that convinces my client's employer that my perception of the most mutually fair and correct negotiating result is a true and correct one.

I begin by collecting and assembling data of all sorts that tend to underlie my perspective, and support my "story" of why my client deserves the many things he or she will be requesting. Since it provides the foundation of your entire case, it is essential that your own initial efforts be devoted to assembling all relevant and material information available in regard to your job situation.

I interview my client again and again to obtain information on his or her health, family, background, aspirations, fears, concerns, and other matters of potential relevance. I also review the events surrounding the loss of the client's job, asking, "Why do you think you were terminated?" Quite often these interview sessions take the form of an interrogation of sorts. What gradually emerges from this series of interviews is "the story," that is, what my client and I will use as the central theme of our discussions.

In your own preparations, you should record for your own review, or review by your attorney, every conceivable piece of evidence that might support:

- Your sense, belief, or understanding that you are *entitled to more*, or better, severance payments and benefits. (Such evidence may include promises made, agreements entered into, assurances given, established company practices, the treatment others have received, or any claims you may have against the employer for unpaid monies or unfulfilled promises.)
- Your view that you have been *treated wrongfully*, such as being treated in some illegal, discriminatory manner, harassed, unfairly passed over for promotions, or even chosen for termination for a reason that is wrong or illegal. (Evidence in this case may include any claims you may have for violation of laws relating to equal treatment under the law.)
- Your contention that the termination, the offered transition assistance, and the terms of the severance offer (that is, the conditions or requirements of its effectiveness) are *fundamentally unfair* for some sound reason.
- Your contention that *your needs and those of your family* for the additional payments and benefits that you will be requesting are of a natural, reasonable, and understandable nature. (Such needs may be as varied as the financial expense of kids in college, or parents in elder care, or the medical bills for physical problems of your own, especially if related to or exacerbated by your work.) These four elements of your story—*entitlement, wrongful treatment, fundamental fairness, and need*—are the four most common elements of our arguments for increased severance payments and benefits. The facts we look for are the facts that will naturally and forcefully support any one, two, three, or four of these arguments at the negotiating table.

2. Choice of Target

One of the most important choices you will make in negotiating your severance is that of your initial "target." By this term I mean that person to whom your initial request for reconsideration and negotiation will be addressed. If there is one thing most people, and their attorneys, do wrong in the severance negotiation process, it is to address their requests and concerns to the designated Human Resources representative or member of the general counsel's staff who is assigned to take care of their severance matter. That is, these employees and their attorneys make the mistake of doing as they are told.

Human Resources Is Not Your Friend. Typically, a client will tell me that a certain person, say, Mary Higgins of Human Resources, was present when he was told of his impending termination by his direct supervisor, whom we'll call Rachel Smith. At that meeting Rachel and Mary advised the client that Mary would be taking care of all details, and that he should hurry up and sign his papers and submit them to her. My client almost always tells me that Mary is the person to call to arrange a meeting.

Virtually every day, consulting firms, management-side law firms, and even insurance companies selling "employment liability insurance policies" offer seminars and workshops that will show employers, just like yours, various tactics and strategies designed to lower overall severance costs and, of greater interest to me, lower lawsuit-related risks. These seminars all teach the same simple thing: keep the employee in the hands of Human Resources staff and away from everyone else. It's no coincidence that almost every large company handles terminations in the way that I described above, with Rachel and Mary as my examples.

The reason is simple: Mary is taught, in good part by attending these seminars and workshops, how to manipulate you into signing almost anything, how to tell you that she empathizes with your predicament and will help you in the future find reemployment (and in every other way), and how to tell you the biggest untruth of the severance experience: that your severance is not negotiable. Sadly, most people thank Mary for her empathy, sign whatever she asks them to sign, and then leave quickly, quietly, and with far less severance moneys and benefits than they might otherwise negotiate. The main motivator used by the employer here is usually shame, shame, shame. But you should not take Mary's treatment personally, because as she would be the first to tell you, "This is not personal. This is business."

Identify Your Target. When first told of your impending termination, you should sit back and consider this question: who is the one person in your company, above all others, who fits the following description best?

- This individual has the authority to direct Human Resources (or any other department for that matter) to make a significant expenditure.
- This individual is at least vaguely aware of who you are or what your contributions have done for the company, or he or she may know close "friends" of yours in senior management and therefore could be inclined to "take good care" of you if asked to do so.
- This individual is a good "politician," sensitive to the appearance of being in control, and would not enjoy being brought into a dispute, a deposition, or a disaster-in-the-making.

In your thinking about this question, start at the very top of senior management and move down the chain of command only if you have a good reason to do so. On whose desk do you stop with these thoughts in mind? That is probably your best "initial target."

Changing the Dynamics of Motivation. Let's talk a bit about motivation. In the normal course of events, Human Resources and the general counsel staff get big gold stars for getting terminated employees out the door quickly, quietly, and inexpensively. Conversely, if they allow employees to move slowly, make a fuss, or negotiate for more than the absolute minimum transition assistance, they get demerits in the minds of those higher up. No one likes demerits in their file.

But imagine a scenario in which you write a letter detailing your predicament, your problem, your improper or illegal treatment, your significant needs, and the moral suasion that those needs may represent, and drop it on the desk or indeed the very lap of the CEO. The CEO then directs that same Human Resources representative, Mary, to "take care of this." She will be only too happy to do so for him or her. That is, the motivation to do well by you, although not too well, is now in place.

I know that this scenario is often the very scenario that plays out in the offices of senior management who receive letters like the one I suggest you consider sending. I know this because I represent them, too, when they are terminated. I asked one CEO whom I recently represented in severance negotiations how he came to choose me to represent him in this matter. He said, "Remember when you represented Paul Smithers when he was terminated? Well, you wrote a letter to me, and I read it, and I said to myself, "Gee, I sure would like someone to write a letter like this one on my behalf if I ever got terminated."

Motivation Is Personal. The idea of choosing an initial "target" is to get yourself, and your need to negotiate your severance, to those individuals who can direct others to do so. As noted in chapter 4, "Your Focus: Motivation and Perceived Interests," you can safely presume that senior management cares more about themselves than they do about the company, and will do whatever is necessary to protect themselves from any possible risks that they perceive. In approaching that initial more powerful target, you initiate that perception of risk in the target's mind that will provide you leverage, with which you can later negotiate to your best ability and in your best interests. Then, during the course of negotiations, keep in touch with your target and maintain that leverage as needed.

3. Recognition of Respective Interests

Negotiation of any matter requires the mutual recognition of respective interests and the addressing of those interests in a mutually satisfactory manner. Anything less than that is not a negotiation and will not lead to a resolution of the issues at hand. In a severance negotiation, the primary interests of the parties are as follows:

- The employee wants to secure those aspects of a severance package that will most enhance his or her prospects for a secure future, or at least to survive the coming employment transition. While that will be, for the vast majority, first and foremost, the most money possible, it is not limited to money. The many other considerations should all support and be conducive to future employment, future business opportunity, and future retirement. (In later chapters I go into much more detail and offer no fewer than 116 different items that may be of importance to employees.)

- The employer wants to protect the working productivity of the company. This is reflected in concerns about severance package cost, effect of precedent, confidentiality, and nondisparagement, and avoiding the costs, disruption, and possible loss entailed by conflict or litigation.
- The chosen "target" wants to ensure that the problem before him or her does not become a problem for him or her. No senior executive wishes to be seen as failing to anticipate a problem or to be the one to allow it to become a problem beyond control.

Bear in mind the message of chapter 4: negotiation is a matter of motivation, and *motivation is essentially personal.*

It is important to realize that some interests of the parties diverge, while other interests converge. For example, when the subject is the number of dollars to be paid in the compensation component of the package, the respective interests diverge; when the negative effects of litigation come into view, the respective interests converge. Likewise, it is in both you and your employer's respective interests to avoid negative publicity, which can harm career and corporate image. It is easy to see how identification of true respective interests can assist in resolution: You can support convergent interests and attempt to craft truly win-win solutions.

It is also a very powerful negotiating tool to identify, understand, and appreciate what the other side considers important, so that it can be either denied, granted, or substituted through use of your own creativity. Through all of this don't focus too much on what you want; focus, instead, on what the other side wants.

4. Establishing Negotiating Partners

While it may sound naive to many, in each of my negotiations I do my very best to establish a negotiating rapport with the employer involved, a relationship of mutual trust and respect, a sense that we are negotiating partners, not adversaries. There are two reasons for this. First, I view negotiations in a business context, in which both sides should emerge victorious. I believe that through compromise and creativity, many combinations of outcomes exist that are pleasing to both sides. Thus I see the negotiators, ideally, as negotiating partners in this search for the most mutually satisfying outcomes.

Second, I encourage the concept of negotiating partners, because, quite simply, it works! Keeping a lid on the urge to predominate keeps potential emotions and ego clashes to a minimum, which, in turn, encourages true, sound, lasting resolution. To put it another way, encouraging a sense of common purpose leads to the achievement of common goals. Try it for yourself. It does work.

It is in no one's interests (except perhaps certain lawyers without enough business) to permit the development of personal animosities, power struggles, ego clashes, or their eventual progeny, litigation battles. For those truly interested in business productivity, the concept of negotiating partners comes easily.

How do you cultivate a negotiating partner? Well, it comes about in many small ways: through courtesy, respect, and recognition of mutual concerns. I also consider very carefully who it is I may be coming into contact with, and try to figure out what I may have in common with this individual. Kids are the first thing I always think about. Once you start talking about your children, and theirs, and the funny, touching, and inspirational things kids do all the time, well, all of a sudden you have a "buddy" in the room. This goes, too, for vacation spots, where you grew up, common interests, such as fishing, sports, or books. In casual conversation, search for common experiences: I remember talking at length with one man, who happened to be on the other side of the negotiating table, about heart disease, and how my mother and his had both been stricken quite young. The conversation did a lot for our relationship; in fact, we're friends to this day.

No matter what your or your negotiating partner's gender, race, ethnic heritage, socioeconomic status, or educational level might be, you both have red blood in your veins and indubitably share a concern for kids and health, enjoyment of recreational activities, worries about the stock market, and have other experiences in common. If you use discussion of these topics to develop a rapport early on with the other side, you will probably find your negotiations will move along much more quickly and smoothly.

Ten Tips for Direct Negotiation

If you plan to be involved directly in your own severance negotiations, without using an attorney, keep in mind:

1. **This negotiation is not personal, but business.** Of course, the negotiation is important to you. Your efforts are geared toward maximizing your compensation and benefits, but this is essentially a business transaction. While you may be negotiating with people who have been your friends, and who may remain friends, this discussion is about a business transaction. To your very best abilities, separate it from your personal feelings, at least for the moment.

2. **Do your homework; first determine your severance market value.** It is essential to do whatever you can to ensure that your severance request is within a credible range. Speak to others who have gone through severance from your company or your industry. Be prepared to cite figures for the amounts given to others. For more information on this point, see chapter 19, "How Much Should You Ask For? The Emerging Severance Standards."

3. **You set the price.** In this negotiation you're the seller. Your employer wants you to agree to leave, changing the status quo, without risk or repercussion. He or she is hoping that the price you set at which you will do just that will not be too high. Simply stated, severance negotiations are discussions about that price. You are setting the price.

4. **You are negotiating on behalf of your family.** Remember you are not negotiating just for yourself. Almost no one is very good at negotiating for themselves. We are all more effective when we are negotiating for others. Bear in mind a very good part of your work efforts—including this negotiation—is for the welfare, security, and health of your family as well as yourself. Keep their pictures in your mind during your discussions. Some people say it helps them to put a family picture in their shirt or suit pocket, and to touch it unobtrusively during face-to-face discussions.

5. **Stress entitlement, wrongful treatment, fairness, and need.** These four things are very persuasive in severance discussions and form the basis for your leverage in negotiation. Be prepared to discuss your claims, your basis for them, and your willingness to address your negotiating counterpart's point of view as well.

6. **Focus all thoughts and discussions on your goals.** Your negotiation has one purpose: to achieve your goals, which you have deter-

mined beforehand. In all events steer clear of discussions about extraneous matters, whether they be related to your performance, the company's difficult finances, your emotions or your negotiating partner's, or even his or her expressions of sympathy or commiseration. Keep moving forward, continually, with your agenda: your goal list and your employer's agreement to it.

7. **Prepare a list of alternative requests.** At the same time, it is important to have prepared this second list to break stalemates or offer as a second option when your first requests are turned down. Your negotiation goals, and substitute goals, should be clear in your mind, and you should be ready to clearly express them.

8. **Be prepared for the question, "Why should you get severance?"** Unless provided for in a contract, no one is legally entitled to severance, but many people—especially you—have earned it by your contributions, need it, and should receive it. Be prepared to be questioned about this, and be confident of your answers. Reread item 5, above.

9. **Maintain an upbeat mood.** Negotiating can be stressful, even harrowing. Negotiators can try to overpower you, intimidate or even frighten you, and make you feel guilty. Maintain an upbeat, positive, pleasant demeanor, posture, and tone no matter how you feel inside. Frowns, growls, yelling, and sarcasm will get you nowhere.

10. **At conclusion, insist upon written confirmation.** As you arrive at points of agreement, write them down. Don't rely on your memory or the memory of your employer. At the conclusion of each session, ask that all points of agreement be confirmed. Signatures are not necessary; even two copies of the same list on a scribble pad are preferable to memory.

5. Assessing Negotiation Leverage

The concept of leverage calls to mind the big stick, properly positioned, which is used to move the big weight. Leverage in negotiation is the relative strength of position, initially provided by the circumstances, properly observed, carefully developed, and skillfully manipulated. The good negotiator is one who makes maximum use of available leverage, and who creates the perception of greater leverage than exists in reality. Perception does, indeed, count.

Leverage is found in the strength of arguments for severance you bring to the attention of your employer. The four legal bases of argument, and the additional, moral basis, set forth in the next few paragraphs, are your most potent sources of leverage.

The risk of a claim depends on its quality and power, and the arguments made to support it. Remember that the arguments will be based on five fundamental notions: entitlement, wrongful treatment, violation of statute, unfairness, and need.

6. Focus on Legal Theory

As law students learn the ways of the profession, they are trained to think in terms of legal theory. This is so because the legal system is built of legal theories, to which facts of particular cases are applied. Sometimes alternative theories, and even opposing theories, are made applicable to a single set of circumstances. Your own unique situation will help you determine which "rule" is more applicable to you.

The basic reason we negotiate is to clarify issues and reach understandings, and we create a written agreement to confirm those understandings. When a good lawyer negotiates, and drafts a proposed settlement agreement, he or she keeps legal theories in mind and "molds" the unique points of mutual understanding around the infrastructure of legal theory.

This is all done to reach understandings of benefit to the client, and to confirm those understandings in such a way as to ensure enforceability in case the employer later breaks his or her word, experiences changed circumstances, or has a good-faith disagreement with the client. While less essential for the client, attorneys utilize legal theory to support claims and to defend against those claims raised by their employers.

Each of the four elements of argument to support claims in severance negotiation, to enhance the perception of risk to management should resolution not take place, correspond with a certain element of the law:

- Arguments of *entitlement* are based in legal concepts of "contract" and thus lend themselves quite readily to a lawyer's understanding of risk and basis in lawsuit.
- Arguments of *wrongful treatment* are based in either what is termed "tort law" or the law of damages of one person by another, either negligently or intentionally. Such arguments may also be based in the violation of one of the many federal, state, and local laws that

regulate conduct in the workplace, including those prohibiting the many forms of illegal discrimination.

- Arguments of *fundamental unfairness* are, based in the legal concept of "equity," a form of law that gives judges the authority to "do justice" even when no other basis in law exists.
- Additionally, arguments of *need* are essentially arguments without legal basis but are based in moral values, which are persuasive to some and unpersuasive to others. Even those not persuaded by moral arguments, though, are often reluctant to be seen so in public, because of their acute understanding of what that makes others think of them.

7. Choosing End Goals

Your choice of goals for your severance negotiation is more important than any other decision you will make. You should make this choice only after careful deliberations and consideration, but *before* entering into active severance negotiations. *Goals should set the direction of your efforts, not vice versa.* All of your efforts should be goal-driven.

In the next part, "What to Ask For," I lay out for you the five first, essential requests, the ten next-most-valuable requests, and finally, 101 additional possible requests. While you may have others on your mind, and each time I represent a client I learn one or two more, chances are your concerns are somewhere to be found on one of those three lists. While your goal list should include, perhaps, four, five, six, or maybe seven items of concern and value for you, you should be aware of alternatives that may cushion the disappointment of losing out on one or more of your primary requests. You should always be very clear as to your goals. Have your goal list available always, at the tip of your tongue. For some, the removal of a "noncomplete" restriction may be primary, for others greater severance monies, and for still others the agreement that enables the employee to continue to work as a consultant. Your future is your only true guide. When you know what you want, and you are clear, focused, and determined to get what you want, there is an almost magical way in which negotiators follow the thoughts, arguments, and goals of the most focused, determined, prepared negotiating partner. It is what some refer to as "the force of will itself." May this force be with you. If you are prepared, there is a much higher likelihood that it will.

8. Developing the Negotiating Strategy

My dictionary defines "strategy" as the "skillful management in getting the better of an adversary or attaining an end." It is the planned deployment of your available resources with a goal in mind. Strategy in severance negotiations comprises: deciding upon your end goals; choosing the best "target"; analyzing those claims you may have, and the arguments you may have in support of those claims; and presenting those claims and arguments in a way that will produce the motivation necessary to get you the goals you desire from your chosen "target."

The general strategy I recommend—the one that is usually successful for my clients—is the following:

- Send your target a letter outlining the unacceptability of the termination offer you have received, the reasons for its unacceptability, and the general elements of an acceptable resolution. In that letter raise all the elements of leverage—entitlement, wrongful treatment, unfairness, and need—that are applicable to your situation. Also stress your target's personal involvement in these circumstances if there is a factual basis for it (for example, "you promised me," or "your assistance in resolving this matter appears necessary").

- Suggest a face-to-face meeting with your employer to discuss a resolution of the differences, Note your preference for a reasonable and nonadversarial resolution and departure. Don't be either surprised or disappointed if your target doesn't attend but sends a surrogate to your meeting. Your target is there in effect, and you should keep him apprised of the status of your case throughout the negotiation process.

- At your meeting, outline your arguments and elements of leverage once again, and present your list of goals. Have with you a written list of your goals, to be given to your negotiating partner at the end of the meeting, so that he or she cannot forget or misunderstand any one or more of the goals you have requested. Follow up with a written confirmation of each item agreed to, and, if necessary, make a request for another meeting to resolve all unresolved points.

This simple strategy can be modified for your particular circumstances, and with your unique claims and arguments in mind. It is the strategy that has worked most of the time, for most of my clients, in obtaining most of the things they have requested. It is quite simple in its approach but effective in its results. Feel free to try it and to modify it as necessary.

Incidentally, I always prefer face-to-face negotiating whenever it can be arranged, even if I have to travel to faraway places to do so. I find that employers (like most of us) find it hardest to say no to someone who is sitting in front of them, less difficult to say no over the telephone, and easiest to say no in a letter.

Ten Tips for Attorney-Assisted Negotiation

If you choose to use an attorney to represent you or assist you in your severance negotiations, you should use such help wisely. Talk with your attorney until you have accomplished each of the following to your satisfaction.

1. **Your negotiation goals must be firmly established in your mind.** You should be able to recite these goals without notes in a series of simple, clear sentences. You also must be absolutely certain of your "bottom line," that is, your minimally acceptable goals. Always bear in mind that your negotiating session would not be taking place if your employer's representative did not want to work out a resolution with you. You and your attorney must be sure of your goals between yourselves if you are to communicate them to your employer in your negotiations.

2. **Your overall negotiation strategy should be clear in your mind.** Are you asking for "X" and prepared to take "$1/2$ X"? Are you prepared to take less now in exchange for more later? Is one aspect of your package absolutely sacred or perhaps nothing more than a point you'd give up without regret? It's often a good idea to prepare a separate list of items you believe are available to you, but which you are willing to sacrifice. Keep this list alongside the one containing key items you really want.

3. **Your attorney should set the ground rules for the severance before it begins.** These ground rules should be hammered out with the opposing counsel or other employer's representative and, preferably, put in writing. They include:

- the overall *purpose of the meeting* (that is, what you and your attorney hope will be achieved by its conclusion)
- the *specific topics* to be discussed
- whether the *principals (clients) will negotiate directly*
- the assurance that the *principals will not be cross-examined* by the attorneys
- *whether notes or a recording will be kept*
- alternatively, whether what is said is to be *"off the record"*
- whether there exist *any time constraints or other limitations* on the meeting
- whether the parties in the room are *authorized to make agreements*

You should be familiar with each and every one of the ground rules.

4. **At the meeting, the attorney is "in charge."** You are the client and, as such, are ultimately the one who must approve all strategy, goals, and steps you and your attorney will take. But in negotiation, unless you and your attorney have agreed to make an exception, you must accept your attorney's authority. Never, ever disagree openly with your attorney during a negotiating session. If necessary, ask that you be permitted a moment alone with your attorney to review and discuss a few items. Any question or dispute you have with how the process is unfolding you should share privately with your attorney.

5. **Inform your attorney of any topic you do not want raised at your negotiation session or fear the other side will bring up.** It doesn't matter how sensitive the topic might be. Indeed, the more sensitive the topic, the more important it is that your attorney be aware of your concern.

6. **Avoid negative emotions.** This is essentially a business transaction. Therefore, you should not show expressions of anger, disappointment, betrayal, and any other negative emotions, if at all possible, unless truly appropriate and/or planned by you and your attorney.

7. **Don't be in a hurry to make compromises and concessions.** Once made, compromises and concessions are next to impossible to withdraw. If you believe strongly that an immediate show of good faith is necessary, and it requires that you express a willingness to compromise, first count slowly to ten, then express your willingness to compromise, but do not agree to the compromise itself. If possible, ask the other side to suggest the necessary compromise. Try not to take the

step of actual compromise unless your strategy, goals, and attorney all point in this direction.

8. **At the meeting, you can request to speak with your attorney privately.** Such a request is appropriate if you have a question about what is happening, or about something that just happened or is not happening, or if things don't seem to be going your way.

9. **Never agree to anything unless your "insides" are comfortable with the decision.**

10. **Never agree to anything unless your attorney agrees with the decision.**

By following these ten steps, you're preparing yourself for a more focused, effective, productive negotiating session in which you and your attorney are working together to achieve your success.

9. Engagement

As I mentioned before, entering into active negotiations of any kind is not as formalistic or ritualistic a process as some books on the subject would have you believe. I have negotiated contracts, disputes, and settlements of all kinds to a successful conclusion in my firm's office, in my "negotiating partner's" office, on a crosstown bus (while standing), over the telephone, over dinner, through letters, and once, believe it or not, in a swimming pool.

The place, time, and style of negotiations are not, to my mind, nearly as important as is the overall sense that (1) I understand the critical issues, (2) I am prepared to the point of comfort in discussing those issues, and (3) I am reasonably aware of my (or my client's) bottom line, that point beyond which I cannot cede the essential points of discussion. If, for example, the first offer of severance regarding salary continuation is initially expected to be at least $50,000, but the negotiating partner instead suggests no more than $5,000, I make it clear to this negotiating partner that we are entering negotiating territory from which a resolution through compromise is not to be reasonably expected. And I cannot be clear with the other side unless I am, first, clear with myself.

Start high? Move slowly lower? Prepare to walk if you don't get your way? I am a very strong proponent of a style of negotiating that is commonly referred to as "principled" negotiating. Put simply, principled negotiating addresses concerns, and the rationales for those concerns, rather than numbers.

As an example, if my client will need no less than $35,000 to move back to her former residence, from which she moved to take this job just three months ago, at the request of this same employer who is now downsizing her, and she is losing her job through no fault of her own, then I cannot see why she should be offered or accept any less. If, for reasons I don't understand and which cannot be explained to me with some sort of rationale, the company refuses to grant this concession, I do not give up but see if other funds, whatever they may be called, are available for the purpose. If there aren't any, I look for some item of negotiating value to my client that I may substitute in my negotiations with the employer. I may even suggest to my negotiating counterpart that for resolution to take place, I need him or her to give some reasonable credence to my client's legitimate concerns, and to see how they can be addressed. This posture works more often than not. The point is: in asking for items, address concerns, for they are far less contentious than numbers, make negotiation a mutual addressing of concerns, and are far more productive in the long run. This is one more reason to focus on your negotiating partner's motivation and perceived interests throughout negotiations, as discussed in chapter 4.

Your best strategy for severance negotiation is to be prepared with: your requests, the rationales for your requests, the claims and arguments to back up those requests, your alternative requests (should your initial ones be denied), and a good idea of the goals of your negotiating counterpart and how you may be able to satisfy them. Never think you will overcome your negotiating counterpart completely and walk away happy with all you wanted; you won't. Be prepared to give as well as receive.

Some believe that there are tricks to negotiating and suggest specific tactics designed to help you prevail. I generally believe that concentrating on these methods is counterproductive. Instead, having a good sense of the leverage available to you at each and every step, as well as continually reviewing the eight points raised earlier in this chapter, to the point of comfort, confidence, and clarity in your own mind, is the best way to increase your chances for success.

Always accept success and postpone failure. By that I mean you should accept those points on which you have been successful, and agree to reconsider those on which you have not prevailed—*yet*. I have found that while preparation may be number one in negotiation, perseverance is surely a close second.

10. Confirmation

A close third in importance, after preparation and perseverance, is confirmation. You must make a prompt and accurate confirmation of the points of resolution achieved in severance negotiation. I have learned time and time again that what has been so laboriously achieved is all for naught if not promptly confirmed in content and tone for later review and reference. Memories fade; circumstances change; goodwill can evaporate. Don't let that happen to you.

In fact, the absence of prompt confirmation by my negotiating partners has many times resulted in my regaining points I had lost in the course of negotiations. Therefore, throughout your own negotiations, it is your job to do the following:

- Take notes of each request made and the response given.
- Jot down each point about which your negotiating partner says, "I'll have to get back to you on that."
- Make sure each item on your agenda is raised during negotiations.
- Suggest your employer reconsider points not agreed to.
- If a stalemate occurs on a particular point, agree to come back to it later, and proceed to the next one.
- Toward the conclusion of the meeting, review your notes with your negotiating partner, and start to discuss the details of the concepts agreed upon.
- At the end of the meeting, either prepare a memo of points agreed upon, for both sides to initial, or suggest that you will confirm for all parties in a memo the progress to date.
- If points remain open, make a list of them as well, and set a time for the next resolution meeting or telephone conference to address them.
- Immediately after the meeting, prepare your confirmation memo and send it, for your counterpart to initial and return.
- If you and your employer have reached a verbal agreement on all possible points, volunteer to prepare the first draft of the formal agreement to be signed, even if it's just a letter or memo. If you are the first to generate a draft, you will have the first opportunity to fill in the crucial details.

• • •

As we have seen, severance negotiation is a process, not an event. Principled negotiation—the mutual recognition of respective interests and concerns—is the negotiation method best suited to success in this process, and to the strategy I have set out here. I have analyzed for you the ten stages in that process, based on hundreds of cases I have successfully negotiated, and some I have unsuccessfully negotiated as well. Each is a complete stage unto itself but is also interrelated with every other stage. Of the ten stages in the severance negotiation process, eight are matters of preparation. Remember that careful, thorough, focused, thoughtful preparation—all directed by your goals—is key to your success. Perseverance is second only to preparation in importance, and prompt, clear confirmation ranks a close third. These are the basic concepts I keep in mind throughout any severance discussion, and you should do the same.

PART V

What
to Ask
For

15

How Much Can You *Really* Negotiate?

A bashful beggar has an empty purse.
—Hungarian proverb

Perhaps the question most commonly asked of me in preparation for severance negotiations is, "How much can I *really* negotiate?" My prospective clients almost always put special emphasis on the word "really," and their lips are tightened, giving the impression that they are skeptical that there is much negotiability at all, especially in this era of daily announcements about corporate downsizings and restructurings.

This question is in fact right on target, because the very first and most crucial issue to resolve in any negotiation is just that—the scope of the negotiation itself. One must ascertain precisely what limits there are on the topics to be discussed and on the reasonable requests that can be made regarding these.

My answer to this question is always a two-part one: there are almost always *more topics open to discussion in severance negotiations than you'd think*, and there's almost always *more room to negotiate on each topic than you'd expect*. This is the most important message of this book: do not needlessly limit yourself in your severance negotiations.

> Employees at almost every level needlessly limit themselves in their sever-
> ance negotiations regarding both the scope of discussions with and the
> extent of their requests to employers. The degree of "negotiability" in
> these areas is getting greater and greater each year.

Often, though, before I get into discussions with clients about the limits of severance negotiations, another question is frequently posed to me: "What do you think the chances are that I could keep my job?" Since this is a more pressing question, and its answer, at least for some, may affect their view of later negotiations, I will address it first.

A. What Are the Chances I Can Keep My Job? (or Preventing Severance)

The answer to this question depends upon the unique facts and circumstances of each employee's situation, as well as the negotiating skills of the employee or his or her attorney. However, with only a very few exceptions, my clients and I have been unable to reverse a termination decision once made by those in authority. In very few cases we have been successful in reversing decisions or obtaining in-house transfer.

The few exceptions I have been involved in each entailed the manipulation of superiors in what is, essentially, the hardball game of corporate politics. Those with access to upper management or board members have the best chance of being able to undo a termination decision.

In my experience, *the chance of reversing a termination decision is largely dependent on the context in which it arises.* As discussed in chapter 6, context in severance is often a predictor of negotiations. If severance initially arises from claims by an employee that his or her employer (or other employees) engaged in some form of misconduct (illegal discrimination, harassment, or retaliation for reporting these things), the chance of keeping one's job is greatest. Where severance involves large groups (downsizing, restructuring, outsourcing, and so on), the opportunity for reversal of decision is diminished but still there. Where the severance starts with a personality clash, company politics, or the like, the chance of reversal is almost nonexistent.

If you are considering attempting to reverse a termination forced upon you, no matter what the particulars are, *the earlier you attempt reversal the better.* While decisions are fresh, they are easier to change.

B. The Scope of Discussions

There are perhaps two dozen or so topics that commonly come up in severance negotiations, but there are innumerable topics that you can bring up to address your own particular needs. Almost every time I represent a new client, I find some new item of importance to that client to consider in our requests. Over the years I've kept a list of these issues, which is my own true list of "severance secrets," and they can be found in chapter 18, "Customize Your Requests: The 101 True 'Severance Secrets.' "

But there's no substitute for creativity, and your own circumstances should dictate what you ask for in your severance negotiations. To help you brainstorm on this point, here are the categories of requests I use in analyzing the needs of each of my own clients.

1. "Reward Alternatives"

It's a given that most people think almost exclusively of money as the number one request to be raised. To be sure, money is at the heart of all severance negotiations. But money is not the only matter to discuss; a broader notion of potential severance awards is necessary. I call this approach "reward alternatives." Because many aspects of daily existence other than money make life more enjoyable, I often raise them in severance negotiations. Examples include:

- Will the employee be permitted to retain samples of his work in a portfolio?
- Will the employer commit to an agreed text of a "departure statement," public announcement, and positive reference to provide a positive "spin" on the separation?
- Will outplacement or educational assistance be provided?
- Can the employee retain her computer, or retain her car until lease expires?
- If the employee contemplates opening his own business, will the employer agree to purchase the new business's goods or services?
- Will the company provide additional pension benefits?

Your own list of reward alternatives, each of which is appropriate and advantageous in your case, is limited only by your own circumstances and creativity.

Asking your employer to substitute reward alternatives for "King Cash" can help you foster successful negotiations, as well. You can use them quite effectively to break a stalemate in discussion of requests your employer considers too expensive. While reward alternatives are often of great value to the employee, they may cost the employer little, if anything. And though they may not directly help you pay the bills, they can sometimes prove more valuable than money itself.

2. "Risk Limiters"

In assessing almost every business transaction, successful business-people look not only at the potential rewards of the deal but at the potential risks, or "downside," as well. In personal affairs, such as employment issues, the very same business executives tend to all but ignore the importance of risk identification, assessment, and allocation. In all of my executive employment-related negotiations, whether on issues of employment, compensation, or severance, I stress to my clients that the elimination (or at least minimization) of risk in their employment relations is at least as important or even more important than the aggregation of reward itself.

While we all recognize, intuitively, that employment relations entail a multitude of risks, identification of these risks may seem difficult. To identify employment "risks," I use a simple yet powerful tool: I prepare a list of employment "rewards," with employment itself at the top, and then place the phrase "loss of" before each item on the list.

When engaged in severance negotiations, I frequently request risk limiters when attempting to gain additional compensation and "reward alternatives" appear to have been exhausted. Examples of risk limiters I have successfully negotiated in these circumstances include the following:

- In the event of the employee's death before all severance payments have been paid, the remaining payments will be made to the employee's estate (risk: loss of payments that will safeguard your family).
- The employer's severance obligations are guaranteed by a parent company, or a personal guarantee is provided by the employer's owner(s) (risk: loss of payment).
- The employer releases the employee from all claims and obligations (risk: loss of resolution, that is, continuation of conflict).
- Any restrictions on future freedoms are deleted, such as restrictive covenants, covenants not to compete, or agreements not to solicit other employees (risk: loss of freedom to move on).
- The employer promises not to disparage the employee (risk: loss of good name and reputation).

None of these is a request for money, but each is a request for a very valuable thing, the loss of which could be devastating to you, depending on your future plans.

C. The Depth of Requests

After I'm asked, "What should I ask for?" the next question posed to me is almost always, "How much [of that thing] can I ask for?" My usual answer is quite simply, "No doubt, probably more than you're comfortable asking for." In negotiating severance, most people tend to *underestimate* their own negotiating strength. And even among those who accurately assess their own leverage, most tend to *underplay* their negotiating hand. To protect yourself, and to provide for your loved ones, it's necessary to both assess and apply the leverage that's available to you. Let's explore how.

1. Assessing Leverage
The primary point for you to keep in mind here is that the assessment of your available leverage is in fact an art, perhaps intuitive more than anything else, and must take into account every pertinent fact available to you.

Ask yourself, "What is my employer sensitive to?" All bosses have their Achilles' heels, their sensitive points, their concerns for how their own superiors may react to any errors they've made. As discussed in chapter 4, negotiation is a matter of motivation, and motivation is personal. Assessing your leverage in severance negotiation is a process of imagining yourself in your employer's shoes and determining how "far" you can push your employer to give you what you want.

Assessing leverage is using your intuition, your instincts, as well as all of the smarts you can muster to imagine what will motivate and how far that motivation will take you. Since you know the company and the various members of senior management best, along with the mood and morale of the staff, and perhaps the insecurities, the idiosyncrasies, and the interpersonal dynamics of your employer, it is your judgment that you'll have to rely on in the end. Just don't underestimate your potential leverage. Remember, if the other side is willing to give some concession, it's willing to give.

I find the art of assessing leverage to be perhaps the most difficult, fun, amorphous, and interesting aspect of negotiation. It is not done once, but continually, at each step you take, as you study and consider each reaction, until all of your negotiation efforts are complete.

2. Applying Leverage

Application of leverage, on the other hand, is more focused; it is essentially a choice of who is to be the best target for your efforts, and what sort of presentation that individual will find most appealing. Who is both actually authorized and potentially motivated to provide the kinds and amount of transition assistance you and your family will need? What arguments will be most convincing? How should you present a request—in person, by letter, or perhaps both? How should you respond to initial rejection? Questions of applying leverage are here brought into play and will be reviewed in depth in upcoming chapters.

16

The Five First Essential Requests

> I know the answer! The answer lies within the heart of
> mankind! The answer is twelve? I think I'm in the wrong
> building.
>
> —Charlie Brown
> (*Peanuts* character)

Without a doubt, almost every client who comes to me for assistance
in negotiating severance seeks help, first, with this very simple question:
"What should I ask for?" While each person's facts, circumstances,
needs, and leverage are unique, there are five essential items that each
and every person *must* consider asking for, as far as I am concerned.
Even if one or more of these essential five don't apply to your present
circumstances, you should think of them as the "must-ask's" of severance
negotiating, and keep them in mind as you go through this experience.

1. King Cash
This is the one item, and the only item, that I don't need to suggest to
anyone considering their buyout or severance offer. It's always there,
in the forefront. In fact, for many people, this is the *only thing* that they
are thinking about. But even for those who seek nothing but increased
severance moneys, there's more here than meets the eye.

In most cases, severance moneys are provided in the form of continuing salary payments. That is, you continue to receive paychecks, just as
you do now, for some set period of time, such as four months or
twenty-three weeks, after which payments will cease. Those employers
offering what are commonly called buyout packages more commonly
provide one single lump-sum payment. Each of these severance payment schemes has its own advantages and disadvantages.

Continued salary payments carry with them the possibility that, for some reason or another, the payments will stop prematurely. I call this payment risk. One client of mine lost his very considerable severance—two years of continued salary—when his former company declared bankruptcy. Another client of mine had her continued salary payments abruptly stop after her company decided that she had breached her obligation to them (namely, not to divulge to anyone the amount of her severance package). Another disadvantage of continued salary payments as the form of severance is that, at least in some states, such payments may disqualify you for unemployment insurance benefits while you receive them.

Some companies also include a provision in severance agreements that stops your continuing salary payments when you find another job or stop looking for one. (This concept is referred to as "mitigation of severance" and is discussed in greater detail in chapter 29.) This represents a kind of built-in payment risk. Despite its disadvantages, though, taking severance in the form of continuing salary payment is attractive to some terminated employees, for it gives them a sense of security to be receiving an ongoing source of support while they are out there seeking a new position.

On the other hand, money in the pocket is worth a lot. Lump-sum payment of buyout or severance moneys is quite attractive to many. One significant risk entailed in this form of severance receipt, though, is that of lumped taxation. That is, lump-sum payment of severance moneys may put you in a higher tax bracket one year and thus result in a lower overall benefit to you. For this reason, when lump-sum payment is offered to one of my clients, especially within the last few months of a calendar year, I often ask that a significant part (perhaps one-half) be paid shortly *before December 31*, and the remainder (in this example, the other one-half) be paid shortly *after January 1*.

As to the amount of salary payments or lump-sum payments you should ask for, see chapter 19, "How Much Should You Ask For? The Emerging Severance Standards." Remember that severance can be customized to your particular situation, so don't be afraid to ask for any combination of salary continuation and lump-sum payment that would suit you best.

2. Continued "Crucial" Employee Benefits

The second of the five essential severance requests is the continuation of employment benefits, especially those that are of special value to you and your family. This request is granted most often in cases of continued salary payments and usually continues for the same period of time as future salary payments. It is very rare that employee benefits are continued for terminated employees who receive a lump-sum payment of severance moneys. In fact, don't be surprised if your employer makes that very point in its severance proposal: you may either take a lump-sum payment of moneys or take continued salary payments along with continuation of benefits for the same period, but you can't take a lump-sum payment and continue to receive benefits. Human Resources will often put it to you this way: "Either you're on the books, or you're off the books."

The employment-related benefits most commonly considered by my clients to be crucial benefits are health insurance coverage, as well as life and disability insurance coverages. As to health insurance coverage, the federal COBRA law (for Consolidated Omnibus Budget Reconciliation Act of 1985) provides in general terms that companies employing fifty or more employees must permit their departing employees to continue on with whatever employer-provided health insurance benefits they provide to others for a period of eighteen months after termination. The one condition is that the terminated employee must pay the full premium costs, plus an additional 2 percent as an administrative fee.

Bear in mind that this is only what the law *requires*. Feel free to request adaptations of the COBRA-mandated rights should they be more favorable to you, such as having your employer pick up the tab for the premiums; the law does not require that you pay if the employer is willing to do so. Likewise, so long as the insurer consents, there's nothing to stop your employer from permitting you to stay on its health program for a period longer than eighteen months or from continuing to pay for your health insurance or health costs.

While there's no federal law (or state law, to my knowledge) that applies in the same way to life insurance coverage or disability insurance coverage, there's nothing stopping your employer from requesting the insurer's consent to keep you on the program or from agreeing to pay for substitute coverage for you on an individual coverage policy. This may be of special importance to you if you have one or more serious, preexisting conditions that can make it difficult for you to obtain insurance coverage elsewhere.

For some, more uncommon employer-provided benefits are the most important. One that comes to mind is continued tuition assistance for employees and their families, especially for those with kids either in or about to enter college. Another is continued matching of the employee's charitable contributions. This last one was especially important to one of my clients whose employment was terminated after only two years through a considerable five-year commitment he had made to the alumni fund-raising campaign of his business school. Without the match he had anticipated, he was to be responsible for a far larger outlay of money than he'd anticipated. You can see from these examples how certain benefits can be customized to suit other's needs. Use that knowledge to get the best settlement for yourself.

3. Pro Rata Bonus

Perhaps the most dramatic shift in the field of employee compensation throughout the 1980s and 1990s has been the simultaneous rise in both incidence and significance of pay-for-performance plans. More and more employees at a wider range of corporate (and even not-for-profit) enterprises are seeing their overall compensation become dependent upon their own job success, the success of their departments or divisions, and even of their companies. A larger proportion of overall income is increasingly represented by bonus or incentive compensation. In some industries, it has become the rule that base salaries are considered only a small proportion of anticipated overall compensation.

This has happened for good reasons. Incentive compensation provides just that: incentive, or motivation, for employees to work harder, longer, smarter, and leaner. Many studies also suggest that incentive compensation programs, if designed correctly, foster a team mentality and increase positive, cooperative efforts throughout a company or organization. Keeping base salaries lower also permits employers to keep a lid on fixed overhead, and results, therefore, in increased ability to weather periodic hard times. But bonus programs, as compared to fixed salaries with annual percentage increases, are also known to result in a greater incidence of employee-employer disputes.

What do you do if a good part of the annual income you anticipated this year was to be in the form of bonus, you were employed for, say, ten of the twelve months of the company's bonus year, and you were just let go? Quite simply, you do what so many others merely think about, but few actually do: you request that, as part of your severance package, you be given ten-twelfths of your anticipated bonus amount. That is, you suggest that this money be paid to you on a pro rata basis in accordance with the time you gave to your employer this present bonus year.

In doing so, you can safely anticipate receiving the stock response that "we only give a bonus to those who are employed on the official bonus day." Or perhaps you will hear this common reply: "That is not our policy, and we are not prepared to set precedent." Be ready, though, with one or more of the available responses that are entirely rational, reasonable, and very possibly sufficient to get you what you want:

- If your termination has not been brought about by either your own misconduct or poor performance, your argument is simple: "Fair is fair." You were attracted to the position because of its bonus potential, you remained for that reason, and neither you nor your family has done anything to be punished by not receiving ten-twelfths of the bonus.
- Tell your employer that you will maintain confidentiality about this matter, so there should be no reason to fear setting a precedent. Suggest, as well, that you are aware that precedent in this regard has already been set, which, in all probability, it has—numerous times.
- Remind your negotiating partner that nowhere is it written that you are obliged to grant your employer a release of all liabilities, which include your bonus; nor is it your own general policy to do so without some good reason.
- Stress the frequency with which precedents are set. You might tell your employer: "Life is nothing but a string of new precedents. Where good reason exists, precedent is nothing more than the first time a good thing was done." Or: "By letting me go without any misconduct or poor performance on my part, you have already set a precedent."

And there are many other good, rational, and reasonable responses as well. Don't be afraid to be bold, for boldness is often what carries the day. Using just the rationales noted above, I have even been successful in my requests that pro rata bonuses be paid *prospectively*, that is, not just until the day of termination but for the future as well—through the projected period of salary continuation. You can do the same.

4. Pension Accommodations
Quite often I hear a client express something like the following: "I've just been terminated, but I'm only eight months away from my fifty-fifth birthday, when my entitlement to lifetime, company-paid medical cov-

erage would have kicked in. Is there some way I could get this?" A second example would be this: "I've just received my termination notice, effective next month. With just fourteen more months of service, I would have been entitled to the more advantageous treatment under the "rule of seventy" in our pension program. Is there something we could do here?" Requests such as these I call pension accommodations, even if they don't actually involve pensions. Those relating solely to retirement status are often called "bridge to retirement" requests. Regardless of name, they are invariably of great importance and value.

These examples and other, similar requests—for, say, an upward calculation in your number of years on the job, in the calculation of your age, or perhaps in your average salary level over the past five years—can very substantially increase your interests in any number of your employer's plans, including the retirement, deferred compensation, pension, health, 401(k) contribution, or other long-term compensation plan.

Asking for a pension accommodation might provide you and your family with additional financial benefits over years, or even decades, to an extent greater than any other severance-related request. Be aware also that these requests are met in many more instances than you might imagine. Sometimes the employer is offering severance in the form of continuing salary payments for four months, but the employee needs, say, eight more months of employment to qualify for a big step up in pension calculations. The employer may agree to a request that the four additional months of salary payments be provided on a half-time basis, so that the payments will be stretched over the needed eight-month period. A simple accommodation like this could result in tens of thousands, or even hundreds of thousands, of dollars of additional benefit to you and your family.

5. Departure Statement
Because I firmly believe that your future is more important than your past, and that you never know what interesting experience life will provide you, I always strongly encourage my clients to request, as part of their severance or buyout package, a "departure statement" that provides the most positive explanation possible for their departure from the employer. This is similar to what many describe as a reference letter but differs in some important ways. The appendix provides a sample text of a departure statement.

The purpose of the departure statement is to lay the groundwork for your answering, without hesitation or trepidation, the following question raised by a prospective employer: "Why did you leave XYZ company, especially after only eight months on the job?" Or, perhaps, "after thirty-one years of faithful service?" Having a departure statement in your pocket not only will allow you to answer that question without fear of having it disputed by your former employer, but will also permit you to immediately back up your story. Even if you have been assured over and over by a trusted coworker, supervisor, or even your company's CEO that you'll get nothing but the best of references, you must bear in mind that these employees, too, are subject to unanticipated termination. Also, their feelings, perspective, and inclination to be helpful to you could change in the future, for any number of unanticipated circumstances.

In the first draft of your departure statement, set forth in positive fashion precisely how you and your departure would best be described. This draft should be handwritten and submitted as a proposal for review by your employer. It should, if possible, be signed by the company's CEO or some other officer near the very top of management. Ideally, the departure statement will become part of your severance agreement, as an exhibit or attachment. The company should agree to give you the departure statement upon leaving, and provide it to all who make inquiry about your tenure at and departure from the company.

The departure statement should address your positive contributions, and the reason for your departure, if not a problem. If the reason for your departure is a problem, the statement should cite other circumstances that are helpful to you, such as the following:

- Martha's departure from our company came about in the midst of a company-wide reorganization that did not, unfortunately, leave a position available that would take sufficient advantage of her considerable skills and initiative.
- Julius's departure from our company was brought about by a redefinition of the company's corporate vision by its board, which differed in substantive ways from his own very valuable ideas regarding where the company should be headed.
- Len's extraordinary efforts to reorganize and reenergize his division and its operations have been so successful that they have

enabled our company to streamline its management structure beyond our expectations.

Because in every industry everyone seemingly knows everyone else, and because your internal reputation within your company may be as important to your future as your ability to perform well during interviews, I sometimes also ask for an internal departure statement or announcement to be distributed to all company personnel regarding my client's departure. Your reasons for leaving the company may travel farther and faster than you think. Indeed, in negotiating CEO severance, in addition to departure statements, I always insist upon approving the timing and text of internal announcements and press releases.

These days, most companies maintain a strict policy against providing references or letters of recommendation, out of their fear that someone may sue them for either not being positive enough (usually the ex-employee), or being too positive by failing to cite misconduct (usually future employers). Instead, companies will usually provide only confirmation of your employment, dates of your employment tenure, your title(s) held, and, sometimes, your salary range. The request for a departure statement is intended to circumvent that reluctance, by not using the term "reference letter," by providing a more easily accepted rationale, by having legal counsel on both sides give their blessings to the document before it is issued, and by issuing the document at a time of mutual release of liabilities. The value of having in your pocket a firm, positive, supportive departure statement should not be underestimated. My clients often later report to me that they appreciated this aspect of their negotiated severance arrangements far more than they'd expected.

As you approach severance negotiations, it is essential that you consider these five severance requests. Try to predict, to the very best of your ability, the circumstances and events that may come upon you in future weeks and future years, and how these requests may help prepare you for them. You will only have this one chance to secure items that could profoundly affect your future financial well-being. Use it wisely. Prepare and be bold.

17

The Ten Next Most
Valuable Requests

> It is better to know some of the questions than all of the answers.
>
> —James Thurber

As noted earlier, each person's facts, circumstances, needs, values, goals, and priorities are unique, and the objectives in severance negotiating must take into account, and reflect, that uniqueness. Likewise, each and every company will see severance differently, highlighting the viewpoint of its management and reflecting its unique corporate culture.

You may have noticed that of the first five essential requests presented in the previous chapter, four (continuing salary, pro rata bonus, continuing benefits, and pension accommodations) represent types of rewards of employment, and only one (departure statement) represents a mixture of reward and risk limiter. Of the ten next-most-valuable requests set out in this chapter, only four are truly rewards, and six are risk limiters. The essence of the attorney's job is to identify and assess risk in any business transaction, and this chapter should give you a better sense of how that task is accomplished in the context of severance negotiation.

The following "ten next-most-valuable" items are based on my fifteen years of negotiating severance for hundreds of clients.

1. Stock Options and Financial Opportunities
Quite often companies entice employees to come work for them, and secure their retention of these employees with stock options and other, similar financial opportunities. These may include stock options,

warrants, share appreciation rights, phantom stock, along with other financial instruments and measures that ripen, mature, or vest over time. In many cases, though, the unanticipated termination of employment defeats these rewards. Especially if your case is one in which the termination was not due to poor performance or misconduct, you should make a strong argument that you have earned the reward, or that it would have been earned but for the termination, and so the payment, vesting, or maturity should still be granted to you. This can be accomplished in a variety of ways, depending on the reward in question, including the acceleration of vesting dates, the extension of exercise dates, and/or the substitution of other, similar or equally valuable rewards.

You and your attorney should carefully review promised but not rewarded compensation substitutes in preparation for negotiations, and you should always consider asking for delivery on any such promises.

2. Nonmitigation

In the previous chapter, I introduced the concept of "mitigation of severance," which states, in one way or another, that your severance payments end when you find a new job or when you stop looking for one. Be very careful about this issue. If there is no "mitigation" language in your severance agreement, don't raise the subject. But when there is such language in your severance agreement, as is often the case, consider requesting its removal.

Mitigation is, to my mind, essentially a risk limiter for employers. It limits their payments to you by the time you spend between jobs. Right there lies the basis of its unfairness, and the argument most successfully used in response: mitigation is entirely one-sided. In this job loss, it limits the risk of the employer, but the limitation on the number of weeks or months of paid severance does not limit the weeks, months, or years of additional time you may be out of work. I always say to employers, "If you are willing to be fair about this, why don't you just limit everyone's risk . . . just agree to pay severance so long as my client is out of work, *no matter how long that is?*" When they decline that invitation, as they usually do, I then suggest that they make life simpler and fairer for all by agreeing to the continuing payments, and let it go at that. That is, you'll take the risk of underpayment, and they'll take the risk of overpayment. The argument is simple and often works.

When that argument is not successful, I go back once more, and insist, at the least, for what I have come to call "mitigation of mitigation." By this strange phrase, I mean that if my client finds a new job, and that new job pays less than his or her terminated position, then payment of the difference will continue throughout the severance period.

Incidentally, those who are planning on going into their own business should be discreet about this, because failure to look for employment may result in your termination of severance, even if mitigation of severance payments is not explicitly set forth in your severance agreement. Some employers or their legal counsels claim mitigation is implied in every severance agreement. Watch out for snooping on this point by outplacement counselors, who may very likely point out your apparent disinterest in suggested interviews, or the fact that you are openly seeking to establish your own business, by reporting it to management. (See chapter 40, "A Concern About Employer-Provided Outplacement," for more about this phenomenon, which I have seen take place many times.)

3. Freedom from Livelihood Restrictions

Many severance agreements require you to give up one or more aspects of your freedom to make a living in the future. These should never be taken lightly, and you should resist them in almost every case.

Agreeing to certain restrictions of your freedom should pose no problem for you if worded in the agreement in a way that is clearly understood. For example, you could easily agree to "maintain confidentiality about the terms of this agreement, excepting that you can tell your spouse, attorney, accountant, and tax officials about it." Likewise, you should be able to agree to "refrain from publicly disparaging the company and its management."

The most common restrictive covenant (or promise to restrict yourself) is the covenant not to compete, or "noncompete." (This is discussed in greater detail in chapter 21.) Any provision limiting the companies you may later work for, the territories you may work in, or the products or services you may sell can end up denying you your ability to earn a living, and thus must be resisted or limited in every way possible. Beware, especially, of those that deny you the opportunity to compete with the company (1) or any company that may become part of or affiliated with it, (2) in any industry it may later choose to enter,

(3) in any future territory it may choose to enter. Don't assume you are fully aware of the company's future plans. Above all, *never* presume what many of my clients tell me—"These things are never enforceable"—for this is completely wrong. Such limiting factors are enforceable, increasingly so, and you must presume that they are entirely enforceable.

The second most common restriction to be avoided is the covenant not to solicit customers or other employees to leave the company. Each is self-explanatory but more restrictive (and thus dangerous) than it may at first appear. Are we speaking of just current customers or future customers as well? As for solicitation, does it include working for a company that does the soliciting? When it comes to other employees of the company, are we speaking of current employees, future employees, or prospective employees? Be careful of wordings in such clauses, and make it a habit to read these provisions with the broadest terms in mind. Whenever possible you should work to remove or restrict them, in wording and in their effect.

4. Outplacement Services (or Cash in Lieu Thereof)

Over the past fifteen years or so, I've watched in wonder the growth, development, and increasing sophistication of what is now called the outplacement industry. Numerous kinds of outplacement counselors and firms have developed, and many of them have a keen sense for identifying and meeting the needs their clients have during transition out of employment and, one hopes, back into new employment. I've seen outplacement do wonders for many of my clients.

While most large employers utilize the services of outplacement firms in the termination process, many employers don't do so as a rule, unless specifically asked. If you are looking forward to returning to work in a similar capacity, in the same industry, outplacement can provide you with many needed maintenance services, including telephone answering, fax use, message retrieval, office or desk use, and photocopying, along with professional services ranging from résumé preparation to skill review, assessment, and enhancement. I suggest that you request detailed information about the services provided to you as part of your outplacement and, especially, the length of time you can take advantage of those services. Be sure to include in your agreement whether or not that time period can be extended if needed.

If you are not interested in returning to the corporate sector but are considering moving into your own business, it may be wise to consider requesting that your company give you the very same moneys that it would otherwise have devoted to outplacement resources for you.

5. "Parachute" Provisions

Pessimism never pays, but prudence does. What do you think you might do if your continuing severance payments run out, and your savings and other resources become strained? This is not what you want, of course, or even what you expect, but it is a possibility. You know this, and your employer does, too.

For nearly every one of my clients I consider this unlikely but entirely possible scenario, and raise the dreaded "what if" question. For most of my clients, and for you as well, I strongly recommend asking for a provision something like this one: "If the employee does not obtain reemployment by or before the expiration of the salary continuation period under this agreement, the company will either (1) extend continued salary payments on a half-time basis for an extended period of three months, (2) consider the employee for all other available positions, whether or not overqualified, on a temporary basis, (3) in the case of a reorganization or downsizing, grant the employee a 'right of first rehire,' or (4) request of appropriate vendors of the company that the employee be given preferential consideration in all of their upcoming hiring."

While you may find none of these four alternative parachute provisions very appealing, your perspective on that could change should you find yourself without a job months from now. Of course, you may consider substituting one or more alternatives of your own; you're limited only by your creativity. The important thing is to get a sense of what you should try to ask for here, and the ways it may be incorporated into your own severance agreement.

6. Reimbursement for Legal Expenses

Ah, here's a request that's sure to warm the cockles of your good friends in the legal community. Actually, this provision is essentially to your benefit more than to your lawyer's.

You will probably find that your severance agreement will state that you are advised to obtain the advice and counsel of an attorney of your choice to review the proposed agreement, and to assist you in your review and decision to sign it. This is written in there for the employer's benefit, because if there's one readily available and solid defense to a lawsuit claiming that you breached an agreement, it is that you didn't understand what you were signing. The admonition in a severance agreement to obtain legal advice is inserted as a preemptive defense to that argument. It is inserted so that the employer can say, in effect, "We advised you to obtain advice of counsel; now we can't be blamed or penalized if you didn't." And that's a pretty good argument.

But that argument, often propounded by management attorneys, contains the very seed of your usually successful, countervailing argument: "Sure, you advised me to obtain assistance of counsel, but facing unemployment and economic insecurity, I simply could not spend the money that I may later need to make my mortgage payments." It is with this rationale—"if it wasn't for this termination and agreement being thrust upon this employee involuntarily, he wouldn't have to face the expense, which is too much to expect from a person in this circumstance"—that I argue for the employer to reimburse the employee for associated legal costs.

How often are such requests successful? About half of the time, provided: the request is made respectfully; it employs the rationale given above; and it sets an outward range of between $2,500 to $5,000 in large, urban areas, and around half that in other areas.

One employee for whom the answer to this request was a resounding and unequivocal no kept asking questions about the meaning of different provisions in her severance agreement, and kept requesting that each explanation be put in the agreement itself; thus she cost her employer so much in additional legal expense of its own that it finally just gave in and agreed to reimburse her for her own legal expense. She then hired me as her attorney.

7. Message and Mail Forwarding

This very simple request is almost always found to be of considerable practical value to the employee and is generally agreeable to the employer. There's nothing worse than having friends, relatives, coworkers, and prospective new employers all be told, "Oh, Ms. Nussbaum . . . she doesn't work here anymore. No, I have no forwarding address or number, either." Far preferable would be, "Oh, surely, I'll give that message to her promptly." It's a good idea, as well, to "test" this periodically by having someone call and write you, to see the response he or she is given.

While you may likely be told, "Oh, you don't have to worry about that; we'll surely help you in that regard," it's a given that you'll be more likely to have problems that come up promptly corrected if the obligation to provide these services is in writing and therefore more easily enforceable.

8. Payments on Passing

If your severance payments are a lump sum representing months of salary or more, or if they involve continuing salary payments over a considerable period of time, or if your buyout requires you to sign papers now but postpones payment of a large lump sum to you until some later date, your circumstances include one significant risk you may not have considered: your death. In the event of your passing after you sign your agreement, or after your termination, will your family or estate receive your severance moneys? In many cases, when I've raised this point, both my clients and our negotiating counterparts reply, "Gee, I never thought about that, and no one else has raised the issue before."

You work to support yourself and your family. If you agree to give up your job, and any claims you may have against your employer, you've earned your severance moneys. No matter what happens. These moneys should go to your family or your estate if you are not present to collect them. In fact, if you should die, your family may have a far greater need than expected for those continuing salary payments or that lump sum or even those extended benefits.

Every person should consider requesting a provision in his or her severance agreement to this effect. With one notable exception, I have never had this request turned down. Many of my negotiating partners are reluctant at first and tell me, "The agreement already implies that, because its says it's binding on all successors." My retort is simple: "Well, then, you shouldn't have any problem being explicit on the point, and it would make me feel a lot more comfortable if we did include clear language on that point. Imagine if this was your severance and your family; wouldn't you want it clear?" Ask for it, and you'll probably get it. Like life insurance, I hope you'll never need it.

9. Mutuality of Release

One of the primary concerns of your employer in the severance transaction is to obtain from you, at minimal expense, a release of all possible claims you may have against the company. You may say to yourself, "But I have no claims against them, at least none I'm aware of." You're probably right, but in this litigious society, your employer recognizes the significant value of the mere absence of risk, and that is just what a release represents. Well, for the same reasons, you should request a release, too.

Every terminated employee should ask that the release provisions in the severance agreement be made mutual, so that you will not be woken up some Saturday morning by a process server at your door because someone, somehow, for some unknown reason, has decided you did something you should not have, or you failed to do something you should have, and therefore you now owe something, probably money, to your former employer. It's to prevent the possibility of just such an occurrence that I always insist upon release mutuality—which is standard in any settlement of a lawsuit—and it is usually granted.

Incidentally, releases do not work prospectively; they apply only to past acts, occurrences, or events. That is, the signing of a release will not excuse anyone from something that happens in the future. The release will therefore not excuse or deny a claim for later breach of the severance obligations themselves or anything else set forth in the severance agreement.

10. Alternative Dispute Resolution

Like it or not, disputes do occur after severance agreements are signed. Even in instances where the negotiating was entirely nonadversarial, there are sometimes differences of opinion as to the meaning of words, items left out of the agreement because "well, we all understood that was a part of the deal," and even how calculations should be made. When these differences arise, and if they are intractable, the only choice is giving in or going to court. Neither is very appealing, to say the least.

More and more often, businesses are participating in dispute resolution with better, quicker, less expensive, and more confidential approaches, commonly referred to as alternative dispute resolution, or ADR. The first ADR mechanism often considered is mediation, which seeks to bring the parties together to resolve a disagreement through discussion, compromise, and resolution in a nonbinding, nonadversarial way. I have participated in numerous mediation efforts, and I have been amazed at what progress a skilled mediator can achieve, even with the most warring, hot-tempered, angry parties. One mediator I've worked with has been, to my mind, something of a miracle worker in difficult matters.

A second ADR mechanism is arbitration, which is just like a mini-trial in court, except it's not in court, it's not in a courtroom, and it doesn't even have to involve lawyers. Instead, arbitration is a matter of telling your "story," providing your evidence, and having your adversary do the same, in a businesslike setting, before one, two, or three independent, neutral parties, who generally render their decision one or two weeks later. The process, if set up and run well, is much simpler, more cost effective, rapid, and confidential than litigation in resolving conflicts. I've participated in many arbitrations and find them quite preferable to the usual litigation process. Incidentally, the decision of an arbitrator is enforceable in court, and it cannot be appealed, except on very narrow grounds, such as bribery or some decision that is entirely beyond the scope of the matter.

I almost always suggest the inclusion of an ADR-type mechanism for resolution of disputes in every severance agreement I negotiate because of its obvious advantages. Considering the fact that I represent employees only, and employees usually have fewer financial resources with which to sustain a litigation, and less time to wait around for resolution, I find it an attractive alternative to litigation. For the same reasons, though, those who represent employers look at ADR with disfavor. At the same time, increasing numbers of employers are seeing the many advantages of ADR and are using it more that they have in the past. I would suggest that you request it.

•   •   •

In the end, just remember: don't be afraid to ask for anything. So long as requests are made in a respectful manner and accompanied by a rationale, there should be no downside to making them. You will probably regret not asking more than you would regret asking.

18

Customize Your Requests:
The 101 True "Severance Secrets"

> Imagination is more important than knowledge.
> —Albert Einstein

In the two previous chapters, I've set down the fifteen most important, valuable, and commonly requested severance negotiation items. Over and above those more commonly negotiated elements of a severance package, many other items may be considered, and should be considered, depending on your unique circumstances and needs. Most people have no trouble coming up with the items discussed in the two previous chapters. The 101 items in this chapter are those that are almost always missed.

I believe the true "trade secrets" in severance negotiating are found by applying all available leverage to the very unique needs of the departing employee. Each of the following benefits has been won by one or more of my clients. Some proved invaluable. Review the items listed here for applicability to your circumstances:

1. Accrued Vacation
Payments to you for accrued but unused vacation (as well as holidays, sick days, and personal days, depending on company policy) should be paid within thirty days of the submission of the signed severance agreement.

2. Amenities to Continue
The employer may agree to provide you with customary employment-related amenities for a specified period, including use of company facilities, office, and staff without cost.

3. Annuity Purchase
Where some reason exists to believe securing severance payments is necessary, employers (especially in the insurance and financial services fields) have been known to purchase annuity contracts to fund continuing severance payments.

4. Attribution
All future publication of articles, research, and studies to which you have contributed should contain proper attribution to you.

5. Automobile Lease Continuation
When you have used an automobile leased by the employer, request continued use of the vehicle until the lease expires. If this request can't be met or is declined, ask for reimbursement, whether partial or total, for alternative automobile use.

6. Automobile Use
You may ask for continued use of your leased automobile for a specified period, preferably without cost.

7. Bankruptcy—Representation and Personal Obligation
Especially in smaller or weaker companies, in which severance is to be paid out over an extended period, it is wise for you to make two requests: that the employer represent that neither discussions nor arrangements have taken place to put the company under bankruptcy protection; and that if bankruptcy protection is sought before payout is complete, the sum then outstanding to you shall become a joint and several obligation of the company's shareholders.

8. Binding on Successors and Assigns
In these days of rampant consolidations and reorganizations, it's important to make sure that your severance payments and benefits will continue no matter what corporate event takes place. Whether your employer is merged, sells its assets, or participates in some sort of reorganization or combination with another company, its obligations should continue, and your agreement should be expressly clear about that.

9. Bonus—Present Year

If terminated without cause, you should be entitled to the anticipated bonus for the year of termination.

10. Borrowings to Be Repaid

If you have taken an advance or a loan from your employer, you should consider asking for an extended period for repayment. If you have borrowed moneys from your 401(k) plan that must be repaid within sixty days of your leaving the plan, you should consider requesting a loan to do so.

11. Breach Declaration and Cure

It is advisable to request that your employer must notify you in writing if it believes you have breached your obligations under the agreement, setting forth how it believes you have done so, and giving you some stated period of time in which to cure your alleged breach. There is nothing wrong with making this a mutual obligation, as well.

12. Breach—Effect

If your employer breaches its obligations to you under the severance agreement, the release of claims signed by you should be considered void; time periods for you to start legal actions should be considered "frozen" as of the date of breach, and you should be allowed your legal and other costs of enforcing your rights.

13. Breach Provisions—Mutuality

In all respects, the rights of the employer and, you, the employee in event of breach by the other under the severance agreement should be mutual.

14. Calendar Month Modification

When the last date of employment set forth in a severance agreement is at the end of the month (for example, July 29), it is advisable to request a slight extension to the first day or two of the next month (for example, August 1). This usually permits extension of your benefits, such as insurance coverages, for a full calendar month and appears to extend employment and diminish unemployment on a résumé by a full month's time.

15. Class Action: None
Before you agree to drop all claims, your employer should be asked to represent that it knows of no pending or threatened class-action lawsuit against it by a class of employees of which you may be a member.

16. COBRA—Commencement
It is wise to request agreement that COBRA insurance coverage is available by law or will be provided even if unavailable by law, and to agree on the actual date (usually the first day of the month following the month of termination) that COBRA coverage will be available.

17. COBRA—Cost
There is nothing wrong with asking your employer to cover the costs of health insurance coverage during the COBRA period.

18. COBRA—Extension
Likewise, it may be very prudent for you to arrange to receive an extension of the COBRA insurance coverage period (usually for a twelve-month period) in the event that you have not yet secured your next job.

19. COBRA—Family Coverage upon Passing
It may be very smart to arrange for the continued health coverage of family members through COBRA in the event of your death during the COBRA period.

20. Commutation Expense
Since you, as the departing employee, may accept reemployment that requires regular and significant travel on a daily or weekly expense, you should be provided a commutation allowance for six to twelve months, which is analogous to relocation expense.

21. Company Practice(s) Confirmed
Most companies have certain "practices" that are not actual promised benefits or written policies, but only customary practices. One common one is a specific payment or benefit—perhaps a month's salary—upon twenty or thirty years' service. If you are potentially eligible, confirm the practice in your severance agreement and your entitlement to it.

22. Computer Purchase
Used computer equipment has little resale or reuse value. Many companies agree to sell to departing executives the computer equipment—especially laptops—to which they've grown accustomed, at a very reasonable price.

23. Confidentiality—Employee's Breach
You, the employee, should not be considered to have breached confidentiality obligations unless the matters in contention are substantial, or "material," there took place actual, willful dissemination of the substantial material, and some harm to employer did, indeed, take place.

24. Confidentiality—Expiration
Circumstances may suggest the wisdom of a time period for the expiration of confidentiality obligations, such as the desire to write a book in the future.

25. Confidentiality—Personal Exceptions
Your confidentiality obligations should except your attorney, immediate family, appropriate tax authorities, accountant, outplacement counselor, therapists, and doctors.

26. Confidentiality—Résumé Exceptions
The following should not be considered "confidential" in nature: the fact of your employment by the company, the dates of employment, the title(s) or position(s) you held, the responsibilities fulfilled, the names(s) of your supervisor(s) and coworker(s).

27. Confidentiality—Mutual
The employer should be under the same confidentiality requirements and disclosure restrictions as you, the employee. It should also be considered a breach of the employer's confidentiality requirements if its officers or other employees issue, disseminate, or otherwise distribute derogatory statements, negative performance reviews, critical personality opinions, or negative reports or claims or innuendoes about the integrity or honesty of you, the departing employee.

28. Consent to Hire

Senior executives frequently note their inclination to ask their secretaries or assistants to move with them to a new company. If you intend to do so, and your secretary or assistant has not been terminated along with you, consider requesting consent to hire in your severance agreement. Of course, you should seek his or her consent first.

29. Consultancy—Extended Period

Employee and employer sometimes find it advantageous to continue their relationship in a new form of consultancy, in which the former goes from employment to independent contractor status.

30. Consultancy—Location

For purposes of tax reporting, home office deductions, and withholdings, it is frequently especially advantageous for you and your employer to agree that the consultancy location is your residence.

31. Continued Employment Title

During periods of continued salary and benefits provided under a severance agreement, it would cost your employer nothing, but could be of considerable value to you, for résumé and interview purposes, if all were to agree that you still held your title.

32. Cooperation by Employer

The employer is to be requested to cooperate with you, the employee, in matters related to the extension of coverages for pension, tax, insurance, and in the transfer of savings plans.

33. Cooperation in Future

It is often a good idea—for both technical reasons and emotional ones—for you and your employer to agree to cooperate in the future in whatever measures may become necessary to fulfill your respective future obligations to each other, including tax reporting and future inquiries by regulatory authorities.

34. Cooperation with Law

You should insist upon an express provision entitling you to cooperate with any criminal, judicial, or administrative probe, grand jury proceeding, investigation or other demand for information or cooperation with the force of law, including, among others, judicial subpoena and court-ordered discovery.

35. Copyright, Patent Rights, and So Forth
Those who have participated in the creation of written works or inventions during their period of employment may be entitled to either a copyright, a patent, or a share of the proceeds or royalties the employer may later enjoy. If these issues pertain to your position, you should address them in the severance agreement.

36. Credit for Creative Works
If you have made creative contributions to your employer's projects, you should not forget that this is bound to be your last opportunity to secure appropriate creative credits.

37. Deductions—Payroll
When you have substantial legal and job-search expenses, as well as potential cash-flow problems, you may choose to declare a significant number of payroll exemptions to lower withholdings from severance payments.

38. Deferral
To avoid moving into a higher tax bracket, you should consider requesting part or all of the intended severance payment be paid on January 2 of the next calendar year.

39. "Departure"—the Preferred Term
To soften the impact of the severance agreement, I often request that wherever the word "termination" or "separation" or the like is used, the word "departure" be used instead.

40. Departure Reasons
In some cases where I have found the employer reluctant to grant a separate departure statement, I ask that a positive reason for departure be set forth right in the severance agreement, to prevent later public statements to my client's detriment. You may want to do the same.

41. Directed Payments to Escrow

Payments of severance moneys may be paid to an escrow account, instead of to you, the employee, for several reasons, including the employer's need for "deniability." Where employer misconduct is alleged, you may fear direct contact with an abusive employer, or you may have a concern that the employer's financial strength is questionable. Escrow accounts might be something you'd like to discuss under these circumstances.

42. Disclosure—Employer Representation

In entering into the severance agreement, the employer should be asked to make a written representation that it is not withholding from you, the employee, any relevant and material fact or circumstance the knowledge of which might determine whether you enter into the severance agreement.

43. Disclosure Permitted

In all events you should be permitted free disclosure of the facts of your employment, including as examples the fact of your employment by the company, the dates of your employment, positions held, responsibilities of the positions, titles, nature and extent of your achievements, and names of individuals (usually excluding customers) with whom you have worked.

44. Employer Appearances Prohibited

It should be stipulated that, regardless of customary company or industry practices, or provisions in the prior employment contract, the employer will not be authorized or entitled to make applications to, or appearance in, arbitration, judicial, administrative, or criminal proceeding or hearing on behalf of, or in the name of you, the employee, without your prior written consent in each case.

45. "Employer" Defined

For the purposes of the severance agreement, the word "employer" (or "company" or "firm" or similar term) should be defined to include, among others, all offices, directors, employees, agents, consultants, and representatives of the employer, its assigns and successors in interest (that is, merger partners or purchasers of the company) at this time and at all future times.

46. Employment Search Expenses
Employers are frequently quite amenable to providing severed employees with reimbursement, upon presentation of receipts, for employment search expenses such as travel, car rental, hotel expenses, and the like. You may want to think about requesting such reimbursement.

47. Enforcement Expense
Though a double-edged sword, the agreement to require the payments of enforcement expenses (including counsel fees) to the prevailing party in any dispute serves to discourage actions in bad faith.

48. Escrow Agent—Fees, Expenses
Whenever the use of an escrow agent is contemplated, it should be clear that in no event will you, the employee, be liable for fees or expenses related to the escrow agent's services.

49. Escrow—Interest
All interest earned on severance moneys held by an escrow agent should rightfully "follow the moneys," that is, be paid to the party (employee or employer) who is ultimately entitled to the escrowed moneys.

50. Expatriate Tax Indemnity
For those who have served their employers on expatriate assignments, because the employer's accountants frequently perform tax-related calculations, any release given the employer and its agents and representatives should exclude issues related to expatriate taxation, because related problems commonly arise only in later years.

51. First Rehire Right
If you are let go in the course of a downsizing, you may request a "right of first rehire" when circumstances change or improve.

52. Future Activities and Residence
Unless there are provisions or understandings to the contrary, especially if a continuing consultancy exists, it is often wise to insert a written provision stipulating that nothing set forth in the severance agreement restricts the future activities of you or your choice as to place of residence.

53. Future Services to Be Compensated

It should be clear that nothing in the severance agreement requires you to provide future services. Any provision of future services should be for negotiated compensation and subject to a separate written, signed agreement.

54. Insurance—Continuation of Coverage

You should always request continuation of all insurance coverages (including medical, dental, disability, life) for a specified period of time, at the employer's expense, with COBRA not to commence until its conclusion.

55. Insurance—Continued Family Coverage

If coverage for medical insurance is on a family basis, ask for confirmation that the family basis will continue, and ask, while you're at it, for the employer to pick up the cost of family coverage.

56. Insurance—Substitute Programs

If, during the COBRA or extended-coverage period, new or substitute health care options become available to the other employees of the company, they should become available to you also.

57. Legal Expense—Segregation

Quite often the employer will decline legal fee reimbursement, but will agree to segregate from severance moneys a sum to be paid directly to the employee's counsel, thereby avoiding the necessity to withhold taxes from the monies.

58. Legal Representation—Opportunity

In order to prevent claims of lack of understanding used to void release agreements, employers typically insist upon employees' acknowledgment that they have had an opportunity to obtain legal counsel and advice. If you have not had such an opportunity, or cannot afford counsel, send your employer a letter to that effect, to evidence your lack of opportunity.

59. Legal Representation in Employer Business

In the event that you, the employee, are later involved as a witness, deponent, codefendant, or in some other capacity in a lawsuit, legal proceeding, arbitration, judicial or administrative hearing, or criminal probe, relating to the business activities of the employer, or in preparation for such a matter, the employer should be required to reimburse you for your costs of legal representation, travel, and accommodations.

60. Letters Permitted
Because employees sometimes wish to say good-bye to many of their coworkers, but either are denied the opportunity or feel the interaction would be awkward, they sometimes ask the employer's prior approval of letters to be sent to coworkers for this purpose.

61. Likeness and Voice
For an employee with a public persona, whose voice and likeness may be considered a valuable asset, it is important to insist that the employer will no longer be authorized to utilize the employee's likeness and voice for any purpose.

62. Lump-Sum Payment
Employees almost always ask if severance payments can be accelerated into one lump-sum payment. If tax issues are not problematic for you, this request should almost always be made.

63. Matching Gifts
For those whose employers have matching gift programs, it may be wise to consider exercising this right at this time.

64. Modifications—Signed Only
While most severance agreements will state that they may be modified only by a written agreement that is signed by both parties, if yours does not state that, you should request that such a provision be inserted, to prevent later misunderstandings and disputes.

65. "Most Favored Nation" Treatment
If you're a senior executive especially, consider asking your employer to represent in writing that no other executive of equivalent or lesser title has received, is receiving, or will receive severance treatment of greater compensation and benefit level than you have been promised.

66. Name Use

If you are involved in research, reports, surveys, and data compilations, you may want to seek assurances that your name will be used in conjunction with publication. Conversely, if you are participating but without final editing authority, you may insist your name not be used in publication without your prior written approval.

67. No Company Rescission Right

For those forty years of age or older, in order for your release of your employer to be binding on you with regard to possible claims of discrimination, you must be provided with a right to change your mind *after* you sign your agreement. This is commonly referred to as your "seven-day right of rescission." It is suggested that the agreement be explicit that the company has no such corresponding rescission right.

68. Noncompetition Annulled

Reason and fairness dictate that if the employer seeks to terminate your job for reasons other than misconduct, any noncompete covenant previously granted by you as an employee should be annulled, so as to permit gainful reemployment.

69. Noncompetition Limited

Any noncompetition covenant to continue in effect after your departure must be expressly limited to competition with the business activities and entities of the employer as of the date of departure. Business activities begun by the employer after that, and business entities acquired by the employer after that, should not be within the purview of the noncompetition covenant.

70. Nondisparagement

The employer customarily requests that you not disparage the company, its employees and officers, and its products. You should request the same obligation of the employer, in return.

71. No-Suit Covenant—Exception

To be expressly excluded from your promise not to bring claims, charges, complaints, or lawsuits against the employer are claims regarding matters about which you, the employee, have no opportunity to do thorough review, including vested pension benefits, company-administered savings and investment plans, and existing workers' compensation programs.

72. Notices—Copy to Attorney
Copies of all notices to be sent in the future by the employer to you should be sent simultaneously and by the same delivery mode to your legal counsel at an address to be provided.

73. Obligations to Be Voided
The severance agreement should stipulate that if a court should find the employer in material breach of its severance obligations to you, the employee, or to be illegal or against public policy, then your remaining obligations to the employer will be considered void.

74. Outlay Reimbursement
It is not uncommon for employees in the severance process to either forget, ignore, or underappreciate the outlays they have made on behalf of their employer in the course of their work. Common examples are expenses related to travel, entertainment, home telephone, personal car use, and dues and subscriptions. You should carefully consider these and require reimbursement in the severance agreement.

75. Outplacement—Cash in Lieu
Many of my clients have elected to leave the corporate world altogether. Accordingly, they have requested, with considerable success, cash payment in lieu of provision of outplacement services, generally in the range of $3,000 to $9,000.

76. Outplacement—Report Restrictions
If outplacement services are provided by the employer as part of the severance package, the employer should provide to you, the employee, written assurances that the outplacement agency will not prepare or disseminate information or reports on you to the employer or third parties without first providing such information and reports to you for review and consent.

77. Outplacement—Services Provided

Because the employer generally contracts with the outplacement service directly, and the outplacement service will generally not divulge what amenities it offers, it is advisable that the severance agreement list the services actually to be offered, or alternatively, state that it will pay for "all services generally accorded the most senior executives."

78. Overtime Issues

Very few executives consider issues related to overtime, on the presumption that, under applicable law, they are considered exempt from coverage. States vary considerably on this point. As a departing employee, you should speak with your attorney or local state labor department office before failing to consider your possible entitlements for potentially tens of thousands of dollars of legally required compensation.

79. Parent Company Guarantee

In those circumstances where I am concerned about the financial viability of an employer, I request that a larger, more stable parent company guarantee the continuing obligations of the employer. You may want to consider doing the same.

80. Payback Inapplicable to Consultancy

Many severance agreements require reimbursement of severance moneys if the employee is rehired by the employer. You should be sure this is made expressly inapplicable to interim or short-term consultancy arrangements, which are common.

81. Payment—Lump Sum

Payment of severance monies in one lump sum is preferable to most clients, and granted—if requested—perhaps one-third or one-half of the time. If it seems appealing to you, ask for it.

82. Payments to Surviving Spouse or Estate

This is among the most valuable, easy-to-win severance modifications possible: where severance payments are either to continue over a period of time or to be given in a lump-sum payment at a future date, should a departing employee decease before payment, all moneys due the employee will be paid to his or her surviving spouse, immediate family, or estate.

83. Pension Calculations—Avoidance of "Downward Skewer"

Where pension calculations are based upon the final year's compensation or the average compensation for the last few years, take care to ensure that the shortened, final employment year does not downwardly skewer the pension calculations.

84. Pension Calculations to Include Severance

Especially when the payment of severance is in the form of salary continuation, and other forms of benefits are continued, there is every reason for you to request that pension calculations, too, take the continued severance payments into account. This is especially important if you are nearing certain threshold periods of service or an age at which pension benefits commence.

85. Pension Certification—Year End

If pension contributions or calculations are at issue for you, you may want to request that, if possible, the employer will make available to you the preliminary year-end certification of pension plan benefits prepared by the plan's consulting actuary.

86. Personal Property—Return

Where applicable, the employer should be asked to agree to return all personal property of the employee.

87. Personal Service Corporation

If you are contemplating establishing your own consulting or other business, and opening a personal service corporation or limited liability company to do so, there may be a tax advantageous for you to have the option of directing severance payments to that new entity.

88. Personnel File

In almost half the states, employees (while employed) have a right to review their personal files. Either request, in writing, to see your file at this time, or preserve your right to do so later, in your severance agreement.

89. Portfolios

If you are an employee involved in advertising, artistic pursuits, or another creative field, you should request the right to retain a portfolio of all your creative works produced on the job, provided none of these items contain proprietary information or would reasonably be expected to compromise the employer's future strategic plans, or your future career plans.

90. Property—Employer's

If any question exists as to the employer's property that may be in your possession, the employer either should acknowledge that all company property has been returned, or should list those items to be returned, and both you and the employer should agree on when and how you will return the items.

91. Reemployment Efforts

Especially among international companies, I have been successful in getting some employers to agree to specific efforts to help the departing employee regain employment, including contacting major suppliers, related companies, and even competitors. You should consider requests along these lines that could help you in your job-search efforts.

92. References—None

It is now almost universal policy that companies will not provide employment references but will only confirm dates of employment, title, and, sometimes, compensation level. In severance, which is usually not on an entirely "friendly" basis, this policy should be confirmed in the severance agreement.

93. Release Limits

The general release to be provided by you, the employee, to the employer—whether incorporated into the severance agreement or existing as a separate document—should rightfully and expressly not extend to claims for workers' compensation benefits, which are not claims against the employer or claims related to vested pension, welfare, and benefit plans.

94. Relocation Expense
If you, as the departing employee, believe that relocation may become necessary to gain appropriate reemployment, you should request that reimbursement for the costs of relocation be included in the severance package.

95. Re-relocation
No, this is not a typo. Whenever you have relocated in order to initially take a position, coverage of the costs of reverse relocation, or re-relocation, should be requested, and insisted upon especially if severance follows shortly after the job was taken.

96. Signature—Employee Counsel
The employer and its counsel should be requested to accept any notice or communication signed by your counsel as if signed by you, yourself.

97. Unemployment—Not to Be Contested
Regardless of future plans, unanticipated events can happen. Always ask for insertion of a provision that the employer will not contest the application for unemployment insurance benefits, should you make one.

98. Vendor Hiring Prohibitions
To prevent "theft of employees," many large companies require that their vendors sign agreements prohibiting the hiring of company employees by company vendors for a set period (commonly six months) after employment termination. This requirement does not make sense in the severance context. It should be expressly waived.

99. Voice Mail Continuation
Continuation of voice mail services will serve to enhance the perception of you, as the departing employee. Request continuation through reemployment or for a period of three to six months.

100. Withholdings—Lump Sum
Whenever severance payout is made in a lump-sum fashion, you should make the request that it be paid on a basis that would minimize tax withholdings. (That minimum is usually a 28 percent rate for so-called supplemental payments.)

101. Withholdings—New W-4

You, as an employee, may always modify the number of exemptions claimed so as to accurately reflect future tax liabilities. Because you may experience periods of unemployment, and deductible legal expense, I suggest to you, as I do to all my clients, that you submit a new W-4 form, requesting withholdings calculated at the level of nine personal exemptions.

• • •

In designing a list of severance negotiation points, the employee and employee's legal counsel should be limited only by the circumstances and their collective creativity. Every need of the employee, as well as his or her family, should be considered a fair topic for discussion. Indeed, I believe it is a duty of sorts for the employer to consider all these needs in a severance package. It may help attorneys to put themselves in their clients' shoes, and consider each of their clients' many concerns, when compiling lists of requests.

I believe, too, that asking for any accommodation in the severance process is entirely proper, provided the request is accomplished, as I have said before, with a genuine politeness, is accompanied by a reasonable rationale, and is reasonable in amount.

19

How Much Should You Ask For?
The Emerging Severance Standards

> Pay your people the least possible, and you'll get from
> them the same.
>
> —Malcolm Forbes

In my severance negotiations on behalf of executives, I see a certain set of discernible "benefit standards" gradually emerging in a wide variety of industries. These benefit standards reflect an increasing sophistication on the part of Human Resources personnel in their handling of this highly sensitive area of their work. As a general rule, I've noticed that larger companies will usually be more generous with severance, although not always.

These emerging standards are public secrets: they should be well-known to all but are not. Each type of standard discussed in this chapter, from salary through stock options, represents a severance secret your employer wishes you did not know. In each category, you can see how—and to what extent—you may assess and possibly reformulate more accurately any severance package offered to you.

In reviewing these severance standards, though, you must keep in mind that they are yardsticks only. Your initial offer from management, and your own knowledge of your leverage in negotiations, may suggest a lower or a higher request. Don't be shy or frightened in your efforts to gain all that you possibly can.

Bear in mind, too, that you can customize severance; that is, the package you receive should address your particular situation. As an example, if your company provides tuition assistance for children, and you need help with your child's next two semesters' tuition, that may take precedence over some of the other items presented here.

With those considerations in mind, review these standards for the primary severance deal points.

Salary Compensation

Without a doubt, the number of weeks or months of continued salary payments is the primary issue most people are concerned about when it comes to severance. Where employment has been ongoing for a considerable period of time, we can use a multiplier of sorts to calculate general guidelines for salary continuation in severance:

- For senior management, salary compensation increasingly reaches the level of one month per year of service.
- For middle management, continued salary payout of two to three weeks per full year of company service is the current norm.
- For support staff, including secretaries and assistants, one to two weeks per year of service is standard.

In a good number of cases I see employers requiring "mitigation of severance," a cessation of salary payments if and when the terminated employee becomes reemployed. However, there is a trend away from mitigation, as it is increasingly viewed as discouraging reemployment efforts and is difficult to administer as well.

As for bare minimums of salary continuation in severance, I am seeing more and more company policies requiring either two or three months of salary continuation in exchange for signed releases. This is sometimes referred to as "payment in lieu of notice." The figure I see most frequently in overall maximum payouts is two years of salary, except on the most senior management levels, where higher amounts are negotiated without reference to formula and regardless of standards. In that category, I have negotiated "golden parachutes" comprising five years of continued salary and bonus compensation.

Bonus Compensation

I increasingly see bonus compensation treated on a pro rata basis in many businesses. In case of pro rata, the terminated employee is provided a share of bonus, incentive compensation, or profit sharing that would have been anticipated had employment continued throughout the full calculation year.

At the same time, I am seeing a frightful trend in other businesses in the opposite direction. More and more investment, securities, and banking firms require that, in order to qualify for a bonus, an employee must be employed on the very date of bonus distribution. It is, therefore, very upsetting to see wide-scale terminations of many employees in these industries during the very week before bonus payment. This seems especially obscene in those firms where the bonus represents the bulk of compensation, sometimes amounting to two, three, or four times the employee's annual base salary.

Pension and Retirement "Accommodations"

Perhaps of greatest significance to middle-aged and older workers are pension and retirement rights. Many people have remained with one company for twenty, thirty, forty, or more years just to ensure their own comfortable retirement. To lose all or a substantial part of that anticipated benefit because of involuntary termination a few years or even a few months short of full vesting hits people in a way that nothing else does.

In cases of executive employees in their late fifties and sixties, for whom there may not be another opportunity to vest in successor pension or other benefit plans, I see a new and increasing willingness by employers to adjust upward both the number of years of employment and true age as bases for calculation of future pension payout. Those who fear either long-term difficulty or complete inability to return to the workforce can request to accelerate commencement of their pension payout.

Increasingly common, also, is a measure called "bridging to retirement," by which an employee's period of salary continuation during severance is not paid out on a full-time basis but is instead stretched out through smaller payments to reach a minimum retirement age or period of service. For example, instead of paying a salary continuation for six months, on a full-salary basis, the same amount of money may be paid to the severed employee on a one-third-salary basis over eighteen months. By this method, employment is "bridged" to the necessary attainment of service or age.

Many companies will greet such requests for pension accommodations with a knee-jerk reaction, saying, "This cannot be done, according to our pension plan." Experience has taught me that that exclamation is often not to be taken seriously. At each such response I ask for the name of the plan administrator and immediately send him or her a letter stating that we have been advised by management (either the general counsel' office or Human Resources) that the accommodations we need are expressly forbidden by the written terms of the plan. Frequently, I soon receive a letter expressing just the opposite to be true.

While pension and retirement accommodations such as these have not yet become standard, the willingness of management to give serious consideration to such requests, where fair, is now quite common.

Additional discussion of pension benefits at the time of severance is to be found in chapter 20.

Outplacement Assistance

Barely known a mere decade ago, the provision of outplacement assistance has become almost an expectation in severance agreements. Outplacement assistance is now truly a standard severance benefit. However, the duration of outplacement assistance, the level of that assistance, and the option of the employer providing cash payment in lieu of outplacement assistance may or may not be open to discussion in your case. It all depends on your employer's flexibility on this issue.

A minimum of three months' outplacement is now almost universal when it comes to the duration of this benefit. I also often see outplacement granted for six months. Less commonly do I see more provided. It is the rare employee who receives a continuation of outplacement through reemployment.

The level of outplacement most commonly provided is the "basic level," which includes career assessment and counseling, telephone answering, résumé preparation, as well as a buffet of seminars on such topics as stress management, networking, financial resource planning, and self-employment counseling. However, senior executives are commonly afforded "senior level" treatment in outplacement, which generally includes use of a private office, secretarial service (sometimes private), personal counseling and "grooming" sessions (often including personality and appearance assessment), as well as focused introduction to appropriate executive search consultants.

For those who don't need outplacement assistance, including severed employees contemplating self-employment or retirement, receipt of cash payment in lieu of outplacement assistance—generally $3,000 to $9,000, depending on your level—is worth asking for since I see it agreed to more and more commonly by employers.

A particular concern about confidentiality in the course of outplacement assistance is explained in chapter 40.

Agreed Departure Statement

Employees are almost universally concerned about having a good cover story when speaking with prospective employers, executive recruiters, coworkers, and even friends and family members about the job they are leaving. This is made even more important by the requirement set forth in most every severance agreement that "the employee shall not divulge to any parties (other than immediate family, accountant, and attorney) either the fact of this severance agreement or its terms." What's a terminated person to say?

At least 80 percent of employers are now willing to work with the terminated employee toward preparation of a mutually agreeable departure statement, which allows the company to avoid being put in a bad light and still permits the executive to retain his or her dignity and self-respect when explaining the separation to others. Unless the employer is especially paranoid or vengeful, an agreed statement of departure represents a "win-win" resolution for both the employer and the employee that doesn't cost a dime.

A sample text of an agreed departure statement may be found in the appendix.

Uncontested Unemployment

Another concession of sorts I see more and more frequently is when management agrees, in writing, not to contest any application for unemployment insurance benefits made by the employee. This provides added assurance to the employee facing potentially difficult financial times, with very little cost to the employer. Because the great percentage of severance cases are, in fact, involuntary, unemployment compensation makes sense.

States vary in their laws regarding whether they will pay out unemployment payments to you if you are also receiving weekly or monthly severance payments. Some states will not provide such compensation if you receive a lump-sum severance payment. You would be wise to consult the Labor Department of Unemployment Division in your home state.

Chapter 39, "Eligibility for Unemployment Benefits," provides further elaboration on this subject.

Accrued Vacation and Personal Days

It is the law in most states that, upon employment termination, an employee is entitled to compensation for accrued, but unused, vacation and personal leave days. This is not universal, however, and may be optional in your jurisdiction. (In New York, for example, the right to accrued unused vacation days is limited to those making less than $30,000 per year.) In actuality, many employees are not paid for these days, or if a severance package of any kind is offered, it is worded in such a way as to deny the employee this compensation, by stating that the package offered covers any and all such accrued days. In my experience, employers seek at first to deny this compensation, but most will eventually provide it.

Mutual Releases

Virtually every severance package requires the employee to release from every kind of liability ever conceived, and to be conceived, the employer-company, its subsidiary companies, parent companies, board members, officers, employees, directors, agents, managers, affiliates, shareholders, successors, and assigns. Few, however, provide for a mutual release by these parties of the employee.

Release of the employee is important for two primary reasons. First, release of the employee gives the employee the same sense of closure and finality sought by the employer, and it is deserved. Second, obtaining a mutuality of release serves to remind the negotiating parties that the employee is an equal member of this negotiating process, and her interests are as important to her as the company's interests are important to it.

It is a good idea to request two exceptions to the release to be given: first, that the release should not include any errors in calculation or collection of moneys due under this agreement. We all make mistakes, and no one should be made to suffer for such errors. Second, the release should not cover matters related to pension or employer savings plan moneys, unless distribution has taken place prior to severance. At the time of signing severance agreements, very few people have had the opportunity to carefully review pension money payments, investments, and their handling, and are therefore not in a position to provide a release in this regard.

When mutuality of release is requested, it is granted some 75 percent of the time. When requested, the two exceptions to the breadth of release stated above are granted 50 percent of the time, and the more likely of the two to be granted, if an employer won't provide both, is the one regarding errors in calculation or collection of moneys.

Further discussion of severance releases is to be found in chapter 42.

Stock Option Acceleration

Last, but surely not least, more and more companies are granting stock options to all levels of employees, right down to the clerical staff. This is something that was unheard of even five years ago. According to the many articles I've read, this proliferation of awarding stock options is due in large measure to the widespread discovery of the many positive effects of options' profit sharing on employee morale, longevity on the job, and productivity. Stock option grants also are not reflected as operating costs on a business balance sheet and therefore may be considered as nearly without cost to the employer.

Stock options may have one date (or event) on which they are deemed to be vested, one date (or event) on which they may be exercised, and a certain, preset price at which they can be purchased. Certain other restrictions (such as loss upon employment termination) or benefits (loans available to help employees finance their stock purchases) may also exist. Upon learning of impending severance, I ask each of my clients to review all facts and dates relevant to their stock option rights, and to review them with me.

Because stock options are often so valuable to the employee and so relatively low in cost to the employer, more and more companies are viewing requests for stock option acceleration in a positive light.

Stock options at time of severance are more fully explained in chapter 22.

• • •

That covers the basics. Remember to use these standards as minimums, only, and do not substitute them for your assessment of leverage in negotiation, and your use of that leverage to gain every payment and benefit potentially available to you. Always keep in mind, as well, that you can customize your severance package. Outline your and your family's needs and priorities, and negotiate accordingly. If there is a special concern that I did not cover here, turn to the next chapter where we'll concentrate on more specialized issues.

20

Pension and Insurance

> A promise made is a debt unpaid.
> —Robert W. Service

With this chapter, I begin to address a series of topics that, excepting the issue of compensation, are among those of greatest concern for terminated employees, especially executives. They stand out among other concerns both for their considerable importance to certain departing employees and for their need for comprehensive discussion, as well. The topics to be covered in succeeding chapters—pension, insurance, restrictive covenants, stock options, defamation, ownership of ideas, confidentiality and trade secrets, continuing consultancies, Form U-5 statements—are all related to your future security, and each may represent one part of your plan for your future security.

These topics also serve as a bridge from the "old" to the "new." They cover aspects of the transition out of the former job and into future employment.

The Importance of Pension and Insurance

It is in all probability not necessary for me to tell you how important are the protections of earned pension benefits and the continuation of various insurance coverages. These two items represent the primary methods by which people in our society reduce the various risks, both large and small, in their personal lives. Indeed, these two items—pension and insurance—may be the main reasons that some people do not go into business for themselves but instead remain with a larger group or company. While job security, itself, always represented personal security—some companies used to go so far as to maintain policies of "no layoffs—ever"—now these two items have come to represent the best one might expect in this regard.

However, pension and insurance are also two of the most expensive employee benefits for employers, and their motivation to reduce these costs is quite intense. They can be somewhat open-ended financial commitments: depending upon the pension plan or insurance policy, the employer's required contribution, premium, deductible, outlay, and similar forms of expense may be unending, at least while the employee covered by it remains alive. Such unfunded "contingent liability" is a very hot topic these days in the valuation of companies, and a subject of increasing concern to government regulators. Employers have every reason to reduce risk to themselves, and to their profits, but they have no legal basis for risking the health and welfare of their employees.

It is just this tension between substantial risk to the employee and substantial risk to the employer that brings about the need to negotiate these topics in severance, as well as employment. (Incidentally, when I use the word "pension," I mean it in its broadest sense, to include profit-sharing, employer-savings, and other retirement-related programs.)

Assessment of Coverages and Needs

The first task before you, without question, is to prepare a list of the pension and insurance benefits you believe are now available to you and therefore represent likely candidates for your negotiating efforts to protect or continue. This may require the assistance of your spouse, accountant, or even Human Resources representatives at your company. Start with your pension: have you received a report from your pension plan administrator during the previous year, outlining for you the status of your benefits, your degree of vesting in the company plan, and the form of investments in which your pension is held? If so, place it in your "crucial benefits" file. If not, ask your Human Resources representative or your boss who your pension plan administrator is, and contact him or her, requesting a report covering the topics I have listed above. Very frequently this report is readily available and titled "Summary of Plan" or "Summary Plan Description."

It is also a very good idea to find out if you would soon be entering a higher vesting level anytime within the next year or two. Perhaps your company increases its contribution, or your right to retire earlier, upon your attainment of a certain number of years of service, age, or both. It would be tragic to miss a significant increase in pension rights if your job ends involuntarily only days or weeks prematurely.

Regarding insurance coverages, prepare a list of each of the insurance coverages made available to you by your employer, possibly including coverages (or contributions) for health, life, disability, and even automobile. Next, alongside each listed coverage, set down the applicable coverage limits, the premium and your share of that, the deductible, and any other pertinent elements of coverage, cost, or limitation. Have you paid your entire yearly deductible? Will a new policy require the payment of an entirely new deductible? Jot down, as well, the name of any agents or administrators of the policies in question.

Most important, begin to think hard about your needs. If you are single, without children or dependent parents, you probably have no real need for life insurance coverage, at least for now. On the other hand, if you have a serious heart problem or long-term degenerative condition, limited savings, and two children approaching their college years, life insurance and disability insurance continuations may be crucial for you. Assessing your true needs, and balancing them with present coverages, perhaps should be your top priority at this time.

Legal Protections Available

A wide variety of legal protections regarding pensions and insurance is available to employees under both state and federal law. While states vary with respect to the legal protections they offer, federal laws apply to all, uniformly, and generally preempt state laws that may conflict with them. Each of these legal protections sets standards for fair treatment; many also provide specific enforcement mechanisms. If you feel you have been treated unfairly in connection with pension or insurance matters, but do not have legal counsel, a telephone call to your state labor board and/or to the nearest office of the U.S. Department of Labor might be a good place to start to find out about your rights.

The primary federal law that governs most retirement plans, and many health benefit plans as well, is the Employee Retirement Income Security Act, commonly called ERISA. ERISA provides employees in private pension plans with certain protections and regulates, as well, employee benefit plans. By its terms it supersedes state laws that relate to the same topics. The provisions of a severance agreement pertaining to health benefits could be considered an "employee welfare benefit plan" and thus subject to ERISA. ERISA acts to set fair standards for employer pension-type plans and is a far-reaching and exhaustive statute. It even provides for reimbursement of legal fees for employees who must sue to enforce their ERISA-based rights.

In 1985 Congress responded in another way to growing unease felt by many at the specter of loss of health insurance benefits by those downsized, by enacting the "COBRA" statute (which stands for the Consolidated Omnibus Budget Reconciliation Act). Generally, COBRA requires most employers to permit severed employees and their dependents to remain on the company's group health insurance policy up to eighteen months after termination, provided the severed employee reimburses the employer an amount equal to 102 percent of the monthly or quarterly premium. Few are aware of it, but the COBRA continuation period is thirty-six months for widows or widowers, divorced spouses, and dependent children.

Each state has its own version of a labor law, a wage law, a worker safety act, and other employee-protective statutes. Due to the wide variety and complexity of legal protections in this area, I can provide you with only the most general of outlines here. As I mentioned above, check with the U.S. Department of Labor for more details.

"The Plan (or Policy) Will Not Permit That"

In severance negotiations, when it seems appropriate and necessary, I often seek for my clients the continuation or modification of the crucial benefits of pension and insurance. With respect to pensions, the area of "pension accommodation" (discussed in the previous chapter) is probably the most difficult request to achieve. The request for continuation of one or more insurance coverages is also difficult to get, but is granted with greater frequency.

Quite commonly I am advised by my negotiating counterparts in Human Resources or the general counsel's office that the plan (in requests for pension accommodations) or policy (in requests for insurance continuation), itself, prevents the granting of my request, because it applies only to active, full-time employees of the company. In the many instances in which I have pressed my negotiating counterparts on this matter, requesting, for example, that they show me that section and paragraph of the plan or policy that is the basis for denying my request, I find that I am right in my expectations: no such section or paragraph can be located. That is, the plan or policy rarely serves to deny my request, and in most instances in which I pushed the issue to this extent, I find that a generalized reluctance to get involved in matters that seem confusing is at the heart of the refusal to consider my request.

In fact, when seeking pension accommodation, I've found that the most helpful person to contact is the plan administrator himself or herself, as well as the local office of the U.S. Department of Labor, which oversees ERISA compliance. Likewise, when I'm seeking an insurance continuation, the best contacts are those in the customer service units at the insurance companies themselves, as well as those in the state insurance regulator's office. These individuals know the details of the plans and have nothing at stake. As a result, they are wonderful sources of pension and insurance rights information, about both specific policies and regulations.

Negotiation Alternatives

Still, the granting of pension accommodations or insurance continuations is not all that common. When my requests are turned down, with finality, or due to true restrictions in the plans or policies themselves, I always make request for alternatives, or substitutes, including the following:

- That the employer consider you, the employee, on sabbatical, leave, or temporary reassignment, for these limited purposes, so as to make accommodations or continuation possible.
- That the employer purchase for you a replacement insurance policy, with comparable coverages, or pay the premiums for such a policy.
- That the employer provide you with the cash equivalent of the pension benefits lost, as determined by an actuary or by a pension benefit consultant hired for this very purpose.
- That the employer agree to "privately" insure you against loss attributable to costs for "preexisting conditions" until you are covered by insurance under a new policy.
- That the employer delay the severance date until you have suc-

cessfully replaced the lost coverage by joining a membership/ affiliation program under the auspices of such organizations as the American Association of Retired Persons (AARP), B'nai B'rith, the Kiwanis, or your local chapter of the auxiliary fire-fighters.

•   •   •

When negotiating for insurance coverage, keep these alternatives in mind. Often, if you have ready suggestions regarding these complex issues, your employer will be more likely to consider them an option and perhaps agree to one in your case.

21

Noncompetition and Other Restrictive Agreements

> Who has lost his freedom has nothing else to lose.
> —German proverb

Imagine the following scenario: You start working on a new job, in a new city, full of boundless enthusiasm and hope. You've barely finished unpacking. You've started getting to know your new coworkers, and your new life seems just right. One week later, you receive a legal-looking document that says you cannot remain in this job or even this industry. You must leave the industry for a minimum of two years. For many, this is not a bad dream but a reality. It is happening every day. In every city. And it could happen to you.

This is precisely what may transpire if you've signed—knowingly or unknowingly—a document containing language by which you've agreed not to work for a business that competes with your former employer, commonly called a "noncompete agreement." Sometimes these agreements are lengthy and heavily negotiated. Sometimes they are hidden in a paragraph in an otherwise innocuous document, presented to you on your first day on the job by Human Resources personnel, among dozens of other forms that require your signature. Last year, one of the largest mutual fund companies in the United States wrote all top managers and executives—220 in all—and required each to sign one of these agreements or leave the company; 218 signed.

Restrictive Covenants: Danger for the Employee

As competition heats up for the most precious asset in today's businesses—human capital—more and more employers are realizing that their best, brightest, and most valuable employees may be lured away by their direct competitors. To protect their considerable investments in their human capital, to reduce the significant costs of executive search, recruitment, and training, to thwart the possibility of losing precious trade secrets and business plans, and to hamstring their competitors' efforts, many companies are requiring executive employees to sign "restrictive covenants." These are, quite generally, promises that restrict, in some way or other, an employee's future freedom to work.

"Restrictive covenant" is the generic term used for the entire family of promises made by employees to their employers restricting their future freedom. These strong, enforceable restrictions may be embodied in one paragraph or section of a larger employment agreement or, on the other hand, put into a separate, distinct agreement of its own.

Restrictive covenants come in many forms:

- "For six months after I leave my employment here, I will not work in New York, Chicago, or Los Angeles for a firm that directly competes with my employer." (This is the standard "noncompetition agreement.")
- "If I voluntarily leave employment with the company within two years, I will not take employment elsewhere until I have repaid to the company its expenses incurred in my relocation and recruitment." (This is a "payback agreement.")
- "For one year after I leave my employer, I will not attempt to lure away from my employer any of its other employees." (This is commonly called a "nonsolicitation covenant.")
- "I must give my employer at least three months' notice before leaving." (This is the common notice requirement for quitting.)
- "If I receive an offer of outside employment, before I accept that offer of employment, I must give notice to my employer, and provide my employer with an opportunity to match that offer. If my employer matches that offer, I will remain." (This unusual covenant is called an "option to match.")
- A very common restrictive covenant, "At no time will I divulge to any person outside the company its trade secrets or other confidential or proprietary information; nor will I ever publicly disparage the company." (These two statements are called, respectively, a "nondisclosure covenant" and a "nondisparagement covenant. They are operative both during and after employment.)

Noncompetition Agreements

Noncompetition Agreements, commonly referred to as "noncompete's," are arguably the most frequently litigated of the postemployment restrictive agreements. There are two major reasons for this:

First, while executive employment is increasingly a game of musical chairs, companies take quite seriously the head-to-head business competition they face, and see noncompetition agreements as a very real part of coping with that competition. This is especially so in industries where new market campaigns, product development plans, and sales strategies are at stake. The financial impact of the loss of a key employee can be devastating to a company, even more so if it results in strategic advantage to a direct competitor.

Second, a certain emotional component seems to exist, and to rise to an unusually high level, when an employer perceives that an employee has intentionally ignored a significant employment contract provision. At the time of hiring, employers and their prospective hires often labor over noncompetes, and the requirement of one is often cited by the employer to justify the granting of a large "sign-on bonus" or expensive relocation package to an employee as an inducement to come aboard. No one likes to feel they've been slapped in the face, especially when it is done in public. When an agreement like this is infringed upon, it is as if corporate honor has been violated.

Negotiations undertaken to resolve disputes concerning noncompetition agreements are usually between the previous and future employers only, and usually do not directly, or at least centrally, involve the executive to which the noncompete applies. These are often strategic negotiations, and very expensive ones, at that. While most disputes over noncompetes are resolved out of court and the public eye, when they are the subject of litigation, they can be embarrassing to all concerned.

Enforceability of These Provisions: Presumptive

Are these agreements enforceable? Well, yes and no . . . and that's the problem. These cases are enforced by the courts on a case-by-case basis; you're never really sure if yours will be enforced until you're in court. Sometimes seeing things from the employee's view, courts are very reluctant to tell anyone they cannot make a living; this goes against our cultural bias in favor of free enterprise and individual initiative. Sometimes seeing things from the employer's side, however, courts tend to say to the employee, "If you agreed to it, and took a job on that basis, perhaps even accepted a sign-on bonus and relocation moneys, you must live with the restrictions now."

Courts weigh several considerations in these decisions: the effect of enforcement or nonenforcement on the respective parties; the amount of money or other benefit given to the employee for signing the restrictive covenant; whether the employee knew the likely consequences of what he or she was signing; the scope of the restriction. That is, no court will enforce a restriction gained by fraud or one that has elements that are too far-reaching, such as a lifetime restriction or worldwide geographic restriction.

Most restrictive covenants are found coupled with a second contractual device called "injunctive relief." If you should violate the promise you made in your restrictive covenant, this device allows your employer to go to court and request an order "enjoining" (ordering you to halt immediately) any further violation of your covenant. The court could then order you to cease working for your new employer temporarily or permanently. This could put both you, and your next employer, in quite a bind—unable to continue in your present position at least until your period of promised restriction (commonly ranging from six months to two years) is over.

Case History: **Campbell's Soup Versus Heinz:** A very interesting and illustrative example of a restrictive covenant dispute concerned one David O'Neill, formerly the head of the Campbell Soup Company's domestic soup business. In January 1997, the H. J. Heinz Company announced publicly that it had hired O'Neill to run its pet food and tuna businesses. Campbell's sought to enforce noncompetition provisions in its employment contract with O'Neill, which would bar him from working for a competitor for a period of eighteen months following his employment with Campbell's. In this case, the new employer, Heinz, did manufacture soup, but O'Neill was, at least officially, only to oversee pet food and tuna production.

After Campbell's and Heinz's negotiations failed to resolve the dispute, Heinz took the initiative in suing Campbell's. Heinz's suit sought to obtain a judgment declaring as invalid the noncompetition provisions. Campbell's responded with a lawsuit of its own, seeking injunctive relief barring O'Neill from working for Heinz for eighteen months.

The matter was settled in a most elaborate, and probably embarrassing, way:

- O'Neill could not assume his new Heinz position for seven months.
- During the seven-month waiting period, O'Neill could not speak with Heinz employees about business matters, only social ones.
- Once O'Neill assumed his new Heinz position, he was required to keep a daily log of his meetings and conversations, to be monitored by an independent auditor to ensure there was no transfer of trade secrets or confidential information that O'Neill brought from Campbells.
- An independent consultant would assess whether proprietary information regarding Campbell's unique soup-manufacturing technology had been adopted by Heinz.

A Heinz spokesman claimed victory: "Campbell's had to recognize that the eighteen-month noncompetition agreement was unreasonable."

A Campbell's spokesman claimed victory: "Our noncompete agreement should be as binding as one's word. No settlement can remove the stain of Heinz's calculated raid."

O'Neill claimed bewilderment: "I'm glad this is resolved, because it could have gone on in the courts for a long time. . . . I was totally caught by surprise that Campbell would react this way."

Protective Measures Regarding Noncompetition and Restrictive Actions

What should an employee do?

1. Carefully read what you've been given to sign. If it is unclear in any way or, worse, looks like legal nonsense to you, consider having an attorney review it with you.

2. Make sure any restrictive covenant is operative only in the event you leave on a voluntary basis. If you are laid off or fired, future restrictions make little sense. That is, if your present employer no longer wants your services, you should be entitled to work for others.

3. Don't be afraid to ask that any such restriction be removed, for it is a risk of forced unemployment or forced employment outside your chosen field or geographic area, and therefore is beyond the level of risk you feel comfortable with.

4. Consider, as well, asking for reasonable limitations on the restrictive covenant. It could cover a shorter period of time, include a more limited definition of the companies considered in "competition" with yours, or perhaps be operative only during your first year with the employer or phased out over time.

5. Suggest that the restrictions be considered inoperative if your compensation level does not increase by a set percentage yearly, or if you have not been promoted to a certain level by a certain time. After all, if you're coming to a new employer for certain rewards or authority, and they fail to materialize, you should be free to seek your fame and fortune elsewhere.

6. Request that any disputes concerning these provisions be handled by arbitration. Arbitration takes place out of the public eye, generally disallows injunctive relief, and is less potentially disruptive to your career than a lawsuit.

7. Consider not agreeing to take the job if these restrictions are not removed. While this is a drastic consideration, it may make sense in your own case.

• • •

The biggest mistake made by executive employees is not to take restrictive covenants with the utmost of seriousness. Many of my clients tell me, to my own amusement and concern, that "*no* court would enforce *that*." Remember, such sentiments could result in lasting harm to an otherwise bright career. These terms can and very well may be enforced.

22

Stock Options

> Stock option plans reward the executive for doing the
> wrong thing. Instead of asking, "Are we making the right
> decisions?" he asks, "How did we close today?" It is
> encouragement to loot the corporation.
> —Peter Drucker (business philosopher)

Despite sentiments like those expressed above, more and more companies are turning to the distribution of stock options both as part of their regular or basic compensation programs and as incentive compensation to reward unusual effort or results. And they are now used more widely than ever before; major employers such as the Travelers Group, Bank America, and Monsanto distribute stock options to all employees, at all levels.

Stock options can be a very effective motivational tool, because their use encourages employee longevity on the job, boosts morale, and promotes a team mentality. They are quite cost-effective as well. Stock options are, relatively speaking, inexpensive for employers, for they have no direct, out-of-pocket cost and do not represent a balance sheet charge against earnings. Recent accounting-standard changes require only that stock option grants be mentioned in the footnotes of shareholder annual reports.

As the incidence of granting stock options has increased, as well as their rise in importance in overall compensation schemes, the negotiation of issues related to stock options at severance time has increased, too.

Accurate Head Count

If you hold company stock options at the time of severance, the first step you should take is to prepare an accurate, detailed schedule of (1) the number and type of options granted to you, (2) when each may vest, and be exercised, including any dates of expiration, (3) the "strike price" of each, (4) whether financing for the purchase is to be made available, (5) the method of exercise required, if explicit, and (6) whether there exist any conditions, limitations, and restriction on such exercise.

Limitations and Restrictions

Of the six classes of information that you must carefully assemble, as noted above, the most crucial, yet most often missed, is the last: limitations and restrictions on exercise. The most common restrictions on stock option exercise are those related to their loss upon termination of employment. That is, many stock option grants made to employees explicitly state that they may be exercised only during the period of employment and expire automatically upon employment termination. It is this singular restriction that is the most important for us to address here. If you remain free to hold and exercise valuable stock options subsequent to being let go, the next decision—whether to hold or sell—is primarily one of investment and tax consequence, not a legal negotiation decision. Look at your own financial situation and make the decision that best suits you.

Replacement or Substitute

The two most common methods of addressing the potential loss of stock options at severance time are (1) replacement by other, new options, often with different exercise dates or conditions, yet representing similar value, and (2) substitution by other forms of value to you, whether as cash payment, continuing consultant agreement, significant pension accommodation, or the voiding of a noncompete agreement.

Cost to Exercise, Including Taxes

The exercise of stock options at severance time, if deemed of value, often will present you with two significant problems. The first is coming up with the necessary liquid assets (or financing) to purchase the shares available, even if at a substantially lower price than market price. The second problem is the adverse tax consequence that commonly comes upon option exercise.

According to the Internal Revenue Code, when you exercise a stock option, you receive a thing of value; hence you have realized income, and you are to be taxed upon the difference between your purchase price and the then-market value of the stock. When you sell these shares, your additional gain (or loss) is then reassessed and potentially retaxed. Note, though, that all of this income is taxed at the "ordinary income" tax rates, which at this writing may be as high as 39.6 percent. But appreciation on shares held for longer than one year is taxed only at the lower, long-term capital gains rate, which is at the time of this writing only 28 percent and apparently headed even lower by congressional action.

Next Employment—Compensation

Sometimes stock options granted at the time of severance can be exercised only within the period of time before reemployment. If giving up valuable stock option rights is, therefore, a necessary precondition to gaining reemployment, the negotiation of that new employment must take into account the loss of this value. Whether you may lose stock options in this way, or as a result of leaving employment voluntarily after being recruited or "courted," you should give serious consideration to requesting reimbursement of such losses by your former employer or your future employer, as the case may be.

Significant Freedom

Most employers have very significant freedom to grant stock options, to modify or remove existing limitations and restrictions, to replace existing options with new stock options, or to provide valuable alternatives for the loss of stock options. For this reason, the use of options at severance is increasing. One restriction, however, is frequently consent by the board of directors, requiring or at least permitting discussion.

In one severance negotiation I engaged in on behalf of an executive vice president of a major insurance company, management's negotiators proposed scrapping the entire, complicated severance package and substituting in its place one single stock option worth about $1 million. With some minor modifications, the new plan was eventually accepted. This is another example of the flexibility available in severance packages. Keep in mind that your creativity in regard to what your agreement contains may be well rewarded.

23

Defamation and Disparagement

> Who steals my purse steals trash;
> 'tis something, nothing; . . .
> But he that filches from me my good name
> Robs me of that which not enriches him,
> And makes me poor indeed.
>
> —William Shakespeare

Mutual Concerns

As stable, long-term employment has become a thing of the past, many people understandably feel insecure. They worry about the loss of health insurance, about the loss of pension benefits, about not having the job skills that will be necessary ten years from now or maybe even next year. In addition, people now worry more and more about the effect job loss and severance will have on their professional reputations. Will people wonder why she's no longer with the company? Will rumors spread about his performance as a salesman?

Those in senior management worry, too, about the possible effect of negative public relations on the company. Companies want to protect their reputations for integrity and trustworthiness, for selling products or services of excellent quality. The environmentally catastrophic *Exxon Valdez* oil spill in Alaska in 1989 was not a happy experience for Exxon; it tarnished a company image developed and polished over decades with tens of millions of dollars. The same holds true for Texaco in the wake of its race discrimination scandal of 1996. It did not help the image of one of the world's most prestigious cancer treatment centers when, in 1997, one of its surgeons operated on the wrong side of a patient's brain. These developments, and consequent concerns, have led to some new severance policies.

Mutual Remedies

It is now almost a universal occurrence for employers to insist upon "nondisparagement" clauses in severance agreements, in an attempt to limit bad publicity of any kind. An example of one such nondisparagement clause is as follows:

> As further conditions to the Company's performance of this agreement, you agree: (i) not to make any public statement or statements to the press concerning the Company, its business objectives, its management practices, or other sensitive information without approval; (ii) that you shall take no action which would cause the Company or its shareholders, directors, officers, employees, or agents any embarrassment or humiliation or otherwise cause or contribute to the Company's or any such persons being held in disrepute by the general public or the Company's employees, vendors, or customers.

While this example is a bit long-winded and far-reaching, it provides a good illustration of nondisparagement clauses I often see. I can certainly appreciate the concerns expressed. But as an advocate for individual executives, I seek to protect my client's interests in a similar fashion. To be protective of my client, yet at the same time fair and reasonable, I insist only upon mutuality, by insertion of a provision such as this one:

> The nondisparagement obligations of the Employee will be considered mutual in every respect, so that the Company, its shareholders, officers, directors, employees, and agents will be under the same restrictions and obligations regarding nondisparagement and confidentiality to Employee as (s)he is to them.

Such a clause is agreed to in a majority of instances where it is requested.

Truth or Defamation

You may have noticed when reading the first example of a nondisparagement clause that the text of the clause never differentiates between true statements and false statements, but only prohibits "embarrassing" or "humiliating" ones. The absence of such a distinction is telling: even true statements, if embarrassing to the company, will violate the nondisparagement prohibition.

The law provides all parties with protection against false and damaging statements, whether spoken ("slander") or written ("libel"); both are generically referred to as "defamation." A good working definition of "defamation" is "the unprivileged publication of false statements, oral or written, that naturally and proximately result in injury to the reputation, respect, or goodwill of another."

It's good to keep in mind that the law protects everyone from false and damaging statements, whereas nondisparagement clauses protect their intended beneficiaries from all statements—true or false—that are humiliating, embarrassing, or hurtful to image or reputation. It's important to bear in mind, as well, that statements made or written directly to you, but not disseminated to others, are not legally considered defamation or disparagement of you because they have not been publicized to others.

The Departure Statement

Many severed executives and management employees want to ensure that the company they are departing from will not provide a negative "job reference" when requested by a prospective future employer. In general, this worry is usually without foundation since job references are not very common anymore. It is now an almost universal and strictly enforced Human Resources policy and practice that only three things are provided upon the request of a prospective employer: (1) confirmation that you once worked for the company; (2) the dates of your employment, and (3) your position(s) held. It is almost universally forbidden to provide performance appraisals or commentaries, compensation levels, or reasons for departure, at least without the employee's prior consent. With this approach, employers aim to avoid the ever present possibility of a defamation lawsuit.

To address this company concern, and to provide the severed executive with a reasonable and credible cover story of sorts, I always request, as part of severance negotiation, that the parties come to agreement upon the text of a departure statement, to be signed by the departed executive's superior, very senior management, or even the CEO. I discuss this in chapter 16 at greater length and provide a sample departure statement in the appendix.

You Can't Stop Murmurings

Even with mutual nondisparagement clauses, and the agreed text and dissemination of a departure statement, people will talk. You should not take it to heart if, in spite of such a document, you hear that other employees, or even your negotiation partners, have said less-than-flattering things about you. People are prone to gossip and can almost be expected to do so in circumstances such as these. You must do all you can to take this as part of the process and ignore it to the best of your ability.

However, a serious related problem is sometimes seen in cases of "veiled defamation." Veiled defamation consists of statements that could be read either as very serious and harmful in nature or as merely innocuous. For example, I had one client who was terminated for allegedly having "unsavory habits." What these were exactly was never disclosed, but the terminology suggests something that could only be considered very negative. Were we talking about purchase and sale of child pornography or failure to keep his fingernails neatly cut? You can see the issue here. Likewise, termination for "violating company policy" could be considered extremely serious in the securities industry, even fatal to one's career, while the actual conduct in question could be as simple as bringing one's dog to work on the weekend. Veiled defamation can be a very difficult problem to resolve satisfactorily.

What to Do If. . . .

So what should you do if you become aware that members of senior management are either defaming you by false statements or disparaging you in violation of a nondisparagement clause? I suggest you take these steps:

1. **Stay calm under all circumstances.** Negative reactions, outbursts, or retaliation of any kind will only backfire on you. Try to bear in mind how little credence most people give to such murmurings.

2. **Investigate; don't speculate.** If you hear certain things are being said about you, ask who told the person who told you. If you can, find out the specifics on when, where, and how the information got out. Seek facts. Don't jump to conclusions. Ask for specifics.

3. **Don't forget: truth is not defamatory.** It is essential that you bear in mind that truthful statements are not defamatory but may still violate nondisparagement obligations.

4. **Ask recipients for confirmation.** Consider seriously asking people who have personally heard the violations, or seen the written statements against you, for either a witnessed or tape-recorded statement or a confirmation of their observations, preferably in written form. This will serve to separate the reliable witnesses from the nonreliable witnesses, and also discourage a witness from caving to other pressures to change his or her story later.

5. **Collect evidence of damage.** If your career, profession, or reputation was damaged, it is crucial that you (or your lawyer) are prepared with accurate lists of such items as business lost or the sudden disappearance of client referrals. Otherwise, you may have a claim, based on merit, but without significant value. If you lost an interview, a job, clients, or business opportunities as the result of a former employer speaking ill of you, collect proof of these damages. Proof of lost future earnings can be targeted by a good actuary.

6. **Contact an attorney.** Whether you've been wrongly disparaged or wrongfully defamed, a good attorney can assess your claim and enforce your rights. Ask around, or call your local bar association referral service, for an attorney experienced in these matters.

7. **Don't focus on the past.** Regardless of whether you choose legal recourse, you should focus on tomorrow, not yesterday. At this challenging time, you need all of your energies to move positively into the future. Try not to waste any of your valuable resources being angry over what a former employer is now saying. Address the situation legally and move forward.

24

Future Ownership and
Use of Ideas and "Creations"

> I am more of a sponge than an inventor. I absorb ideas
> from every source. My principal business is giving com-
> mercial value to the brilliant but misdirected ideas of
> others.
>
> —Thomas Edison

It is relatively uncommon for severance negotiations to include issues related to the future ownership and use of ideas and creations, or the expression and development of ideas into written, picture, formula, or physical form. In the great majority of cases, severed executives have no such concerns, actual or potential. There are, however, two compelling reasons I include the discussion of this subject here: first, when these issues do, in fact, exist, most people are not aware of them; second, when these issues arise, they are often of major importance and require the most careful, strategic negotiation approach. (Issues related to the use of confidential information and trade secrets—such as chemical formulas and customer lists—are entirely distinct, and I'll discuss them in the next chapter.)

The Law of Ideas and Creations

Before delving into these issues, and their negotiation during severance discussions, I believe a bit of explanation of the applicable law is in order. Ideas come to each of us every day, and we all come up with good ideas concerning all sorts of matters, including ones related to our workplace, all the time—ideas that could result in new products or services; ideas that could identify new customers, clients, or strategic directions; ideas that could lower costs and increase productivity. The law in all jurisdictions treats ideas the same in this way: no one can own an idea. Thus ideas, in and of themselves, have no commercial value. It's just that simple.

But ideas can be expressed and developed, and in their expression or development they begin to take on value, and that value is quite often considerable, and quite often fought over. That's crucial: expression or development of an idea is, in and of itself, of value. We often refer to expressed ideas or developed ideas as "creations." It is when and how an idea is first conceived, and then expressed and developed into a creation, that leads us to our discovery of who probably owns that creation, may profit from it, or may use it for any variety of business purposes.

If you have an idea, you can protect it as your own if you have expressed or developed that idea. In the eyes of the law, you may develop those rights in one of two main ways: by publicly using that creation in a provable way, or by pursuing legally recognized "creation-preservation" procedures regarding it. The latter involves copyright of the creation if it is a literary, musical, or visual one, or patent of the creation if it is an invention, process, formula, or product. Even though many people may have had the same idea as you have had, even if they had the idea before you, your expressing or developing it first, to the point of creation, and your then seeking legal protection of that creation, gives you the protection you need to move forward to enjoy its value in commerce.

In severance negotiations, we most often see issues of this kind arise in cases where people regularly deal with new and valuable ideas that are then commonly expressed and developed: in highly technical industries, such as the computer and software industries; in creative industries such as the toy and fashion industries; and in ground-breaking areas such as the medical/pharmaceutical/biotechnology industries.

Presumption in Favor of Employer Ownership

Ideas you express and develop while you are on the job are, with one general exception (discussed in the next section of this chapter), considered to be assets of the employer. If you conceived of a new process or product while sitting at your desk, using company computers and company time to develop it to the point of a new creation, and the company spent additional considerable sums to develop, perfect, test, and market it, the idea is the company's to exploit and enjoy in the commercial marketplace. This hypothetical example, though, is quite extreme and clear, and thus easy to classify under the legal doctrine known as the "shop right doctrine." The creation in this hypothetical situation is the employer's, no question about it, with the one general exception referred to above.

Another clear example of presumptive employer ownership of an idea is when your employer asks you to come up with a solution to, say, a software "bug," and you do so, and are paid to do so. This is another instance of a clear example of likely employer ownership, commonly called a "work for hire."

Most examples are not as clear as these two are. Sometimes an employee conceived of an idea at home or before employment began, and developed it without company input or assistance entirely on his or her own time. If such facts and circumstances exist and are provable, they would tend to support a contention that the employee, alone, is entitled to own and enjoy the creation's value in the marketplace.

Employee Ownership by Provable Agreement

The one major exception to the rule that the employer is presumptively entitled to ownership of creations developed with its resources, input, and assistance is when the employee and employer have agreed to employee ownership or shared ownership, or use, of the creation.

If the creation was volunteered by the employee to the employer, without apparent expectation that the employee was to be considered its owner, or to receive the fruits of its later commercial exploitation, or payment for its use, and then used by the employer in business, in any contest or negotiation between the employee and employer, it is more than likely that the creation will be considered an asset of the employer only.

If, on the other hand, the employee first approached the employer with a fully developed creation, provably conceived, expressed, and developed outside employment, and offered to the employer for a fee, or percentage of profits, or on some terms then specified or to be negotiated later, it is likely in the long run to be enforceably considered an asset of the employee, to be owned and enjoyed by that employee only in the event he or she leave the company. The most savvy and prudent employees make efforts to establish such a provable situation, either by agreement in writing or by memos or other tangible evidence.

Employee/Creator Precautions

Safeguard your creations by:

1. **Never signing broadly written releases of creative ideas or inventions.** Among the reams of forms and other papers that Human Resources personnel will present to you when you're first hired, you may find a release of this sort that requires your signature. "Just say no." If you are concerned that taking this stance may jeopardize your new job, explain your concern.

2. **Never sharing ideas on a casual basis.** If an idea seems a good one or new to your industry, devote the time it takes to express and develop it, to give it value, before sharing it with your employer.

3. **Always creating dated evidence of your authorship or invention.** Legal copyrighting or patenting is wise. One simple method you can use to show ownership is to mail a fully developed creation to yourself, by certified mail, and not open the envelope upon receiving it. The postmark and the sealed envelope together will tend to provide evidence of authorship. Mailing the creation in similar fashion to a friend, without his or her opening the envelope, is a wise backup measure to take.

4. **Establishing your financial motivations either before or upon submission to your employer.** Send your employer a letter or memo requesting confirmation of your creation and stating your expectation that the employer will not seek to usurp your creator's rights to ownership and commercial exploitation, without agreement as to payment. I also suggest transmittal of this information by provable means, such as certified mail, return receipt, or by hand-delivering it to the employer yourself.

Negotiation in Severance

As noted in earlier sections, one of the first things I do when meeting a new severance client is to conduct an interview of sorts to get to know that individual and understand the relevant facts and circumstances of his or her case. Part of that initial talk is always devoted to issues of this type. The critical facts I want to learn regarding creative ownership are: (1) when the idea was initially conceived; (2) when and how the idea was expressed and developed to the point of "creation"; (3) how the creation was presented to the employer; (4) how the employer contributed to the further development of the creation; (5) whether the employee and the employer agreed on how the creation would be "enjoyed"; (6) what proof exists to establish all of the above-mentioned points.

If I determine with my client's input that issues related to ideas and creations do exist, I then must begin to think strategically: Should we preemptively bring the subject up, seeking clear agreement, if neither the negotiators nor the initial draft agreement broach the subject first? Should we raise an objection if the other side raises the subject in negotiations or in its initial draft agreement?

The strategic choices are all guided by the facts—including our assessment of the likely long-term value of the creation, the apparent strength of proof of employee ownership, and the anticipated future direction of the employee's career. This line of thought is undertaken, of course, in the context of a larger negotiation of considerable importance to the severed executive, and so is guided by the other aspects of the negotiation at hand.

These considerations all help me conclude, with my client, whether and to what extent we may raise the issue in open discussion, or whether I will counsel silence, as I often do for strategic purposes in such circumstances. It is difficult, if not impossible, to detail all parameters of these discussions and decisions here, for the particular facts of each creation and creator are unique and, at the same time, determine strategy. You should simply keep the points I raise here in mind when you discuss issues of creative ownership with your lawyer, but ultimately you will tailor your approach to this issue based on the facts in your case.

Case History: For twenty-two years Jerry had been a senior Human Resource director for a major office furniture manufacturer. His area of expertise was the design and implementation of motivational programs. Over the years, Jerry had created, tested, and perfected a certain motivational seminar for salespeople that was an absolute winner. Survey results proved that salespeople who attended Jerry's seminar averaged a 150 percent increase in customer retention and a 225 percent increase in overall sales. Over time, almost every business unit in the company requested Jerry's seminars. In fact, as other companies heard of Jerry's success, they requested his services, and the company Jerry worked for developed an entire new business unit.

But success has its price. Others in Human Resources began to envy Jerry, and in what I call a political restructuring and severance, Jerry was given termination notice. While it is ironic, irrational, counterproductive, and stupid, every veteran of large organizations will recognize this all-too-common pattern of success-envy-dismissal.

However, Jerry was not too upset over this turn of events. He was fifty-seven years old and fully vested in pension, indeed entitled to early retirement payout, and interested in opening his own consulting/training business. He was comfortable with the company's severance policy of two weeks per year of service, which granted him forty-four weeks of severance pay. There was just one big question that Jerry was concerned about: his future use of his motivational seminars.

Our severance negotiations focused on this one primary issue. Through a comprehensive analysis of the concerns of both parties, we were able to reach a set of terms and conditions under which both sides felt pleased. Jerry was permitted to pay one dollar per year as a "license fee" to sell the seminars, but the company was recognized as the "owner" of this creation. Jerry would present the seminars under his own new company name, but in all advertisements and promotional materials, the words "sponsored by [the company]" were to be prominently displayed. Further, the company reserved the right to reasonably restrict Jerry from selling his training services to potential clients of the company. Last, but not least, if the company ever decided to close down this business unit, Jerry would be entitled to purchase the rights to the seminar, at a price then to be determined by a jointly chosen business appraiser. Jerry went on to pursue a successful business on his own, and the company benefited from his use of "its" seminar. Everyone won.

25

Confidentiality, Proprietary Information, and Trade Secrets

> If the Nile knows your secret, it will soon be known in the desert.
>
> —African proverb

We live in a time many refer to as the "information age," in which data and images fly back and forth between continents in a fraction of a second. Businesspeople are increasingly concerned about how they and their companies may be affected, for good or bad, by the flow of their information to competitors, to the media, to their customers, to their stockholders, and on and on. In many businesses, whoever controls the information controls the power. Therefore, for executives, the collection, management, analysis, and control of information can make or break a career.

At the time of severance negotiations, three issues arise with great frequency that center on the control of information. Though we may speak of these issues as if they were three distinct categories, they do overlap to a considerable degree. They are confidentiality of the agreement, proprietary information, and trade secrets. Let's look at each.

Confidentiality of the Agreement

In almost every severance agreement prepared by the employer, I find a clause providing that the employee must keep confidential both the fact that she or he entered into such an agreement as well as its terms. There are, however, several commonly permitted exceptions to this restriction: the employee can divulge such information to his or her (1) spouse and immediate family, (2) attorney, (3) accountant or tax adviser; and (4) if and when required by law, such as in a court proceeding or upon service of a lawful subpoena.

Here is a good example of such a "confidentiality clause":

> The Employee agrees to keep the existence and the terms of this agreement confidential, except that the Employee may divulge the existence and terms of this agreement to his or her immediate family, legal counsel, financial and tax advisers, and as he or she may be required by operation of law.

The question often arises: is the employee considered in breach of this clause if he or she discusses the terms of the agreement with, for example, the family lawyer, which is expressly permitted, and the lawyer then discusses the agreement with others, which is expressly prohibited? Some confidentiality clauses say that this would be considered a breach of the agreement; others provide that the severed employee must, in the least, caution the "permitted recipients" of their own need to maintain confidentiality. Most confidentiality clauses, though, are silent on this point. It would probably be reasonable to presume that, in those cases, breach of confidentiality by "permitted recipients" would not be considered a breach by the employee in a court of law.

What is the penalty for loose lips? It's high. Quite often severance agreements provide that, in event of breach, the severed employee must return all monetary severance benefits previously paid.

The evident concern of most employers that other employees will find out that severance benefits are potentially available, what types and amounts are potentially available, and to whom it has been made available is a real one that is to be respected, for severance is a matter of negotiation. It's quite effective, and often amusing, to hear the director of Human Resources lecture me on the company policy— which is supposedly never violated—to limit severance payments to six months' salary, *without exception* (that last phrase repeated four times), only then to tell her the names of five former employees (not my own clients, but others with loose lips) who each received between twelve and thirty-six months' base salary as severance. Sort of knocks the wind out of that argument, doesn't it?

As with many "control" issues in severance negotiation, I frequently ask for mutuality; that is, that the employer agree to maintain this matter and all of its details on a confidential basis, along with the employee. This is agreed to in perhaps 75 percent of the cases where I've requested it.

Confidentiality is almost always required. Limitation of information is limitation of risk.

Proprietary Information

"Proprietary Information" may be defined as any information in which a party holds an ownership or other valuable interest. Proprietary information is most commonly available to the public, but originally conceived, gathered, sorted, or reported by a company or person in a way that adds value to it. A good example of proprietary information is a listing of dentists and their addresses assembled from the telephone book. The time and effort taken to assemble it makes it valuable. Indeed, if you called each dentist and asked if he or she was about to buy dental equipment, that additional answer is proprietary information that would be even more valuable.

Proprietary information may also be the formula for a new plastic that is patented: since it is patented, the formula is set out in a public record, for all to see, but its use is limited by law to the patent holder and its licensees. Though dissemination of proprietary information may not, in itself, be a violation of law, it may be guarded against by agreement. Indeed, in many severance agreements, employers require severed employees to agree not to divulge or disseminate information of a proprietary nature.

Trade Secrets

Trade secrets are valuable, secure information that has, for this reason, readily available protection under the law of most states. In New York, the punishment for theft of trade secrets can be quite severe and even lead to imprisonment. One commonly used definition of trade secrets is as follows:

> Any formula, pattern device or compilation of information which is used in one's business and which gives him an opportunity to obtain an advantage over competitors who do not know or use it.

Whether a unit of information is a trade secret depends upon several factors:

- the resources devoted to developing it
- the difficulty others would have in developing it
- the degree of its being known in the business or outside the business
- the value of the information in the business, profession, or trade
- the extent to which its owner guards against its dissemination.

Perhaps the most famous trade secret is the recipe for the Coca-Cola syrup, which has never been patented and is allegedly known by only a handful of individuals. A severance agreement might contain a broadly worded provision covering proprietary information and trade secrets, such as the following:

> The Employee will not, at any time, disclose to others or use for his or her own benefit or the benefit of others any knowledge or information regarding the operation, sales, or finances of the Company, or with respect to confidential, proprietary, secret customer or vendor lists, advertising, marketing or sales practices, plans, processes, techniques, product information, processes, know-how, designs, formulas, development or experimental work, computer programs, data bases, original works of authorship, or business plans. If the employee breaches or threatens to breach his or her obligations under this paragraph, the Company will be entitled, over and above all other remedies, to obtain an order enjoining such breach or threatened breach. Further, in such event, the Employee will be obligated to return to the Company all monetary and other consideration provided to Employee under this agreement and, in addition, to reimburse the Company for its reasonable attorney fees and costs incurred in pursuing any action to enforce this agreement.

Many industries' and companies' ability to survive and compete depends on their successful maintenance of trade secrets. You can see when it comes to severance: the potential loss of valuable information in this way becomes a real risk. As times go on, I see ever greater efforts made by companies to continually increase the penalties faced by departing employees if such vital information is shared. Likewise, the more high-tech, more cutting-edge, or trendsetting a business is, the greater is the risk and the greater the attention to this detail during severance negotiations.

26

For Those Contemplating Continuing Arrangements or Consultancies

> Any new venture goes through the following stages: enthusiasm, complication, disillusionment, search for the guilty, punishment of the innocent, and decoration of those who did nothing.
>
> —anonymous

Over the last few years I've seen a continual increase in the incidence of severance negotiations in which discussions include a continuing business arrangement, or consultancy, between the employee and the employer. As explained in this chapter, these are among the most intricate, and interesting, of my negotiations because they integrate two, and sometimes three, distinct business relationships. Before I address those negotiations, I will address the needs from which they arise.

As a Justification for Continuing Benefits

Continuing consultancies—especially what are often termed "in-house consultancies"—are sometimes little more than a title given to a severed executive so that, despite the termination, he or she may continue to be afforded benefits and insurance coverages. In these circumstances, continuing consultancies are a temporary tool used to overcome the nonnegotiable requirement of some benefit programs that recipients be employed at the present time to enjoy coverage. A departing employee might be called an in-house consultant in name only for a few months following his or her last day to receive life insurance during recuperation from heart surgery or to qualify for early retirement under a retirement or pension plan. In these instances, continuing arrangements are quite easy to negotiate, for little is expected of the severed executive.

"Outsourcing" from Within

One strategy companies have commonly used since the mid-1980s to lower payroll-related overhead is employing contractors to provide the same services as "inside" employees formerly did. In this way, companies look to save money by lowering their benefit costs, gaining flexibility of services, avoiding costs associated with personnel functions (hiring, firing, training, etc.), and by being able to negotiate fees continually in the marketplace for these services. Sometimes the strategy works; sometimes it doesn't. This has been the dynamic underlying many recent corporate downsizings.

Entering into such a continuing consultant arrangement with a severed employee offers the employer the added benefit of gaining a consultant who has knowledge of the company, its operations, and its people. Being severed, yet outsourced, is of potential benefit to the employee as well. The consultancy is a source of income, and for some the more flexible role is one they come to find is preferable to that of full-time employee.

True Consultancies

In perhaps most instances of continuing consultancies I see, there develops through negotiation a true, new relationship. Most commonly, it is a relationship driven, first and foremost, by the company's real and sometimes urgent need to access the unique, special, or rare knowledge, talent, and skills of the severed executive. So why, you may ask, did the severance occur in the first place? Three reasons generally stand out: (1) cost savings (as noted above), (2) political terminations, as discussed in greater detail in chapter 6 (which happen with special frequency following mergers and acquisitions), and (3) employee-initiated transitions.

1. Cost Savings
In circumstances of workforce reduction due to corporate restructuring aimed at cost containment, very often the most senior management recognizes the continuing need for the skills and experience of

the severed employee, but is under extraordinary pressure to cut costs "somewhere, anywhere" from the company's board of directors, its principal shareholders, nervous lenders, or stock analysts who cover either the industry as a whole or the company in particular. This movement toward greater use of contingent workers, who have neither benefits nor expectation of long-term employment, is perhaps the most profound transition under way in employment relationships worldwide. It has given rise to a temporary workforce never seen before.

2. Political Terminations

Merger and acquisition results in new political hierarchies within recently united companies that give rise to dismissals and subsequent consultant relationships.

This was vividly illustrated in a recent merger of retail banks. I represented two individuals—one from each bank—who were severed due to their close affiliations with the nonprevailing side in power struggles in the merged entity. Both were asked to go, but to remain affiliated so that their skills and contacts could be tapped during the completion of the merger. One eventually returned to his department when yet more internal changes took place.

3. Employee-Initiated Transitions

Continuing consultancies also develop when the employee decides to become self-employed. The increase in the number of entrepreneurial consultants, in all industries, has been dramatic. In some cases, the newly solo executive joins an existing group of consultants or advisers.

These continuing arrangements are the most unique arrangements of all and require the highest degree of sensitivity, attention, and strategic thinking. While we need to recognize and address the requirements of the parties in the employment-termination context, and of the same parties' respective interests in the commencement of the continuing relationship, we also must bear in mind the needs of the employee regarding his or her new venture. For example, will the employee be undertaking a solitary venture or become a partner or associate of an ongoing firm? In the former case, there are numerous preliminary questions to be addressed and resolved regarding initial investment, choice of business structure, longer-term commitments (including space and equipment leases), as well as the simultaneous, general overlay of tax considerations. In the latter case, there will be a third, distinct relationship to decipher and develop, and parties whose needs and concerns bear consideration at the same time.

Case History: Brian was brought on board by a regional banking institution to oversee the development of its new on-line banking subsidiary. He had a sterling reputation in the banking industry and had been happily running his own consulting firm for four years when lured back into full-time employment. His coming on board to head up the new subsidiary was frequently cited by stock analysts for their decisions to issue "buy" recommendations for the bank's stock.

Brian's subsidiary was, as expected, off to a successful start, but his success, itself, set off certain infighting among the bank's many territorially minded senior officers. The competing claims for credit for the new success, and for the considerable staff and clout that it inevitably generated, were intense. When the infighting subsided, the die was cast: after only one and one-half years at the helm, Brian's tenure would be cut short by shortsighted, yet controlling, political interests. To all, though, one fact was clear: no one at the bank could match (or had immediate access to) Brian's unique skills, considerable experience, and, most important, his reputation among the stock analysts. Brian had such significant leverage in negotiating severance that most of his severance requests would be honored with little more than a murmur.

Having been through such infighting before, and knowing that the insecurity of his situation had taken a serious toll on his wife, Brian decided that he would return, once and for all, to the world of consulting. The bank's dire need for Brian's continuing services to complete the process he had begun coincided quite well with Brian's own needs for the resources and commitment to restart his consulting career, including: relocation expense, start-up equipment, continued monthly payments for an extended period under a binding contract, and additional amenities, including continuation of insurance coverages.

I helped Brian negotiate a consulting contract that incorporated all of these provisions, as well as a public statement that was to be issued praising Brian's successful completion of his mission at the bank and his continuing oversight of future progress in the subsidiary's operations. The announcement highlighted the fact that Brian would now be available, in addition, to other retail banking institutions for similar start-up missions. This is just exactly what Brian needed to jump-start his new venture.

27

Form U-5 Statements:
Special Concern for Those
in the Securities Industry

> Never cut what you can untie.
>
> —Joseph Joubert (French essayist)

The securities industry is a highly regulated one. Governmental agencies, particularly the federal Securities and Exchange Commission (SEC), and numerous state agencies keep a tight rein on industry practices and personnel. This is one of the reasons that U.S. markets are generally trusted worldwide. The industry, itself, also devotes considerable effort and resources to self-regulation. One important focus of these constant regulatory efforts is the identification and elimination from the industry's ranks of those whose character and integrity are not deemed to meet acceptable standards. But how can we assess character and integrity? Prior conduct is the primary identifying factor.

Form U-5 Termination Notice

Rule 345.17 of the New York Stock Exchange and Rule 214 of the National Futures Association each require their respective member firms to file with a central depository a certain form called the "Uniform Termination Notice for Securities Industry Registration," commonly called a "Form U-5," whenever the employment of a registered representative is terminated. This applies whether the registered representative quit, was fired, or was terminated for another reason, such as the dissolution of the firm itself. Information from these U-5 Forms is publicly available, to both potential customers and prospective employers. The forms contain facts and circumstances of both the employee's tenure and termination from the reporting firm.

Item 12 of the Form U-5 requires identification of a "Reason for Termination," listing the available choices as: "Voluntary," "Deceased," "Permitted to Resign," "Discharged," or "Other." For the last three of these categories, an explanation is required. On the surface, this form provides all potential future employers with the reason and circumstances of termination for any registered securities representative. Both the form and its purpose seem clear and sensible. But, in practice, problems are plentiful.

Repercussions in Severance Negotiations

According to the written "Form U-5 Instructions," "amendments" to Item 12 (Reasons for Termination) answers are strictly prohibited. That is, once an employer states why a person's employment was terminated, that reason should never change.

I am, therefore, always concerned about potentially defamatory remarks being made in Item 12 in severance negotiations for registered representatives in the securities industry because negative references can instantly and irretrievably ruin an otherwise bright, promising career. Especially if they state, imply, or suggest an "integrity" concern.

Resultant Disputes and Difficulties

The Securities and Exchange Commission and the various federal courts have come to realize that securities firms are in something of a bind: they are pressured to reveal employees who have engaged in misconduct, yet fearful of defamation suits by the same employees. Since these regulatory filings are considered quasi-governmental, most courts give the Form U-5 a "qualified privilege" in the law. This means that what is stated in the Form U-5 cannot be the basis of legal liability in a lawsuit, *provided* that the allegedly defamatory statement is not motivated by malice. If, on the other hand, malice or vindictiveness form the motivation for the statement, defamation—and liability for enforceable damages—may be found to exist. (Some courts have given Form U-5 statements an absolute privilege, that is, without the condition noted above. This is, though, the minority view; most federal and state courts grant only the more restrictive "qualified" privilege.)

The number of such lawsuits and arbitration proceedings is on a dramatic increase. In one well-publicized example in 1996, Merrill Lynch was held liable to a former commodities broker for $2.1 million in damages due to U-5 defamation. According to the *New York Times*, the case was brought by a former Merrill Lynch employee who said Merrill Lynch had wrongfully accused her of concealing investor complaints and hiding the fact that a termination notice from a former employer contended she had been discharged because of "dishonesty." The $2.1 million award was made to her by an arbitration panel of the National Association of Securities Dealers.

The Problem with Vague Generalities

The problem with the present circumstance is that many securities employers are seeking a compromise solution of sorts, which unfortunately serves only to make the situation worse. To satisfy regulators, and avoid lawsuits, and sometimes to be vindictive without liability, more and more securities employers are putting statements in U-5 Forms that are vague. In the long run, I believe, this is good for no one. For example, I know of one case in which a securities firm stated that a former employee was "in violation of financial controls," which surely has an ominous ring to it. The "violation": he had used his company credit card some $200 over the authorized limit. I was involved in another case in which a former employee was reported to be "under departmental review" when, in fact, only the size of his future bonus amount was being considered. Clarity is an essential component of any good relationship, business or otherwise; vague generalities are good for no one, except the lawyers.

• • •

While severance negotiations initially seem primarily concerned about monetary issues, very often matters of special concern arise in the process. These matters may be of greater significance to you for they can affect your long-term prospects and goals. Indeed, negotiation of the severance issues of special concern may entail long-term consideration of your reputation, your inventions, your creations, and even your finances later in life—issues of considerable importance. Consider all of these issues carefully as you prepare to meet your employer at the bargaining table.

PART VI

What Your
Employer Will
Ask of You
and How
to Respond
to Each Request

28

Release and Waiver
of Employee's Claims

> The weak can never forgive. Forgiveness is the attribute
> of the strong.
>
> —Mahatma Gandhi

In this section of the book, I present the most commonly seen items in a severance agreement and, depending on your circumstances, your possible responses. No matter what request you see in a severance agreement—and I've seen some highly unpredictable ones—don't get either upset, excited, or depressed. First, it may be a mistake. Second, your negotiating counterpart may just be testing the waters. Third, what you see may be a reflection of some very bad experience your negotiating partner may have experienced. Above all, show that you recognize the validity of the issue raised. Don't call it crazy, stupid, or misplaced, even if you believe it is. Call it "interesting" until you understand it better. Seek out the other party's concerns, and concentrate on finding out where the request comes from, and what it will take to address it.

If there is one thing that your employer will invariably seek in entering into a severance agreement with you, it is your release of the employer from all possible sources of liability and your waiver of all possible claims you may have. This is the essence of the severance transaction and, some would say, its very reason for being. It is not at all rare for a severance agreement to be titled "Severance and Release Agreement."

The Request

The release provision in a severance agreement is usually drafted to include every possible kind of potential liability. These liabilities might include:

> Any and all actions, causes of action, claims, demands, damages, rights, remedies, and liabilities of whatsoever kind or character, in law or equity, suspected or unsuspected, past or present, that the Employee has ever had, may now have, or may later assert, including but not limited to, and whether or not related to, his employment by or the performance of any services to or on behalf of the Company or the termination of that employment and those services, from the beginning of time to the effective date hereof.

The parties who are intended to be released from any of these claims are quite comprehensive. They will be defined as "releasees," and will include:

> The Company, its parents, subsidiaries, and affiliates, affiliated persons, partnerships, and corporations, including, without limitation, successors and assigns, and all of their past and present directors, officers, consultants, agents, representatives, attorneys, shareholders, employees, employee benefits plans, and plan fiduciaries.

To be sure that the release and waiver cover all possible laws that the employer could have violated, they are usually spelled out like this:

> Any claims arising out of or related to any federal, state, and/or local labor or civil rights laws including, without limitation, the federal Civil Rights Acts of 1866, 1871, 1964, and 1991, the Age Discrimination in Employment Act of 1967, as amended by, inter alia, the Older Workers Benefit Protection Act of 1990, the Workers' Adjustment and Retraining Notification Act, the Employee Retirement Income Security Act of 1974, the Consolidated Omnibus Budget Reconciliation Act of 1985, the Americans with Disabilities Act of 1990, the Fair Labor Standards

Act of 1938, the New Jersey Law Against Discrimination, the New York State Labor Law, the New York State Wage and Hours Laws, as each may have been amended from time to time.

Your Response

Unless unusual circumstances exist, it is entirely fair and appropriate that the employer receive the release from liabilities it seeks, with certain limitations. These limitations, preferably set forth in writing, should include the following:

1. The release should expressly exclude any liabilities arising out of the violation of the severance agreement itself.

2. The release should also exclude pending workers' compensation or other insurance claims.

3. The release should expressly exclude claims related to vested benefit, welfare, or pension plans.

4. You will note that the release provision quoted above releases all company shareholders. This would be reasonable in a closely held corporation but entirely inappropriate in a publicly held one.

5. I always request the inclusion of a simple sentence that states, "The employee shall be released from all claims and liabilities to the same extent that the employer has been released by the terms of this agreement."

29

Mitigation

> Change is inevitable, except from a vending machine.
>
> —bumper sticker

As noted in earlier chapters, one of the primary items that may become an issue in your severance negotiations is your employer's insistence that your continuing salary payments be "mitigated," that is, that they will come to a halt if you either take a new position or stop looking for one.

The Request

Mitigation provisions in many severance agreements look like this:

> Even though you are entitled to receive continued salary payments for a period of forty-eight weeks following the effective date of this agreement, you shall be required, however, to make a good faith effort to obtain substitute employment during this period, and to mitigate the amount of any payments you would otherwise be entitled to pursuant to this agreement. You shall report to the Company the start date of any new employment, your failure to do so to be deemed a substantial breach of this agreement, entitling the Company to the immediate return of all severance moneys it has paid to you, as well as legal expenses incurred in collecting these amounts.

A far simpler version would be this:

> Your separation benefits and pay will stop if you become employed, or if you stop looking for employment for any reason.

Your Response

Based upon my working through hundreds of these severance agreements, and seeing the experiences of my clients, I know there are very good reasons to object to the notion of mitigation of severance. As a general rule I suggest that all my clients argue strenuously against the notion. Here are some of those reasons:

1. It's not fair because it's not mutual; that is, it only works one way. Would your employer "feel bad" if you were offered twenty-four weeks of continuing salary payments as your severance, and it took you two years to gain reemployment? If your employer is concerned about "windfalls," does it not understand your concern about "financial downfalls"? There should be mutual risk limitation or none.

2. No one should be denied payments for taking a new job or discouraged in any way from doing so. By setting things up in such a way that you will no longer receive continued salary payments when you take your next job, you are being discouraged from taking your next job.

3. Mitigation carries with it an implied obligation for you to continue making good-faith efforts to land a new job, and management's right to terminate your continuing salary if it believes you are not. Who will police this? This sets things up on a win-lose basis, in which adversarial relations are more probable than not.

4. What might happen if the new job does not work out? Will severance payments resume? That would be unlikely, thus discouraging you from trying out a risky position in, say, a start-up company.

5. What if you are considering trying your hand at opening your own business? Most mitigation provisions would make this impossible, except upon the loss of continuing salary payments and benefits.

6. A few of my clients have confidentially shared with outplacement counselors their interest in starting a new business, or having a child, or staying home with their present children, or just taking some time to travel and reconsider things, only to have these thoughts transmitted to their former employers. Severance should not be lost in this way, and outplacement counselors should not be forced to dishonor confidences by turning on those who have shared them.

7. At the very minimum, "mitigation should be mitigated." That is, if you take a new position that provides, say, only two-thirds of your previous compensation, you should be entitled to maintain one-third of your continuing salary payments until they are set to expire.

30

Confidentiality

> He who has once burnt his mouth always blows his soup.
> —German proverb

It may surprise you, but after release and waiver, and then mitigation of continuing payments, the subject that comes up the most in severance negotiations, and is often the most sensitive, is confidentiality. Confidentiality in this context is most commonly limited to confidentiality about the fact of the agreement and the terms of the agreement.

The Request

A typical confidentiality provision in a severance agreement is the following:

> The existence and terms of this separation agreement shall be strictly confidential and shall not be disclosed by you, your family members or representatives, to anyone or any entity, for any reason or under any circumstances, except to your attorneys, governmental agencies that require this information, and except as may be required by a court order.

Your Response

Confidentiality is both noble and reasonable, so long as it provides you with reasonable room to move. There are several limitations that you should request:

1. You should surely be entitled to share information about this agreement and its terms with those with a good reason to know: your immediate family, your attorney, your accountant and financial planner; perhaps also your outplacement counselor and any doctor and professional therapist whose services you might use.

2. Any employer that insists you must be responsible if these excepted individuals then turn around and disclose this information would have a good point. You should always be discreet about the fact and terms of your severance, and ask others to be so, too. Bear in mind, though, that in my fifteen years or so of negotiating severance, I'm not sure I've heard one complaint of someone's representative breaching a promise not to do so.

3. It should be clear that, in all events, you are to be permitted to disclose to all others the fact of your employment by the company, the dates of your employment, the title(s) you held, the responsibilities you shouldered, and your general salary range.

4. You must be free to comply with orders to divulge such information if such orders have the force of law behind them. These would include lawful subpoenas, notices of deposition, and summonses to appear at agency hearings. Don't be surprised if your employer requires immediate notice of your receipt of any such legal requirement.

5. I always ask for mutuality, because I believe there is always a real value to maintaining confidentiality about problems.

6. Every now and then I see a confidentiality provision that requires a very severe penalty to the employee in the event the promise of confidentiality is broken, even in an incidental, accidental way. The mere use of the word "settled" in a conversation should not require the repayment of all severance payments to date and the termination of future payments. Perhaps this would make sense for a material breach such as publication of critical information to the media, but for an incidental breach, it is uncalled for, unreasonable, and should be resisted.

7. It may be best, after some period of time, perhaps three years, to let confidentiality provisions expire, according to your agreement. Sooner or later all restrictions may no longer serve any useful purpose.

31

Return of the Employer's "Property"

Don't wrestle with pigs; you get dirty and they enjoy it.
—anonymous

The Request

A fairly standard and usually noncontroversial provision in most severance agreements is the requirement that you return to the employer
all of the employer's property. This provision, in and of itself, engen-
ders little discussion but must be taken very seriously, for considerable
negative repercussions may take place if it is not.

A technical and encompassing provision would be the following:

> You are obligated to surrender and hereby acknowledge that
> you have surrendered or will surrender to the Company's
> counsel on or before the effective date of this agreement, any
> and all papers, contracts, drafts, data, records, plans, proposals,
> photographs, tape recordings, video recordings, other elec-
> tronic recordings, and other information, documents, or prop-
> erty, including any copies thereof, related to the Company in
> your possession or under your control, including but not lim-
> ited to any such items in the possession or under the control of
> your attorneys, agents, or representatives.

The rationale underlying this provision is self-evident: the company
should have what belongs to it. Certain limitations, conditions, and
permutations may apply.

Your Response

Consider carefully whether any one or more of these provisions may be applicable to your circumstances.

1. I always ask that provisions such as these be made mutual. The company should agree, as well, to promptly return to you any and all property of yours that it has in its possession or that may come into its possession.

2. You may want to negotiate your continued use of company property that has special relevance to you. For example, if you have used a company-leased car, it may be in everyone's interests for you to continue using it. First, the company may have committed to a long-term lease and have no other use for it. Second, early return of a leased car may require payment of a considerable penalty fee. Third, you may have continued need for the car. Consider negotiating its continued use, if necessary, at your own expense.

3. You may want to consider negotiating the purchase of other company property for which you may have continued use and special affinity, such as your laptop computer or home fax machine. These might be of considerable use to you while searching for a new job or starting your own business, and would likely have little market value as used equipment. Special provision may have to be made for the removal of company-confidential files from the computer's memory.

4. Determining what is the company's property, as opposed to your property, may cause some difficulties. Probably the quintessential example of this is your own Rolodex (whether card or computer type), full of not only the names, telephone numbers, and addresses you assembled over years of work before coming to the company, but also the names, telephone numbers, and addresses you assembled while on the job during these past few years. Who owns this material? The law says that anything you've assembled on company time, using company materials, and with the help of the company secretaries, belongs to the company.

Anything removed from an office upon termination, even assuming for the moment that there will be an opportunity to do so, is highly suspect and could lead to some very ugly accusations. So I suggest that if there is such an opportunity, you take home all items, including your portion of your Rolodex information, make copies at home, and return the original items to the company.

5. If you are in advertising, artistic pursuits, or other creative fields, as an exception to the return-all-property requirement, you should always request the right to retain a portfolio of your work and accomplishments while working for the company. Assure the company, in writing or by way of a right to inspect and approve all portfolio material, that none of the items intended for your portfolio would reasonably be expected to compromise any present or presently anticipated future strategic plans.

6. Upon your return of all company property in your possession, custody, or control, and the possession, custody, or control of your attorneys, agents, and representatives, request a statement in writing, perhaps as part of the severance agreement, acknowledging that the company knows of no company property that it believes you have retained, and that the company knows of no property of yours in its possession.

32

Nondisparagement

> You can uncover what your enemy fears most by observing the means he uses to frighten you.
>
> —Eric Hoffer (author, essayist)

The Request

Almost every employer has a concern that terminated employees will speak badly of the company and people who still work there. When I see a nondisparagement clause in a severance agreement, I usually assume that one of two things is going on: stock language, standard in the severance agreements prepared by their Human Resources or general counsel's office; or some special circumstance exists, some real concern emanating from the upper levels, that my client has the ability to "hurt" the name, reputation, or fortune of other, high-level executives if she spoke her mind to the board of directors, the media, or other company executives. One possibility is innocuous; the other is very sensitive. In either event, I willingly accept nondisparagement provisions, with few comments to my negotiating partner, with most of my comments and suggestions addressed to my client.

A common nondisparagement clause will read like this:

> The Employee agrees not to make any negative or disparaging statements, allegations, accusations, or comments of any kind to any person or entity against or regarding the Company, its officers, employees, contractors, employees, Board of Directors, attorneys, agents, representatives, parents, subsidiaries, affiliates, principals, partners, or shareholders, or to take any actions which might foreseeably affect the public image, reputation, or name of any of these parties in a negative manner.

Your Response

As noted above, the response I have for my negotiating partner is usually quite simple, embodied in only the first item noted below. The remainder of my comments and suggestions are for my client primarily.

1. If anything in the nondisparagement provision seems very unusual, pointed, or out of place, I may request a slight modification to limit its character and make it more reasonable. Barring such an element, which is not present in the provision quoted above, I will generally refrain from comment on a nondisparagement clause, except for my usual refrain in these matters: please make it mutual, so that it applies to the employer to the same extent it applies to the employee.

The one comment I may get from my negotiating partner is that it is much easier to control the words of one person (the employee) than it is to control the words of, perhaps, tens of thousands of people (the company). My usual retort is to say that I agree wholeheartedly, as I suspect he will agree with my belief that the lips of ten thousand people saying bad things about one person can do more damage. The result: usually a knowing grin and an agreement to make the provision mutual.

2. For you, I can only advise you that it is always best to refrain, to the extent humanly possible, from bad-mouthing former employers, just as it is a good idea to refrain from bad-mouthing anyone. It only makes you look bad in the eyes of others.

3. Perhaps of greatest import in this area is that no court will listen seriously for more than a few seconds to any complaint about a slight comment, a "he's a jerk" type remark, or "They don't know what they're doing" muse in a bar, restaurant, or on a golf course. It just won't happen. This is what we call in the law by the Latin phrase "de minimus," or as they say on the street, "no big thing."

33

Beware of Restrictive Covenants

> Change your dwelling place often, for the sweetness of
> life consists in variety.
>
> —Arabian proverb

Making severance assistance conditional on a promise to restrict
yourself, perhaps very seriously, in how you make a living is just not
right. I would not advise you or anyone to sign an agreement with such
a provision in it.

The Request

"Restrictive covenants" are promises to restrict yourself. In business, we
see them in employment agreements, and we see them as well in severance agreements. Most judges in most jurisdictions will enforce them if
(1) they were truly "bargained for," meaning you were free not to
enter into the promise, and you got something for it; (2) they are reasonable in scope and effect; and (3) you understood what you were
signing. They are more commonly enforced in East Coast states, but
they are always considered on a case-by-case basis; that is, no attorney
can ever tell you with definiteness if yours will be enforced, enforced
partially, or not enforced at all. However, you must presume that they
are entirely enforceable.

As noted in chapter 21, there are several types of restrictive
covenants, but three are most frequently seen in severance agreements: (1) covenant not to compete (casually referred to as a "noncompete"), (2) covenant not to solicit, serve, or divert customers, and
(3) covenant not to solicit or hire employees. A typical set of restrictive
covenants was placed into a proposed severance agreement of a client
of mine in the securities industry:

For a period of one (1) year after the termination of my employment for any reason or for such period that I am receiving payments from the Company in the form of compensation (e.g., separation pay) and/or benefits, whichever is longer, I agree that I will not engage in or render consulting or other services to any current client of the Company, or any prospective client, i.e., any entity with which the Company is actively negotiating with or soliciting business from at the time of my termination. As used herein, the word "engage" means to participate directly or indirectly as a sole proprietor, agent, employee, officer, director, stockholder, partner, or in any other capacity whatsoever, on my own behalf or on behalf of any other entity.

I further agree that for the period set forth above, I will not directly or indirectly interfere with, disrupt, or attempt to interfere with or disrupt, the Company's relationship, contractual or otherwise, with its employees, or engage in the solicitation or inducement of its employees, customers, or suppliers to breach, modify, or terminate any agreement(s) or relationship(s) that they may have with the Company.

My opinion is quite clear: this will stop my client from working practically anywhere in the securities industry, and especially in the function he has engaged in for the past twelve years, without the very real possibility of being hauled into court with two or three days' notice. That is because, due to technical, legal reasons, most of these agreements are enforceable prospectively, that is, the aggrieved party can ask a court to order, or enjoin, the employee from violating the covenant, stopping him from continuing with a new job. The language in a severance agreement that provides for this authority sounds just like this:

I agree that the Company may, in addition to pursuing any other remedies that it may have at law or in equity, obtain an injunction against me from any court having jurisdiction over the matter, restraining any violations of these covenants by me.

What really happens with these things, if you sign them, is that your next employment will be tentative at best and disastrous at worst. That is because, in effect, these restrictive covenants have three parties to them: you; your former employer; and every employer in the world you may want to work for during your restricted period. More and more employers—out of concern for being involved in lawsuits—are asking for assurances that you haven't signed any such covenant, and if you did, they are asking to see it, as a precondition for employment.

Your Response

1. You want this clause removed. Your first response can be: "If you don't want me working for you anymore, why do you care that I work for someone else? Surely if I was valuable to anyone, you would want me to stay. If I'm a poor performer, surely you'd want me on your competitor's payroll."

2. Your second argument to get this language withdrawn: "This is nearly punitive. I haven't done anything wrong. If you were looking to make an enemy out of someone, the best way would be to make them unemployed, and then go ahead and make them unemployable. This can't be intentional." If your employer says, "I don't want to pay you severance while you're working for my competitor," offer to mitigate, that is, stop taking your severance the minute you're reemployed, IF it's by a competitor.

3. If you're still unsuccessful in your efforts to remove the provision, try to either restrict its breadth or ask for a specific list of companies the employer considers customers and competitors, and certain personnel it is concerned about your taking with you.

4. If all else fails, just insist upon the inclusion of one sentence that says, "Regardless of any confidentiality provisions in this agreement, I will be free to show just this one provision to prospective employers so that they may assess whether their work, their customers, and my work for them will violate its terms."

PART VII

If
Negotiations
Fail

34

There Are No Guarantees

> Trust in Allah, but tie your camel.
>
> —Arabian proverb

In the course of my experience negotiating severance matters over a period of fifteen years or so, only in a very small percentage of instances have I seen an employee negotiating in good faith, with good intentions, and with a good mind, fail to achieve some measure of fair treatment and benefit. Still, there are no guarantees that your efforts in these matters will be successful or even without harm. Your understanding of that fact is very important.

As noted in previous chapters, *negotiations are never predictable.* For reasons related to the negotiations, or for reasons totally unrelated, the employer may walk away from the negotiating table. Sometimes an employer may withdraw an offer sitting "on the table" without notice, or good cause, even when such a move seems to be against the employer's interests. While you may be able to plan every step you take in negotiation, reactions to each of your moves are unpredictable.

Further, I have seen efforts to achieve benefit in employment matters cause harm. This has happened because *someone's "wrong button" was pushed,* and when it was, retaliation came about. The act of standing tall, and letting your thoughts and desires be publicly expressed, is threatening to some. With others, simply denying them absolute authority and control is tantamount to direct challenge, and good cause for "war." Retaliation could take the form of a legal suit (or countersuit, if a lawsuit is already pending) or intentional harm to future career moves of the employee who is departing.

My biggest concerns arise when a prospective client comes to me expressing his or her absolute confidence that "my employer never goes to court; it always settles. It's afraid of bad publicity, and this will be a big case. Negotiation will be easy." Though it's never easy dealing with the problems of others, ease of the negotiation is not my concern; it's the difficulties and problems I foresee in helping this particular individual that concern me.

First, this overly confident type of sentiment suggests to me that the prospective client believes that he or she understands well both the severance negotiation process and the likely outcome of that process in his or her case. Since I don't believe anyone can be confident of either matter, I am starting out with a very different prospective than that of my client. To my mind, clients of this type tend to be relatively close-minded to discussions and suggestions that might otherwise be of significant benefit to them and their case. Second, it is these "overconfident" clients who are most likely to become disappointed and angry if things don't initially proceed as smoothly as they'd expected. They then start blaming others, which is always counterproductive.

Circumstances change, too. While a company may have awarded its last ten severed employees one full year of continued salary as severance, a new CEO, or a cost-reduction program, or a new board policy on severance, or any number of things could produce an outcome different from the one expected or traditionally given.

35

Beware of Withdrawn Offers and Counterclaims

Who rides a tiger cannot dismount.

—Chinese proverb

As I said in the previous chapter, severance negotiations, like all negotiations, are inherently unpredictable. While we may prepare, plan, and project in order to achieve an outcome, the actual outcome can never be predicted with any sort of accuracy. I have two great concerns relative to the process that I always share with each of my clients: the possibilities of withdrawn offers and counterclaims.

These two potential risks are of great concern to me because each represents a kind of loss, or step backward, for my client. It is as if our efforts, in the end, not only did not prove helpful but in fact proved harmful. In the name of education and thoughtful consideration of this process, I discuss these risks here. You will want to factor them into your decision whether to move ahead with your severance negotiations or not.

A. Withdrawal of Offer

When an offer of severance (or anything else, for that matter) is made, whether verbally or in writing, the basic tenets of the law of contracts provide that the offer may be withdrawn at any time by the party making the offer (called the "offeror") until such time as it is accepted by the party to whom it is addressed (called the "offeree"). Further, if the offeree (recipient) openly rejects the offer made, the offer is then considered to be extinguished, or made dead forever, unless later revived by the offeror.

There are two general exceptions to this basic rule. The first exists if some law requires that the offer remain open for a specified period of time. As an example, federal law requires this in the case of a public company that makes an offer to its shareholders to buy its stock back; the offer must be held open for a specified period or at a specified price. The law in many states also requires that certain prize contests or sweepstakes offerings be kept open for a certain period as well.

As to this first general exception, no law requires your severance offer be left on the table for any specified period of time. But one federal law—the Age Discrimination in Employment Act (ADEA)—does stipulate that any release signed by a person over the age of forty will not protect the employer from claims of age bias unless the employee had an opportunity lasting at least twenty-one days to consider the offer. Does this require that the offer remain on the table that long? No, but if the employer seeks release of all claims, and ADEA claims are very sensitive ones for employers, then the offer must be on the table for at least twenty-one days. Does this still allow you to accept the offer in less than twenty-one days? Yes. Certain other laws give different periods for consideration, but this twenty-one-day period is what I see most often. A different federal law—the Older Workers Benefit Protection Act (OWBPA), which applies to employees who are among a group or class of employees being urged to accept early retirement or other reduced-benefit plan—requires a forty-five-day consideration period.

If these periods of time are stated in the severance proposal, it is in these periods that we review, consider, and negotiate. I have many times requested limited extensions—say, two or three weeks—where they were needed, and I have never been turned down. But if you request an extension of time, and it is granted, request that the agreement to extend be put in writing.

The second general exception to the basic rule that an offer is revocable at any time is to be found in basic contract law: if the offer, by its own terms, states that it will be kept open and available for acceptance for a certain period of time, then it must be.

As to the second general exception, the severance offer letter, or proposal, itself, must be carefully reviewed, preferably by legal counsel, to determine if its language requires the offer to be kept "alive" for any specified period. For example, it might say, "This offer may be considered and accepted for a period of twenty-one days from your receipt of it." If it does not, you are on notice that the severance offer or proposal made may be withdrawn, at any time, without notice.

Bear in mind that an offer, by its own terms, may dictate in what manner it may be accepted. This may be by certified or registered mail, by hand-delivery, by facsimile, or by service upon a specified individual. If an offer is silent regarding the manner in which it may be accepted, it may be accepted in any manner that is reasonable under the circumstances. The offeree delivering his or her acceptance of an offer of severance, though, would be wise to deliver such acceptance in a manner that can later be easily proven, by Federal Express receipt, for one example.

It is important that you also understand that not everyone always follows the dictates of the law or even does what they've agreed to do. That is, even if your employer makes an offer of severance to you, and you accept that severance offer, in precisely the manner in which acceptance must be made, that does not always mean that your employer will then honor its word and pay you what has been agreed.

Every agreement and all laws are based, first, on good faith and, second, on their enforceability under the law. We live together in society in contemplation of good faith by most others, but we all know that we sometimes must unfortunately proceed to court to enforce agreements. It's happened to my clients. It's happened to me. It could happen to you.

B. Counterclaims

One caveat is always in order when you consider making a request for additional severance payments or benefits, or raising and enforcing a severance-related claim: your employer may raise and seek to enforce a claim against you, by what attorneys call a counterclaim.

Counterclaims need not necessarily be related to the original claim. For example, you may raise a claim based upon your supervisor's refusal to pay to you moneys due for reimbursement of expenses; in response, your employer could raise a claim against you either that your expense reimbursements in the past were overpaid to you (a related counterclaim) or that you caused damage to company equipment during improper personal use (an unrelated counterclaim).

While counterclaims are rare in the area of severance negotiations, they do at times take place. When they do arise, it is most frequently in the form of claims that an employee: (1) breached a restrictive covenant or covenant not to compete; (2) committed theft (or improper distribution) of protected business secrets; (3) improperly competed with the employer or the employer's business opportunities. You must consider whether there exists any possible basis for such counterclaims in actions you may have taken before you go into severance negotiations.

Employers also sometimes raise the specter of possible counterclaims as a strategic tool in severance negotiation. Several times I have witnessed an employee refrain from continuing with a reasonable severance request or valid claim in the face of the threat of counterclaim.

Attorneys often fail to remind clients of a secondary risk of counterclaim: if a lawsuit is commenced by the employee, he or she can later decide to withdraw or abandon it, but this is not the case if a counterclaim is asserted. Withdrawal of the entire case in such circumstances requires the employer's consent as well.

Last, but not least, I have seen a few employers get so emotional about a request for additional severance benefits that they fire the employee on the spot. Two things generally prevent this: the more reasoned understanding that this is business, not personal, and the employer's counsel's understanding that this, in itself, may constitute an illegal retaliation for an employee's seeking to raise and enforce his or her rights.

36

Litigation, Arbitration, Mediation

> When you go into court you are putting your fate into
> the hands of twelve people who weren't smart enough to
> get out of jury duty.
> —Norm Crosby (comedian)

All of us have some familiarity with litigation and arbitration, whether through personal experience, the experience of others, or media portrayals. Litigation and arbitration related to severance matters entail very little substantive difference from other litigation and arbitration. Those differences that do set severance disputes apart from others come primarily from the employment context of severance, its unique bases in law, and certain matters of procedure related to employment and discrimination law.

Litigation and Arbitration—Shared Characteristics

Litigation and arbitration, in all matters, share certain characteristics:

- They should be avoided if other methods of resolving disputes and claims are available.
- They always entail significant expense, time, and disruption of the everyday workings of organizations and the daily lives of individuals.
- Litigation frequently requires years for completion. While arbitration is a much faster process, it, too, can become protracted.
- They are inherently unpredictable in their processes and results. One possible result of bringing a claim, often overlooked, is the possibility of counterclaim against the employee.
- Very few of those involved in litigation or arbitration are pleased with the overall experience and feel they achieved real "justice."

Attributes of Litigation and Arbitration
in Resolution of Severance Claims

- Because they deal in our case with employment relations, future employment possibilities may be affected by them.
- Many claims involve one or more allegations of discriminatory behavior by the employer (based, for example, on age, gender, disability, or race) and, so, will probably require involvement of one or more federal, state, or local human rights agencies.
- Certain industries, most notably the securities industry, require almost all employment-related disputes to be brought before certain specified forums for arbitrated resolution.
- It is sometimes said that two kinds of cases exact the greatest emotional toll from participants: divorce matters and employment matters. I would concur in this.
- The law relative to severance disputes is extremely dynamic. The law is changing just slightly more slowly than society is changing in its attitudes toward various aspects of the employment relationship. Claims unheard of even five years ago are becoming commonplace today. The concept of "fairness" is surely evolving.

The Legal Bases for Severance Claims
in Litigation or Arbitration

(a). Breach of Contract

In all breach of contract cases, it is our task to set out the basic factual and legal elements of our case. That is, to describe for the court, or arbitrator, that (1) there existed some form of contract (or agreement) between the employee and the employer; (2) the contract was breached by the termination of the employee, either by the fact of the termination, the manner of the termination, or the motivation for the termination; (3) the employee suffered damages as a result of the termination in violation of the contract. Each client's claim is based upon a different set of facts, but each breach of contract claim must fit into this general pattern, and the facts must be shown to support it.

(b). Illegal Workplace Discrimination

Frequently reported to me are facts and circumstances that support a claim that illegal workplace discrimination is the primary cause of, or a major factor in, an employment termination. Various federal, state, and local laws, rules, and regulations make such workplace discrimination illegal. Many, if not most, of these applicable laws also set out enforcement procedures for claimants.

The salient point here is that most of these enforcement procedures, including those set out by the federal Equal Employment Opportunity Commission (EEOC), require that before a lawsuit may be started based upon a claim of illegal workplace discrimination, the claimant must first file and follow up on a complaint with that agency and/or its state or local counterpart. Claimants must file a "charge" of discrimination and first await the determination of the agency's investigative and reporting divisions. It is reported that most state and local agencies, as well as the federal EEOC, are some three to four years backlogged with unfinished cases. The chief concern: deadly delay.

It is for this reason that I often counsel clients with discrimination-based claims to seek resolution through compromise wherever possible, and to consider, as well, and when made absolutely necessary, a lawsuit or arbitration based upon a different legal basis, such as breach of contract or wrongful or retaliatory discharge, if the facts of the matter would support such a claim.

Once the appropriate agency issues a ruling in favor of the claimant, or where no determination is found, but no ruling is made in favor of the employer, the employee becomes free to seek redress in the courts, under either state or federal jurisdiction. At times, especially where the agency's investigative division makes a finding of widespread discrimination, the agency enforcement division will choose to represent the claimant and others similarly situated using its own staff, at no direct charge to the claimant. These cases are quite rare, however, and the agency enforcement division may be entitled to take a percentage of the award, if any, for its efforts, as would a private attorney.

(c). Violation of Basic Fairness or Public Policy

I see more and more cases in which claimants allege that they have been fired for some reason that is so wrong, they have been "wrongfully discharged." Reported cases of these claims include: a man who was fired after he refused to go along with his superior in a money-laundering scheme involving the business that employed them; a client of mine who was fired after she reported to her company's health office that she was dizzy from fumes in her office and was planning to seek assistance from governmental authorities who investigate occupational health and safety; a woman who was fired after telling her boss that she planned to have another child and take standard maternity leave, and refusing to terminate the pregnancy, as her superior had requested.

In these cases, courts have agreed to recognize a valid claim, holding that violations of such fundamental rights as freedom to live a crime-free life, freedom to maintain one's health, and freedom to have children cannot exist without available opportunity for enforcement in the courts. Other courts, in similar cases, have refused to recognize a valid claim under such circumstances, holding instead that it is for the state legislatures and the U.S. Congress to enact laws recognizing such claims if the public policy is to be deemed to be so truly important. This difference between various courts is a source of great uncertainty in this area of the law and makes it difficult to enforce employees' rights.

Arbitration

Arbitration is a simplified, less formal version of the litigation process. It is generally viewed as an alternative to litigation in the courts and is perhaps the oldest version of those many efforts of more recent times to find a workable method of "alternative dispute resolution," or ADR. The rules of engagement in arbitration are generally simplified—so much so that many individuals choose to go through the process without legal counsel.

To engage in the arbitration process, one has to either have agreed previously to go through the process in a contract of sorts, or now agree to submit to the process at the time of the dispute. For example, contracts between movie producers, talent agents, and members of the Screen Actors Guild, one of the primary actors' unions, require that disputes be resolved by arbitration under the auspices of the American Arbitration Association. Many business contracts require arbitration of disputes by the American Arbitration Association or similar bodies. Employment contracts for securities industry employees generally require arbitration under the auspices of the New York Stock

Exchange or the National Association of Securities Dealers. Each of these agencies has its own procedures, fees, and rules of engagement.

One aspect of arbitration that is preferred by virtually all is its speed, unless one side or the other is trying to stall matters. And even in this circumstance, a decision of the arbitrator(s), which is the equivalent of the final judgment of a judge or jury, can usually be achieved in a matter of months. Lawsuits in state or federal courts usually take years to reach a final judgment.

One aspect of arbitration that employee advocates frequently complain about is that it allows very limited opportunity for "discovery," the process by which each side in a dispute "discovers" the facts in the control or possession of the other or of third parties. Employer advocates generally like arbitration for this very reason. Without a broad discovery process, important facts may be unknown until the actual hearing in front of the arbitrator or, for that matter, perhaps never be known. While arbitrators are generally given wide discretion by the relevant rules of engagement to permit (or order) prehearing discovery, historically they have tended to limit discovery rights.

One aspect of arbitration that is frequently preferred by all is that the decision of the arbitrator(s) is, with few exceptions, beyond the reach of an appeal to higher courts, whereas a decision of the judge or jury in a court of law is easily appealable. The grounds for appeal of an arbitrator's ruling are so narrow that most consider them virtually appeal-proof. Grounds for appeal are generally limited to provable claims of undue influence (for example, a bribe) or truly gross error in process (for example, finding a party liable who is not involved in the arbitration). Thus, finality is generally achieved sooner in arbitration than in litigation.

The process of arbitration generally involves five stages: (1) the filing of a demand for arbitration or "statement of claim" with the appropriate arbitration body, and payment of the applicable filing fees; (2) the serving of the demand for arbitration or claim statement upon the adversary; (3) the joint choice of a mutually acceptable arbitrator or panel of arbitrators; (4) a hearing; (5) the rendering of a written decision by the arbitrator or panel. Enforcement of an arbitration award, like enforcement of a court's decision, may require further effort.

More and more employers are requiring arbitration of employment disputes by "in-house" groups or panels, often composed of some members of management, some peers of the claimant. Provided participation in such a panel is generally fair, includes some peer involvement, and does not act to automatically waive other remedies available in law, I generally support these plans. The panel appointed under the Toys-R-Us company program contains a majority of peers and is empowered to overturn or modify any prior management decision. This, not surprisingly, has been quite conducive to good employee morale in that company.

Litigation

The course of the first phase of a lawsuit in litigation is generally as follows: (1) the filing of a summons and complaint with the court, and the payment of filing fees; (2) the serving of the summons and complaint upon the defendant; (3) the answer of the defendant, and the serving of counterclaims, if any, on the plaintiff (the suing party); (4) the serving of the reply, if any, of the plaintiff on the defendant.

At this stage, the longest phase of a litigation—the discovery phase—begins. It is in this phase that the parties engage in the many different methods of "discovering" the facts at issue in the matter, including the "dreaded depositions." While, in theory, the purpose of this phase is to resolve as many factual issues as possible and, thus, shorten the trial, the discovery phase has become the most protracted, frustrating, and expensive part of most lawsuits. It is not uncommon for this phase alone to require years to complete.

The final phase of lawsuits—the trial—rarely happens. Sometimes the parties find reason to settle. Sometimes the lawyers run out of steam because their clients run out of money to finance the continuation of the suit. Most often the judge (or his or her assistants) strongly urge, induce, cajole, and push the attorneys to convince the clients to settle. This urging to settle, which often seems unfair but results in a kind of "rough" justice in its own way, acts to unclog the court system, and also reaches a virtually appeal-proof ending, because a settled case, which is really a kind of agreement of which the judge takes official notice, is not considered a decision of the judge and thus presents almost no basis whatsoever for appeal.

Two aspects of the litigation process bear mentioning here because they are often ignored or discounted by the client who is confident of his or her prevailing in a lawsuit. First is the strong possibility of the postjudgment appeal and collection phases of any suit. In the event a lawsuit goes through the final phase of jury deliberation and verdict, even if that verdict is unambiguously in your favor, your adversary may appeal the decision, entailing additional delay in collection, perhaps lasting years. Also, winning a judgment from a court is not automatically the end; very frequently (especially where the employer is not a large company, or is privately owned, or is in financial distress) a new and lengthy phase of proceedings now becomes necessary: the collection phase. This phase can last as long as all the others combined. Sometimes it even entails employing special legal counsel who are adept at locating, freezing, and seizing the employer's assets sufficient to satisfy the court-provided judgment. The time, expense, and frustration of the appeal and enforcement phases of a lawsuit cannot be underestimated.

The second aspect of the litigation process that many clients ignore or discount is its inherent unpredictability. While, theoretically, a lawsuit has certain, definable stages, starting with service of summons and ending with rendering a verdict, in actuality lawsuits can go on in as many ways as lawyers can dream up, that is, seemingly forever.

I was involved in one lawsuit that involved so many frivolous motions and midsuit appeals on technical points of little relevance or significance that the opposing counsel were fined (called "sanctioned") $10,000 by the court for these interminable delays. In fact, some litigants and their attorneys use these delays strategically, to try to wear out (or bankrupt!) their adversaries. Rarely, if ever, does a litigation proceed smoothly from early stage to later stage to conclusion.

Mediation

Increasingly I see parties in employment-related disputes seek to resolve their issues through mediation, which is a voluntary process of compromise facilitated by a trained person, often not an attorney or judge, who is skilled in bringing warring parties together. Mediation is a process of conciliated resolution; it is the opposite of adversarial proceedings. At any time in this process you are free to do or say whatever you please. And there is no final judgment, as provided in a court or arbitration. The end goal of a mediation is a resolution by compromise. I always feel that if a party has expressed a willingness to attend a mediation, that party has right there and then indicated his or her willingness to compromise. It is truly amazing how a skilled mediator can operate to resolve a matter that no one ever thought could be resolved amicably.

While I strongly support mediation efforts, and believe they will be called upon increasingly in the future, in my experience final resolution through mediation remains a somewhat uncommon event. Also, the dollar amounts of settlements achieved through mediation are significantly lower than those anticipated at the conclusion of an arbitration or litigation. Still, mediation of a dispute is an ideal way of resolving it, and you should give this method of conflict resolution serious consideration.

• • •

When resolution of your severance request and claim is not achieved through negotiation, the door remains open to other avenues: mediation, arbitration, or litigation, each of which entails certain unique advantages and disadvantages, as we have seen. But sometimes no method and no amount of time can bring two disagreeing parties together in agreement over severance. When do you decide to walk away? Let's look at that question next.

37

When It May Be Time to "Walk Away"

The thing is to be able to outlast the trends.
—Paul Anka

Every now and then in my negotiating efforts on behalf of my severance clients, I come to a moment of decision that is best described by the question, "Is it time to walk away?" It's one of the most difficult questions I face in my practice. There are two scenarios in which I usually face this question, and several ways that I arrive at an answer.

The Scenarios

The most common scenario from which this question arises is when the employer says "absolutely, positively no." The employer either denies a request for increased severance payments and benefits or offers no severance package at all. What's the best response to that? Invariably, I decide that my client and I are just asking the wrong person, and that our request should go farther up the power hierarchy in search of a more receptive member of senior management. But then again, sometimes the "absolutely, positively no" is coming from the top.

A second scenario in which the question arises is when my client's and my own efforts to initiate initial negotiations or continued negotiations elicit no response whatsoever. This is a less common scenario, because it is generally considered unwise for the long-term career prospects of any management executive to ignore a situation that might one day explode in his or her face, at which time everyone will say, "How could you let this happen?" Moreover, when management receives a letter written on legal letterhead, especially of a firm that has a healthy reputation for its abilities in the court system, it's hard to ignore it. Still, this does sometimes happen.

The Responses Available

One of the things each of my partners at my law firm makes it a habit to do is to sit around the conference room table to "brainstorm" in situations like this. Have we missed any salient fact in our review of client data? Is there some message we did not pick up from the initial response, is there a possible miscommunication, or maybe even a lost communication? At times, new leverage points, new potential claims, and new approaches arise when we come up with a fresh perspective applied to the facts at hand.

Before any final decisions are made, it's always a good idea to try at least one last letter, sent by hand delivery, Federal Express, or certified mail, return receipt requested, to the company CEO outlining the inadequacy of the pending offer, the dire circumstances that it has caused for you, or the unacceptability of the overall situation, as well as the items of payment and/or benefit necessary to achieve a minimally acceptable settlement with you. That letter should also state quite clearly and emphatically that your only alternatives at this time are either to litigate or to take some other measure that would be in no one's interest.

To Litigate, Arbitrate, or Perhaps Mediate

Absence of some initiation of discussions at this point would surely suggest that the commencement of some aspect of the adversarial process is in order. In only one instance that I can remember did the employer agree, at a time such as this, to enter into the mediation process.

The decision to commence adversarial relations does not need to be made just yet in cases where the employee has a valid claim that is based on one or more of the federal laws making it illegal to discriminate in employment on the basis of age, gender, race, disability, or ethnic heritage. In these cases, the necessity of filing an administrative complaint with the federal Equal Employment Opportunity Commission (EEOC), as a precondition to filing suit complaint in the federal court, provides yet another opportunity to bring your message before responsible people at the higher levels of the employer, with clarity, with minimal expense (there is no filing fee), and with the employer facing the dual requirements of responding and of incurring legal expense. The EEOC also has a mediation program and will, in the right cases, strongly suggest to both sides that participation in that mediation process would be in their respective best interests.

If the decision regarding litigation of claims does arise, it is one that you should not take lightly, given the significant expense, time, effort, attention, and frustration demanded once you begin the process. It is one decision that I never permit my clients to make without very serious consideration of all the difficulties involved, and a written commitment with my firm as to the maintenance of monetary reserves to fund estimated upcoming expenses.

It is also at this time that I review with each of my clients contemplating initiating litigation the very real possibility of the imposition of sanctions (monetary fines) for bringing litigation without what the judge in question believes to be either a good basis in the facts or a good basis in the law.

The Decision to "Walk Away"

If and when the decision is finally made to "drop" the matter, to let things be, to "walk away" without getting what was initially hoped for, there is invariably a sense of disappointment and perhaps even of failure. Coming to the conclusion that either the additional risk, the additional cost, the additional effort, or the additional time devoted will not be justified by the anticipated reward to be gained is no failure, though. It is a business decision, the kind that is made by businesses every single day. It should be made with that perspective in mind.

PART VIII

Post-Negotiation Concerns

38

Bouncing Back and Standing Tall

> Don't carry a grudge. While you're carrying the grudge
> the other guy's out dancing.
>
> —Buddy Hackett (comedian)

Although this book is devoted to assisting you in surviving and perhaps thriving in the severance negotiation process, its greater goal is to set you off on that next phase in the process: getting on with your life. As I've said several times before in this book, and as I frequently counsel my firm's clients, "Your future is more important than your past." Turning that corner—from past to future—is your present job.

My legal practice is one that seeks to serve its clients again and again, within a framework of counsel, support, and guidance. I assist my clients both in preparing for and moving through times of transition. Executives, especially, will move into positions, and out of them, and into new positions, continually. For this reason, I have found that the continuity of my legal/business counseling relations with my clients serves them in the way a periodic tune-up serves a car: as a reminder of what has taken place, as a reconditioning, and as a preparation for what is coming up. These continuing client relations, I find, are extremely productive and conducive to long-term career success.

The severance context is one of the major transitions you face in your career. There are several discreet steps you can take, and should take, to best help you move forward after you've experienced job loss.

A. Get over the Anger

When couples divorce, it is often said that it takes the parties some three years to move beyond the personal angst entailed. In this business divorce—unless you've really saved your pennies or have achieved a very good severance package—you don't have three years to recover. Moving right on also will prevent cobwebs on your résumé and rust in your job skills. While you know these statements are true, you may be thinking that you just don't feel ready to get back out in the job market.

Executive recruiters sometimes tell me, "He's not ready" after meeting with one of my clients. When they say this, they are making the observation that the client has not yet put to rest the intense feelings of resentment and anger resulting from his recent involuntary employment termination. My advice to this client is, "Whatever it takes, get over the anger." I will say the same to you. I know it is difficult, but this anger is the primary impediment to moving on, which should be your primary goal.

But like many things, it's easier to say than do. Getting over anger requires learning the source of anger, putting angry feelings into perspective, and then refocusing your thoughts and energies on productive matters. I recommend support groups, counseling, exercise, and prayer. Whatever helps you get over those intense feelings, do a lot of it.

B. Categorize Your Experience

In chapter 6, I set forth several contexts in which, and from which, severance arises. These range from large-scale downsizings, to performance disputes, to complaints of illegal discrimination or sexual harassment. In conducting intake interviews with my clients, I always find myself slowly fitting each client's experience into one of these categories. Once I do so, I'm more likely to figure out what might take place in the negotiations, and which approach I might choose to take for this client's greatest advantage.

Likewise, it is a very good idea for you to place your severance experience into one of these categories, so that you will be more likely to understand that you are not alone, and be able to convey to interviewers what brought about your involuntary termination and why you are looking for a new position. It is important that you relay this information easily, without providing all the details, because the primary objective for each interview you have is to demonstrate what you can do in the future, not to share all the problems that may have existed in the past. By thinking through and becoming comfortable with the story of your severance experience, you will be more likely to get over this initial hurdle with your interviewers, and on to the new job that may be in your future. Interviewers may want to see that you've learned from your experience, and that you're not likely to get into the same situation should they hire you. So you can expect that. I can also assure you that prospective employers do not want to hire angry people.

If your severance was initiated by a political loss or interpersonal difficulty, or if it is somewhat difficult to explain, it's also a good idea to be prepared with names of people in your former company whom you have spoken with, who are willing and able to serve as "material witnesses" to the problem, and who can and will back up your version of events. This can only enhance your credibility.

If you categorize your experience, you may find, as many of my clients have, that it will also help you come to grips with your feelings of anger and resentment. It is like putting a problem into a box, and affording yourself some peace from it, at least for the time being.

C. Assess Strengths and Weaknesses; Enhance Skills

This is a perfect time to sit back and examine your strengths and weaknesses in your chosen field, and to be quite frank with yourself about what you should focus on improving to prepare the skills for your future advancement. Financial analysis; computer skills; a new language; communication skills; public speaking; networking skills; client acquisition and development. Or perhaps it's a tone-up of your body or other aspects of your physical appearance that you believe is in order.

This is also the perfect time to start improving yourself in the ways that will be of most benefit to you in the future. When you're busy with full-time work, you barely have the time to attend to the things you need to on a daily basis, let alone take future-oriented courses, classes, counseling, or seminars. Take the time now to undertake a new project. One bonus of self-improvement is that it raises your self-esteem. You need to feel in control of yourself, and on top of things, despite recently being treated in a way that may have been totally beyond your control, and which made you feel about two inches tall. Perhaps smaller, especially, you may fear, in the eyes of your loved ones. Efforts at self-improvement help you feel taller, stronger, more in control.

D. Prepare Your Own Marketing Plan

Face it, you're now in the process of selling yourself, to one buyer if you're looking for a job, to many buyers if you're going into business for yourself.

Many of us ignore difficult questions about what would fulfill us because facing the true answers would entail making changes. But since you are already in transition, now is the time to clarify:

- Exactly *what position or role* would make your life most fulfilling?
- *Who is it that would help you* get that position or role, or closer to it?
- *Do you presently have "what it takes"* to be an attractive candidate for that position or role? If not, how will you get the skills, experience, contacts it does in fact take?
- *How will you market yourself?* Networking? Letters? Recruiters?
- *Do you know your worth on the market?* Don't overprice or underprice yourself.

A carefully drawn plan is an essential tool to prepare yourself for the steps ahead and to reach your goal.

E. Get Out There: On the Phone, on the Fax, on the Net

Before you know it, it will be time for you to start getting out there with your résumé and your talents. You are about to embark on an extremely important sales trip. Developing your action plan will help you focus your efforts in the places that will be of most benefit to you. There are many books available to help you in your job search, and the usual networking possibilities are not to be overlooked either. Fully one-third of my clients find their next jobs through friends and colleagues, one-third through executive search firms, and one-third through pure creative effort and pounding the pavement. Explore and follow up on opportunities that all of these avenues offer you.

These days, you will find many job openings listed on companies' Web pages. You will also find job openings through professional or trade organizations. E-mail is becoming perhaps the fastest-growing way to contact employers and communicate about job openings. How you'll come to find your next job is unknown to you at the moment, but it is probably going to be different from the way you found your last one.

Eligibility for
Unemployment Benefits

> The trouble with unemployment is that the minute you
> wake up in the morning you're on the job.
> —"Slappy" White (comedian)

I don't know how many of my clients apply for unemployment insurance benefits, but one thing is for sure: many of them ask me whether they're eligible to receive unemployment benefits, just in case they should decide to apply. I am including the basic information on these benefits here to answer any questions you might have on the subject.

A. State Law and Practice Determine Eligibility

For almost all issues related to unemployment insurance coverage, it is state law that is applicable; federal law coverage of the subject is really quite secondary. This being so, I advise you to consult with your local state labor department for answers to your questions about your particular situation. Since my firm's severance practice is a national one, my colleagues and I always refer these questions to local counsel for their review. My familiarity is primarily with New York law, where my practice is centered. While most states have generally equivalent outlooks and procedures to those of New York State, you should double-check your state's policies if you live elsewhere.

Also know that the clerks at your local unemployment insurance office may not follow the law precisely. They may be more, or less, inclined to offer assistance, on a purely personal basis, and in this hold great sway. Indeed, how you present yourself and answer questions on your initial application influences your application's success above and beyond the applicable law. Always be kind, respectful, and courteous in your approach to the clerks you work with. When it comes to your application, instead of using the word "fired," use "discharged," "terminated," "downsized," or "laid off," if appropriate. Likewise, if you've received a large lump-sum severance payout, unless you really must provide that information, don't reveal it. These small steps can make a big difference as to whether you end up with unemployment insurance in a time of need.

B. Misconduct May Disqualify You

Bear in mind that even if you meet all other criteria for benefit coverage, you may be disqualified from unemployment benefits if you have engaged in certain on-the-job conduct, including:

- frequent absence, lateness, or leaving early;
- insubordination or willful failure to discharge duties;
- refusal to accept a similar position if yours is eliminated;
- certain inappropriate behavior or unacceptable appearance.

Therefore, it is always a good idea to request that a clear statement be included in your severance agreement to the effect that your termination was not due to misconduct on your part.

C. A Resignation May Cost You

As part of perhaps 10 percent of my severance negotiations, the employer requests that the employee submit a written resignation, ostensibly to establish without doubt that the actual termination was accepted without complaint, if not entirely voluntary. Since unemployment insurance benefits are in almost all cases denied to a person who has left his or her job voluntarily, the submission of a resignation may significantly harm your chances for later unemployment benefits. There are, however, precautions you can take in this regard. In cases where the employer insists upon a tendered resignation, I respond by requesting inclusion in the severance agreement of a provision like the following one:

> The submission of Employee's resignation as part of this resolution of differences and disagreements is not to be considered

a voluntary employment termination on the Employee's part. To the contrary, it is an accommodation requested by the Employer only to resolve certain of the issues of this involuntary employment termination. It should not be utilized to deny unemployment insurance benefits, should application be made. Employer agrees that it shall not contest Employee's application for state unemployment insurance benefits, should one be made.

The inclusion of such a provision in a severance agreement should suffice to negate any inference of voluntary termination that submission of a resignation may create.

Even an entirely voluntary resignation should not cost you unemployment benefits if it was justified by such circumstances as harassment (physical, verbal, sexual, or otherwise), conditions that endangered your safety and/or health, your employer's demand that you engage in illegal or unethical activities, or the relocation of your workplace many miles away. In any such circumstance, though, the burden of proof would be on you. Try to promptly gather good evidence and willing witnesses that support your case, for as time passes, this task becomes more and more difficult.

D. The Critical Issue: Are You Really "Severed"?

The critical issue in most states in determining whether you are entitled "to collect" is whether, in fact, you've really been "severed," that is, whether your employment is really terminated. That sounds like quite a simple fact to establish, but it's not. It is often quite confusing.

1. "Last Day of Employment"
If you have received a letter, memo, or other writing that sets down a "termination date," "date of discharge," "last day of employment," or their equivalent, you would seem to have good proof that your employment with that employer is over. Your entitlement to unemployment insurance benefits would be pegged from that date onward. Save any such documentation.

2. Continued Vacation Pay or Provision of Benefits

If, however, you continue to receive installments of vacation pay or are "left on the books" to receive health insurance and other benefits, you will likely be considered not yet discharged, hence ineligible for unemployment benefits.

3. "Salary Continuation" or "Consultancy"

Receiving regularly either "salary continuation" or "consultancy" moneys may disqualify you from unemployment insurance benefits, especially if regular services of any kind from you are required in return. For this reason, in particular, a lump-sum payout of severance moneys due is often preferable to continued payout.

E. Beware of Application Deadlines

Several states have established deadlines for application for unemployment insurance benefits. These deadlines run from the last date of employment and may be as short as thirty or sixty days. If you continue in severance negotiations, or are on a personal leave of absence, or on a period of disability, your failure to timely apply for unemployment benefits may, in itself, make you ineligible. Consult your local or state labor department for these deadlines.

• • •

As you can see from this chapter, your continued relationship with your employer may make you ineligible for unemployment benefits; on the other hand, if you have been discharged, you will probably be able to receive them. However, since qualifying criteria, law, regulations, and rulings do vary from state to state, looking into them before you begin severance negotiating can only help you here. Find out the details of your state's laws.

A Concern About
Employer-Provided Outplacement

No man can serve two masters.

—Matthew 6:24

Case History: I remember discussing with my client, Jennifer, the services that would be provided to her by the outplacement firm hired by her employer. The issue before us was whether she would have a private secretary or merely a telephone-answering and message-forwarding service. At Jennifer's request, I telephoned the outplacement provider and spoke to one of the senior officers of the company.

When I completed my question, there was a moment of silence on the line. I asked if something was wrong. The outplacement officer stated simply, "We cannot divulge that sort of information. We can divulge it only with the client." "All right," I responded, "can you speak with me about it if I have Jennifer sign a letter permitting me to act on her behalf?" Again, there was one of those moments of silence, after which the outplacement officer advised, "No, you don't understand. Jennifer is not our client; her employer is."

A. Increasing Utilization

As noted in chapters 17 and 19, it has become increasingly common for employers to provide professional outplacement services for their employees going through the severance process. In fact, the outplacement industry did not really exist ten or fifteen years ago, but now its use by severed and downsized employees has become the norm. Outplacement agencies generally provide valuable assistance to their clients in many important areas, including career counseling, financial planning, résumé preparation, and instruction on networking techniques. My firm maintains good relations with several outplacement agencies, large and small. But one aspect of the operation of many outplacement providers troubles me, and you should be aware of it.

B. The Concern

The issue that troubles me is that many outplacement agencies make periodic reports on the "progress" of their employee-clients to the latter's former employers. These reports contain, among other items, the number of visits made by an ex-employee to the agency's facilities, an evaluation of emotional state and/or general attitude of the ex-employee, the number and type of interviews attended by the ex-employee, or just a general overview.

In cases where employees have not completed severance negotiations, or where all severance payments have not yet been made, this kind of reporting to former employers can be detrimental to the interests of the ex-employees. If the employee is considering relocating, or starting up his or her own consulting firm, or is in desperate need of emotional closure with respect to the employment termination, this should be kept confidential by the outplacement service providers. Often, however, it is not.

Likewise, if a severed executive is discussing employment with the direct competitor of his or her former employer, that is *the executive's business only*. Especially in cases where the severance agreement contains essential issues of restrictive covenants or trade secrets, the former employer should never be told of potential job discussions. This represents to me an apparently glaring conflict of interest in the outplacement industry that few seem to notice. You should be aware of it and guard against it.

C. The Remedy

For these reasons, and others, I strongly urge every severance client of my firm who is using employer-provided outplacement services to insist upon written guarantees from the outplacement service that no reports—whether written or verbal—on any aspect of the employee's outplacement experience will be provided to the employer, without prior written consent. Alternatively, I urge that all reports be written, and be first provided to my client, and to my office, for prior review, comment, approval, and editing if necessary, before being sent to the employer. Indeed, this is one point of negotiation in my severance negotiations that is often hotly contested by employers, for reasons they usually refuse to discuss with me.

If an outplacement firm will not provide these reasonable assurances, it may not necessarily be an outplacement firm worthy of trust or use.

41

Is Severance Taxable?
Are Related Costs Deductible?

> I have no use for bodyguards, but I have a very special use
> for two highly trained certified public accountants.
> —Elvis Presley

Before I address the topic of taxes, a few cautionary remarks are in order. First, I am not an expert in taxation; you should therefore treat the tax-related information in this chapter as cautionary and tentative only. It should help you formulate your questions and answers to a real tax authority, accountant, or financial planner. Indeed, my discussion of tax issues is limited to the three largest issues only. Second, proper tax analysis must take into account your unique situation. Third, tax laws can be interpreted in a variety of ways and are subject to continual change. For these reasons and others, all questions regarding your personal tax filings and strategies should be addressed to your own tax advisers.

A. Generally, Severance Payments Are Taxable

For many years the proper tax treatment of severance payments was open to question. Many severance recipients (and others) took the position that severance payments were essentially payments made as a replacement for the loss of a valuable right: employment. Because tax law generally treats other repayments for a loss suffered as a nontaxed event—as in the case of a personal injury settlement for the loss of an arm or leg in an auto accident—the argument was set forth that nothing is gained when a loss is repaid and, thus, that severance should be properly nontaxed.

The IRS has always taken the opposite position: that since payroll payments are fully taxable, severance payments, as replacement of salary payments, are likewise properly taxable as well. Until mid-1996, the decisions in the courts were divided.

In August of 1996, Congress revised Section 104 of the Internal Revenue Code to settle the matter: all severance payments are now clearly taxable as income, except for severance payments that are expressly, and with factual support, allocated to the reimbursement of actual medical expense, whether past, present, or future. To the extent allocated to future medical expense, such as for treatment of ulcers, or pursuant to a company's self-insurance for medical problems of its personnel, severance is nontaxed.

B. Other Severance Benefits May Not Be Taxable

Other benefits received as part of severance packages may not be properly taxable or reported by employers as taxable. Depending upon the item, and the circumstances, other severance benefits may or may not be properly taxable:

- *Continued insurance coverages:* usually not taxable.
- *Outplacement services:* usually not taxable.
- *Stock options:* usually taxable at time of exercise.
- *Education benefits:* usually not taxable for upgrading of work-related skills, but taxable if used to learn a new trade or profession.
- *Reimbursement of relocation expenses:* generally taxable.
- *Legal and accounting fees:* generally not taxable, because the expenditures would likely be proper business expenses for you.
- *Car lease payments:* probably properly taxable, but not commonly reported as income by employers.

C. Deferral Advantage Is Often Available

Perhaps the most commonly used tax strategy is to defer the taxation of income by deferring its receipt. In severance matters, this deferral advantage is made available in four distinct ways:

1. I sometimes request that a portion or all of the severance payments be put off to the next calendar year. While money in the pocket is worth a lot, deferring receipt of income by weeks or months may defer tax payments by a year or more. In the interim, the additional moneys will be available to you.

2. I am sometimes in a position to request that my client be given the option to defer or accelerate receipt of future severance payments so as to manipulate income to more closely match deductible losses and unusually high deductible expenses, such as legal fees.

3. I have negotiated the redirection of payments to deferred compensation programs so as to move income taxation forward into later retirement years.

4. I usually recommend that my client complete and sign a new IRS W-4 form, entitled "Employee's Withholding Allowance Certificate," to declare the proper levels of withholding at nine personal exemptions. (At the time of this writing, nine personal exemptions are the maximum number an individual taxpayer may claim without having to immediate file a report of the claim to the IRS.) Whether employers should or must comply with such W-4 submissions is not easy to establish in all instances, for the relevant regulations are not at all easy to comprehend or follow. A few employers have insisted that they are required to withhold at a 28 percent rate, as a "special distribution." While the law is not so clear, I still recommend that my clients make this change on their W-4's.

The effect of this new level of exemptions is twofold. First, it takes into account probable and significant employment-related deductible expenses you will have in the year of severance—including thousands (or tens of thousands) of dollars in legal, accounting, and investment-related services. Second, it places more moneys in your hands, making more cash readily available when critical needs arise. While this may, admittedly, result in later imposition of additional taxes, by way of penalties and interest, that cost may well be worth the additional peace of mind you will gain during this period of transition.

42

"Getting Out" of
Waivers and Releases

> The art of prophecy is very difficult, especially with respect
> to the future.
>
> —Mark Twain

At the conclusion of nearly every severance negotiation, the parties
sign a severance agreement, separation agreement, or similar document, which sets down the elements and conditions of the agreed severance package. Either as part of that document or as a separate
companion document, you will be required to sign an agreement to
give up any and all claims you may now have, or may in the future
have, against your employer, and all parties "related" to your
employer, in exchange for your package. We commonly refer to these
as "waivers and releases."

A. Broad Coverage

A good example of a waiver and release form appears in the appendix.
This sample is a bit unusual in that it does not specifically list all of
the many persons released by the usual provision. Most such provisions list, as well, all past, present, and future company officers,
directors, employees, agents, shareholders, subsidiaries, affiliates, representatives, attorneys, predecessors, successors, assigns, and all persons, firms, and corporations acting by, through, or in concert with
any of them or with whom any of them is now or may hereafter be affiliated. As you can see, no one is forgotten. The release also covers all
claims, suits, laws, contracts, subjects, damages, rights, remedies, and

charges that a lawyer can think of, past or present, suspected or unsuspected, related to employment or otherwise.

So with all these parties protected and all these claims waived, are there any exceptions, loopholes, or ways out should you change your mind? Yes. The primary reasons that people use to base their breaches of waivers and releases are discussed in this chapter. Bear in mind, though, that the law will presume that an instrument or agreement you have signed is to be valid and enforceable. Any effort to negate it will usually be a tough battle.

B. Express Exceptions

Sometimes the parties agree to remove certain items from the coverage of the waiver/release as a matter of negotiation, to preserve the rights of the terminated executive for possible use under certain, later circumstances. A common example came up in a severance negotiation I recently worked on. Because my client had previously gotten injured on the job and was still undergoing medical treatments, it was only sensible (and prudent) to permit him to continue requesting payments from the company's workers' compensation insurer if continued medical treatments were to become necessary, and to bring his claim to court if wrongfully denied. Thus pending workers' compensation claims were expressly excepted.

Additionally, and of greater consequence and relevance, any rights with regard to vested benefits in company pension plans and company savings and investment plans are commonly excepted from the release. These benefits are excluded from the waiver/release for a very good reason: at time of severance, employees do not have the time, expertise, or opportunity to arrange for an audit of past company conduct with respect to pensions, savings plans, and the like. For this reason, the federal ERISA law makes such releases and waivers of vested benefits all but unenforceable. If you've signed a waiver and release that doesn't include language specifically excluding these benefits, and believe your former employer may have incorrectly or inappropriately handled your pension, profit-sharing, or other employer-contributed plan, you may be in luck. Consult an attorney, preferably one with ERISA or benefit-claim experience, or consider filing a complaint with the federal EEOC.

C. Seven-Day Revocation Period

Several state and federal laws, including the Older Workers Benefit Protection Act (OWBPA), which protects those over forty years old, provide that after you sign a waiver and release, you have seven calendar days to change your mind and revoke that agreement. Because of these laws, many employers place a seven-day revocation period into their waiver/release forms, just as a safety measure, even if not required by law. Some even require that before you are paid any severance moneys, you give written notice of "nonrevocation" seven or more days after your written acceptance.

If you wish to revoke, though, you usually have to give your employer written revocation notice. If your waiver/release does not contain language specifically providing a seven-day revocation period, you may not have such an option.

D. Readily Understandable

As a general rule of law, and as a specific requirement under several state and federal laws, including OWBPA, your waiver/release must be readily understandable to the average individual. If it is written in a form that is not easily understood or is deceptive, it may not be enforceable.

E. "Consideration" Required

As a general legal requirement of any agreement, including an agreement not to sue, your employer must offer you something of value, called "consideration" in legal theory, in exchange for your waiver. (This is also a requirement of several laws, including OWBPA.) If you are part of a general reduction in force (RIF), you must receive some "extra consideration," above and beyond your usual employment compensation policy, to constitute "consideration" for your waiver/release.

F. Benefit of Legal Counsel

Almost every separation or severance agreement I've seen states quite clearly that you are advised to obtain the assistance of legal counsel before you sign the agreement. This is to ensure against later possible claims by the employee that he or she did not understand the meaning or ramifications of what was signed. If such a warning was not included in your waiver/release, or if you were denied the opportunity to gain assistance of legal counsel, your waiver/release may be subject to defeat. Bear in mind that this "advice" to get legal counsel is really in the employer's self-protective interests.

G. Necessary Exception: Enforcement of the Separation Agreement Itself

One point often misunderstood is that the waiver/release of rights should not cover any later need to enforce the provisions of your separation agreement itself. That is, your waiver/release should except any and all claims that you never received your severance payments, or that your employer failed to honor any of its other severance-related obligations. Even if such a provision is missing from your waiver/release, failure to pay severance payments may represent failure of "consideration," as noted above.

The general topic of default, or breach, of severance agreements by either employee or employer is discussed in chapter 43, "Breach of the Severance Agreement—by Either Side."

H. Fixed Review Period

To be a valid waiver/release of claims under most federal antidiscrimination laws, your document must provide that you have twenty-one days (forty-five days to satisfy OWBPA) to review and consider the severance/separation offer. If not, your waiver/release may be invalid. Bear in mind that you do not have to take so much time to consider the severance package offered to you, but only that the time period is available to you. Know, as well, that you may request an extension of this period, but if you do so, *please,* get your employer to "sign off" on it in writing.

Not all severance agreements are required to have a twenty-one- or forty-five-day review period. Those that have no bearing on or relation to federal or state laws have no such requirement.

I. Claim of Duress

It is asked of me at times, "If I signed this waiver/release because I needed the money so badly, or I signed it because I was in dire need, or there was some other deadline or pressure facing me, can I later claim it was signed under duress and is therefore not binding or enforceable?" Though many of my clients have been in difficult financial straits or in a very uncomfortable position with moneys due, this is not a claim I have ever put forward or one that, to my knowledge, others have used with success. So I would advise you not to use it in your own case.

That said, if a claim exists that is reasonably beyond the scope of the waiver/release, or that arguably fits into an exception noted above, its pressing or filing should receive full consideration.

43

Breach of the Severance Agreement— by Either Side

> An acre of performance is worth the whole Land of Promise.
> —James Howell

What happens if either I or my employer doesn't honor the severance agreement?" Of all the questions my clients ask about the severance process, this is the one I am perhaps most reluctant to answer. That's because the events and circumstances that are likely to take place following breach of the severance agreement—whether by the employer or the employee—are so varied and so unpredictable. Likewise, the ways in which contracts are dishonored are innumerable. For these reasons and others, the number of possible results is great.

Nevertheless, in this chapter I will summarize for you the most common occurrences when a severance agreement is dishonored. In very simplified form, my discussion will present the main points of general contract law relevant to breach of severance agreements and the practical and common consequences of each. You must bear in mind, though, that these are general rules, and that the laws of your own state and locality must be followed.

A. Types of Obligations: To Perform or to Refrain

Both employer and employee have certain obligations in every severance agreement. Some obligations involve performing a task. For example, the employer often must pay severance moneys and cooperate with COBRA insurance coverage; the employee commonly must return company property and sometimes must provide a written resignation. These are affirmative duties.

On the other hand, certain obligations require the parties to refrain from doing certain things. The employer must often agree not to make an objection to any application for unemployment insurance benefits, and must refrain from making public comments detrimental to the employee's career. The employee often must not at any future time initiate lawsuits against the company and its officials, and must not divulge company trade secrets to others.

In my experience, the most common claims against employers in this context are related to their alleged failure to pay all severance moneys; next in line are claims of breach of the obligations of confidentiality and nondisparagement against the employee. The most common claims against employees in this context relate to alleged breach of covenants of noncompetition and those restricting future employment.

Be true to your obligations or face the consequences. By breaking severance obligations, you are sure to incite negative consequences.

B. Apparent Breach: Notice of Default; Time to Cure

As a general legal matter, and as an obligation set down in most severance agreements, if either employer or employee believes the other has failed to honor obligations, whether they are obligations to perform or to refrain, this belief should be communicated clearly to the apparently defaulting party, in writing. (A sample notice of default is included in the appendix.)

Exactly how this should be done (that is, to whom this letter should be sent, at what address, by what mode of delivery) is usually set out in detail in the severance agreement. (For an example of such a notice provision, see Paragraph 12 of the "Sample 'Long-Form' Severance Agreement, Waiver, and Release" in the appendix.)

If the required form, content, and recipient of the default notice is not set out in the severance agreement, then care and clarity are the rules. By "care" I mean that the severance agreement should be carefully read to look for all possible parties to notify and all possible addresses noted. Notice of default should be sent to all such recipients and addresses.

By "clarity," I mean just that. Be clear about what was required, and what was not provided. For example: "Paragraph 4(b) of our severance agreement requires payment of $10,000 to be made to me, at my home address, no later than February 9, 1997. Today is February 16, 1997, and no such check has been received." Or: "Paragraph 11(e)(i) sets forth that the company is to refrain from making objection to my application for unemployment insurance application. However, I today received a written notice from my local unemployment benefits office, a copy of which is attached, indicating quite clearly that the company is contesting my application."

There are two primary reasons to require a clear notice in the case of apparent default. First, this lets the other side know of your belief that it is in default, which gives that party an opportunity to look into the matter. Many times I find that innocent mistakes were made: a check was misdirected by a postal carrier, a check was received by a client's ten-year-old son but not placed in the usual mail spot, or a new bookkeeper was not notified about the severance payment requirement and therefore failed to prepare and transmit the necessary severance check.

Second, a notice of default gives the apparently defaulting party an opportunity to correct, or "cure," the default if in fact it has not followed through on the agreed-upon action. With little or no damage yet done, acknowledgment and correction of an error are the best way to handle such a problem.

It is for this reason that your notice of default should include a statement such as this: "If I am incorrect in my belief that you have not honored your obligation to me, please let me know, as soon as possible, in writing. If I am correct, please contact me immediately if you intend to cure this default."

Sending out a default notice is more important today than ever before. For courts are increasingly applying financial sanctions or penalties against parties who initiate lawsuits without first making such a good-faith effort to resolve disputes.

C. Types of Contract Breach:
Material Breach Versus Substantial Performance

There is an essential legal distinction between "material breach," which means that an essential part of an agreement was not carried out, and "substantial performance," which signifies that the essential parts of the agreement were in fact performed. They are opposites. In determining whether one or the other exists, some suggest that you ask the question, "Would I have entered into this agreement had I known that the breach in question was to take place?"

For an example of an employer material breach, let's suppose that you released your employer from all actual and potential claims, that you agreed to refrain from working in your field of expertise for two years, and that you took a lower-paying and less prestigious position in another field to honor this obligation. Suppose, further, that your employer stopped making agreed severance payments after the first few of twenty-four payments due you, and that your notice of default to the employer elicited no response. This would represent a "material" breach by your employer, probably entitling you to seek both (1) a declaration that your further obligations and your release are void ("rescission" of the contract), and (2) the financial damages you may have suffered by taking a position outside of your field ("compensatory damage"). If we modify the example to suppose that all payments were made, but the employer was six weeks late in providing you with an agreed "departure statement," this would likely be considered an immaterial breach, permitting you, at most, to seek reimbursement for your lost salary on the first position lost as a result.

Now let's look at employee breach. Suppose you did everything you were obligated to do under your severance agreement, but that you violated your "nondisparagement" clause by casually telling people in your industry that the company CEO was a heavy whiskey drinker, which was true, and that she frequently took four-hour liquid lunches, which was also true. This would probably be considered a breach of your nondisparagement clause but an immaterial breach of the overall agreement, not to be considered sufficient basis for halting the severance payments still due you. On the other hand, suppose your transgression was the transfer to your former employer's direct competitor of vital trade secrets about strategic business plans and secret customer lists. This would surely constitute a material breach of your severance agreement, upon which the cessation of future severance payments would be properly based, as well as a substantial claim for compensatory (resulting) financial damages suffered by your employer.

The laws, legal doctrines, and judges of each state set out what damages can be based upon what actions, but this general distinction flows through the laws of most, if not all, jurisdictions. Bear in mind that this discussion is a "primer" of sorts and presents legal matters in only the most simplified form.

D. Choices of Remedy: Damages, Rescission, or Injunction

In the event a party does commit a material breach of its severance-agreement obligations, the aggrieved party must elect what course to take to redress grievances. This is a strategic choice, to be made upon weighing, first, the goals to be achieved. In some states, alternative bases of suit, or duplicative bases for suit, may be brought simultaneously. There are many ways to bring a lawsuit, but the following three are the most common in these circumstances.

1. Damages

The most common lawsuit is one for damages; that is, the plaintiff (party bringing the suit) charges that the defendant has failed to honor his or her end of the bargain, and that plaintiff has, therefore, suffered certain financial damages.

Implicit in such lawsuits are positions that the agreement is and was valid, and that the plaintiff will complete his or her end of the bargain if this has not yet been done. These two points are critical to consider before seeking damages. Either side—employer or employee—may seek damages for material breach.

2. Rescission

In the case of "rescission," you file a claim that states that the other party has failed to honor its obligations to you, and you therefore seek the court's agreement that you may consider the agreement null and void.

Such a declaration would free the plaintiff from having to perform his or her end of the agreement in any additional way, but would free the defendant in the same way. Either side—employer or employee—may seek rescission in the event of material breach.

3. Injunction

A lawsuit seeking an "injunction" is filed with the objective of obtaining a court order to halt a certain activity. In organized labor circumstances, it is commonly heard that a court will "enjoin" picketing too close to a store entrance, for example, or a boycott of an innocent third party.

In severance circumstances, courts are frequently asked to enjoin such employee activities as:

- disparagement of the employer or its officers;
- breach of confidentiality;
- breach of a restrictive covenant limiting employment or of a non-competition clause;
- dissemination of trade secrets;
- breach of a continuing fiduciary obligation or relationship.

It is quite common—indeed, it is almost the rule—that a severance agreement expressly grants to the employer the employee's consent to injunctive remedies on the employer's behalf. It is extremely rare, although not unheard of, for a severance agreement to give an employee the unfettered right to seek injunctive relief from a court. Nothing prevents an aggrieved employee from doing so, however.

Injunctive relief is sought in two general steps. First, a party seeks temporary relief, often called a temporary restraining order (or TRO), asking the court to order the allegedly violating behavior to be halted temporarily until a hearing can be held at which both sides may be heard. These TRO's are granted quite frequently on minimal proof, but they last only a short time, usually a matter of weeks.

Second, and more important, is the judge's decision regarding extension of the TRO until the results of a full trial—possibly years away—are in. This is, essentially, the crux of the affair, for it drastically alters the rights of the parties and hence negotiation leverage.

E. The Likelihood of Settlement

Our discussion of the breach of a severance agreement, and the consequences of such a breach, is to be considered in the context of eventual settlement, for ninety-nine of one hundred cases of every kind are resolved this way. Ideally, settlement of claims is achieved shortly after claims are presented, discussed, evaluated, and negotiated, with minimum expenditure of time, energy, attention, and legal expense.

Settlement is easier to propose than achieve. Bear in mind that this is a *settlement of a breached settlement* (that is, the severance agreement, itself, is a settlement of sorts). In such a situation, trust and consequent willingness to trust are to be presumed in short supply. While some cases do indeed go to trial and result in a clear "winner," even in these cases few if any of the parties really ever feel they have won anything.

I look at most litigation as a boxing match in which endurance is primary, strength of argument is secondary, and both parties usually leave the ring battered and bruised. Endurance is almost always an employer-side advantage, although skillful manipulation of the media under certain circumstances can serve to minimize that advantage or even turn it around to the employee's favor.

44

Employer Bankruptcy

> Bankruptcy is a legal proceeding in which you put your
> money in your pants pocket and give your coat to your
> creditors.
>
> —Joey Adams (comedian)

Question: After I sign my severance agreement, will I lose severance benefits if my employer goes bankrupt? *Answer:* Absolutely. Severance payments and benefits can be lost, or at least severely diminished, as a result of the employer's subsequent bankruptcy. Two clients of mine— both senior executives of an apparel manufacturer—lost most of two years of continued salary payments in this way. But there are certain prudent things you may be able to do to protect yourself or limit your risk in such a situation.

A. Bankruptcy 101

Bankruptcy is an area of the law that is meant to help all parties concerned with a failing or failed business—creditors, lenders, employees, owners, tax authorities, and others—deal with the practical problems such a case caused. In a nutshell, bankruptcy occurs when there's just not enough money to satisfy the competing demands of those who are due or are going to be due money from a company. Capitalism anticipates that business failures will take place, and our legal system has established a separate category of special laws, special courts, and special judges to deal with the problems that arise.

In short, the laws state that a bankruptcy judge will appoint a bankruptcy trustee to oversee either the "reorganization" of the business declaring bankruptcy, to restart it, or its dissolution and financial dismemberment, and distribution of its assets to creditors. The day that a bankruptcy petition is filed with the court requesting court intervention—either voluntarily by the business owners or involuntarily by one or more of its creditors—the business comes under the bankruptcy court's special umbrella of protection. All lawsuits, proceedings, collection efforts, and the like must be halted while the bankruptcy court takes over. Incidentally, bankruptcy law is federal law and so preempts all otherwise applicable state and local laws. The objective of the process is to do what's best for all, in light of the limited assets available, and the competing and overwhelming demands on those assets.

B. The Trustee's Right to "Reject Contracts"

There are three overriding aspects of bankruptcy law and procedure that most directly concern severance negotiations. The first, and most important, is the bankruptcy trustee's duty to review all ongoing contracts and arrangements of the company, and his or her right to reject, or void, those he or she considers unduly burdensome or not in the best interests of the bankrupt estate, which may be loosely defined as the interests of all combined.

A severance (or employment separation) agreement is a contract that usually surfaces in the discussion of such rejection, and a likely candidate for rejection. So if your company declares bankruptcy, your severance agreement may be voided by the trustee. If this happens to you, take your place in a line of creditors who must make an application to the trustee explaining why they deserve to get paid, and how much.

The other two aspects of bankruptcy that most directly affect severance benefits are the trustees' right to "reverse," and preferences and priorities.

C. The Trustee's Right to "Reverse" Transactions

The bankruptcy trustee is also authorized to reverse transactions in which the bankrupt concern has taken part, generally for a period of ninety days prior to the date the bankruptcy petition was filed. Thus severance benefits and payments received during this ninety-day period may be directed, by court order, to be returned to the bankrupt estate. You can in effect be asked to return money you've received and possibly already spent. Obviously, this can cause severe problems for you.

To make matters worse, if you were one of the "insiders" who ran the company—that is, a company officer or high-level executive—any payments, benefits, or property you received from the company for a *full year* before the petition filing date are subject to seizure for return to the bankrupt estate. This is intended to protect creditors from senior management looting the estate in anticipation of the filing of a bankruptcy petition.

D. Preferences, Priorities, and Payouts

When the bankruptcy trustee gets a firm handle on the various assets and interests comprising the bankrupt estate, it is then time for his or her consideration of distribution of available assets to and among those who have filed and proven their claims. (The court must first acquiesce.)

The order of payment goes like this: First come the costs of administering the estate, including running the company if it has resumed operation. Next, creditors are listed in a certain priority order, with secured creditors at top and unsecured general creditors at bottom. (Secured creditors have given credit, goods, or services only after having filed public-record instruments, such as mortgages or liens-of-records. Employees never do that.) Claims for wages due are commonly somewhat in the middle. Payouts then are made to creditors, to the extent moneys are available, quite often at a discount to the actual amount due and owing. You've no doubt heard of creditors getting paid "twenty cents on the dollar."

E. Severance Strategies

If you think your soon-to-be-ex-employer may be headed down the path of bankruptcy, there are certain prudent courses of action I suggest you consider to minimize your exposure:

1. Take Your Lump-Sum Payment

Requesting all of your severance moneys up front, in one lump, is the best first step. While you may not be able to predict if, and when, a bankruptcy petition will be filed, at least this affords you an opportunity to get paid before the ninety-day (or one-year) period of "take back" may start. With this in mind, it may even prove worthwhile for you to offer the employer a discount in exchange for lump-sum payout.

2. Shorten the Payout Period

If lump-sum severance payout is not available, the next best step is to request a shortened term for payout. To whatever extent you may avoid participation in the bankruptcy process, you'll come out ahead. If part of your payment is received "clear" of the ninety-day (or one-year) reversal period, the balance owed to you may eventually be paid to you, as a general creditor, at a reduced rate.

3. Delay the Termination Itself

One smart strategy, utilized especially where bankruptcy appears quite inevitable, is to hold off on your termination papers until after the bankruptcy petition is filed. While this may seem counterintuitive, it has several potential advantages. First, severance claims related to work done or deals made "postpetition" are afforded administrative priority and thus paid on an ongoing basis; waiting for payment with other creditors until the end of the process may not be necessary. Second, administrative claims are often afforded full payment, while other claims frequently are not. Third, unsecured claims are capable of satisfaction by transfer of assets or stock, both at times of dubious value; administrative claims, on the other hand, must be paid in cash, by law.

4. Other "Security" Measures

To further protect yourself from the effects of the bankruptcy process, you can request that your employer take certain additional measures. Your employer might purchase an annuity with your name as beneficiary, place moneys into escrow, or prepay your insurance premiums, tuition payments, and the like. Before making any of these requests, you should evaluate it in the special context in which it arises.

•   •   •

The specter of bankruptcy of the employer looms over every severance package that entails payments and benefits afforded over time. Potential bankruptcy of the employer is a reality; if it may reasonably be expected to take place, all available prudent steps should be taken to avoid its risks.

45

Rollovers, Reinvestments, and Replacements

> I detest life insurance agents; they always argue that someday I shall die, which is not so.
> —Stephen B. Leacock (1869–1944)

At the time of employment termination and transition, there is much for you to attend to. One of the most important is the rollover, reinvestment, and replacement of your pension, savings, and insurance plans. While these matters are technically outside the purview of severance negotiations, they are matters of significant post-negotiation concern that frequently call for my involvement as legal representative.

This chapter will serve only to briefly highlight the areas of primary concern. I strongly suggest that you speak with your pension administrator, your benefits manager, and your own accountant and financial adviser about the specifics of your plans, as well as your rights and options where they are concerned, along with how each of these may impact upon your personal financial goals and taxes.

401(k) Plans

These tax-deferred savings plans have grown in popularity to the degree that more of my clients participate in them than they do in formal company pension plans. Though your 401(k) plan is funded primarily by you, the transition out of your current employment will require that you elect to do one of the following within sixty days of leaving:

- roll the moneys over into an IRA account of your own; or
- roll the moneys over into a 401(k) plan administered by your next employer; or
- leave the moneys in your former employer's 401(k) plan if the plan permits continued participation by former employees; or
- take a distribution of some or all of the 401(k) moneys, in which case
  - *your employer will have to deduct 20 percent for withholding, and*
  - *you will be liable for a 10 percent penalty if you are under the age of fifty-nine and a half.*

You must bear in mind that any moneys made payable to you, that is, distributed to your name instead of to a rollover account custodian, will be taxed and penalized, no matter how short a time it remains in your possession. Many of my clients with company-sponsored 401(k) plans set up an individual IRA account at a brokerage house only as a temporary holding account, to hold their 401(k) moneys until they know what their future plans are, thus avoiding the required 20 percent withholding, the 10 percent penalty, and resultant income taxation.

Note that whether your company makes a 401(k) contribution on your behalf for the year in question is usually determined by the plan. However, "accommodations" in determining your "last day on the books for 401(k) purposes" are commonly part of severance negotiations.

Pension Plans

Upon request, your Human Resources representative can provide you with the name and telephone number of your company pension plan administrator, from whom you can obtain answers to all questions you may have about vesting, balances, and payment options. You should be sure to request a copy of the pension program's Summary Plan Description, as well as a copy of your most recent year-end benefits statement. You should also make it your business to fully understand the rights, benefits, and disadvantages that are applicable to taking "early retirement."

If your pension plan gives its participants the option of taking a lump-sum payment upon termination of employment, you might consider it very seriously. This option would permit you to take control over how you want to invest your pension moneys, something many people find very appealing.

Remember that pension accommodations and "bridge to retirement" provisions are very valuable and commonly granted severance negotiation requests.

Stock Plans

Many companies use a variety of vehicles to make stock ownership a valuable benefit, a motivational device, and sometimes even a requirement to hold senior executive positions. These include:

- Employee Stock Ownership Plans (ESOPs), through which employees, as a group and through trustees, take on a significant ownership position in the company.
- Stock Purchase Plans, by which employees are usually permitted to buy company stock at reduced price.
- Stock Appreciation Rights agreements, through which employees are rewarded for an increase in company stock price.
- Incentive Stock Options, which are awarded for meeting specified performance standards.

Each plan will have its own exercise prices, holding periods, policies, restrictions, and tax implications. Your immediate task is to gather information about each such plan or program you are eligible to participate in from the company benefits officer, and to take note of all applicable deadlines.

As noted in earlier chapters, accommodations in stock option programs, in particular, are commonly requested and granted during severance negotiations. Indeed, in some cases I've seen the manipulation of these programs constitute the greatest proportion of benefits in the total severance package.

Insurance Programs

As discussed in earlier chapters, continuation of employer-sponsored health insurance coverage is possible in most companies employing fifty or more employees under a federal law nicknamed COBRA.

Continuation is permitted for up to eighteen months and, under certain, limited conditions, can be extended for an additional year. In any continuation, though, the law provides that the employee, not the employer, is obligated to pay the premiums plus a small administrative handling charge. In severance negotiations, however, it's commonly requested that the employer agree to take on the cost of COBRA coverage continuation.

Life insurance and disability insurance are the two next most common insurance that will very likely require replacement coverage. No federal, state, or local laws of which I am aware require that the employer arrange for coverage continuation for life or disability policies. That said, you should consider requesting—especially where health considerations would support the argument of critical need—continued coverage through the employer plan, at least until you can arrange substitute coverage, either individually or as part of a group. Many people join affinity groups at this time to gain eligibility to participate in their group insurance programs.

· · ·

Review and consider each of these critical items with your own personal financial planner and/or accountant. Then negotiate extension, reimbursement, and accommodation of these items during the severance negotiation process as suits your situation best.

46

Conclusion: Severance Negotiating . . .
and Your Empowerment Beyond

> Tomorrow is the most important thing in life. Comes
> into us at midnight very clean. It's perfect when it arrives
> and it puts itself into our hands. It hopes we've learned
> something from yesterday.
>
> —John Wayne

Living your life and planning your life both require some sense of
continuity, some things you can count on, some sense of security. In
the old days, until perhaps 1985, job security was a function of
seniority. If you performed on the job, you could generally count on
keeping your job and rising through the ranks as new positions
opened up for which you were interested and suited. But seniority as a
source of job security is now gone, long gone, and it's not likely to
return again.

Continual workplace negotiation has taken the place of seniority as
today's primary source of job security. Job security must now be continually negotiated: while getting into the job, while on the job, and,
most especially, while on the way out of a job. To the extent that you
can learn to negotiate for yourself in the workplace, you will develop
some degree of job security.

When you are facing involuntary job loss—whether you've been
fired, downsized, or laid off—negotiating with the very people who've
just let you go is definitely not easy. Addressing these seemingly powerful people, without any perceived leverage and while you're in a relative state of shock, can be a daunting proposition. This book is
intended to assist you with that task. It is designed to help you level the
playing field and gain the true sense, in your heart, mind, and gut, that

there is a very good severance deal out there for you waiting to be negotiated.

But negotiating a good (or even better) severance package is just the beginning. For this process is a learning experience about workplace negotiating, for today, and about achieving job security, in the future. It is also an experience from which you will learn to discover some of your hidden negotiating potential, so as to unleash, exhibit, and effectively sell and enjoy your true worth in the employment marketplace. And that will do even better and better things for you.

Let me share a story with you: One of my clients, whom I'll call Charlie, was a professional who'd worked for decades for a company that he had helped establish, and in which, he'd been led to believe, he had an ownership interest. The ownership paperwork, though, had never been completed. His boss/partner always treated him without respect.

Over time Charlie developed a debilitating illness that limited his mobility and muscular coordination; though his speech was somewhat halting, his mind was as sharp and focused as ever. His mobility was accomplished by motorized wheelchair. Despite his physical problems, Charlie would travel to work a few days a week at the office with the help of an attendant, and he worked at home, too. One day his boss/partner ordered that no more paychecks or expense reimbursements be issued to Charlie. When Charlie met with him to discuss the matter, all he was told was he was now "worth less than nothing."

Over the course of a few months, Charlie and I managed to convince his boss/partner that Charlie was, indeed, worth far more than "less than nothing." Through skillful use of the few documents available to us, cooperating coworkers as witnesses, state and federal laws protecting employees in these situations, and whatever leverage was available to us, the tide was slowly turned in Charlie's favor, and his boss/partner became the one initiating requests for meetings with him. A reasonable, respectful, dignified settlement of all issues was under way.

In a conversation with Charlie's wife, she told me that his doctor, following a regular monthly checkup, remarked to Charlie that his vital signs and physical appearance were the best they'd been in years, representing a remarkable improvement over his condition of late. Charlie's doctor asked him what was new in his life, and Charlie ascribed his newfound health and well-being to the satisfaction, exhilaration, and esteem-building side effects of finally standing up and confronting "wrong," and seeing "wrong" run away.

Reading this book, using its lessons and suggestions to your own benefit, will give you a leg up, a sense of real personal empowerment, in the severance negotiating process. Taking the information and inspiration put into this book, and putting it to good use in your own life, is the next, intended step toward learning what you need to learn to achieve greater job security. Now, you will be able to negotiate job security as well as or even better than almost anyone else you know, including your boss or HR representative.

This process works; I know it does. I developed it, and I use it every day and so do my clients, all over the world. Learn it, internalize it, and use it to bring about your best possible severance package and your greatest future job security. Your workplace is a negotiating place, today more than ever, and you've now got the knowledge, perspective, and know-how to succeed as never before.

⋮ Appendix

Sample Letters of Nonacceptance
of Termination Terms

> Writing is easy. All you do is sit staring at a blank sheet of
> paper until the drops of blood form on your forehead.
> —Gene Fowler

> The right to be heard does not automatically include the
> right to be taken seriously.
> —Hubert Humphrey

In the following letters, which I helped write, two of my clients indicate that they do not—and will not—accept the terms of their termination, with or without the separation package offered. Of course, the particular facts in each letter have been altered to preclude identification of the parties.

In both cases, employers responded to these letters by offering significantly enhanced severance packages and agreeing to enter into comprehensive severance package discussions. In both cases, the higher-ups to whom the letters were addressed did not, themselves, participate in the reopened severance negotiations. Instead, the newly "invigorated"—and now apparently motivated—personnel from Human Resources and the general counsel's office indicated, for the first time, a strong interest in accommodating the concerns expressed.

[Sample Nonacceptance Letter A]
MEMORANDUM

To: Mr. John Bigler, Remington Stores CEO
From: Jennifer Adams, Fashion Club Director, Chicago
Date: May 12, 1992
Subject: Direct Appeal for Intervention

Dear Mr. Bigler:

I write this memorandum directly to you mindful that, in doing so, I bypass regular channels. Appeals through regular channels available to me have been attempted, to no avail. I take this step as the last resort of a faithful Remington employee about to be terminated for unsubstantiated reasons.

I also write with all sincerity that I just turned sixty-eight years of age, with many years of good business experience and judgment, quite confident and competent in my work. In my fourteen years as an executive of Remington Stores I have devoted all of my energies and extensive contacts in the Chicago community and in Fort Wayne, as well, to the benefit of Remington. All of my performance reviews have been overall either "good" or "very good." Not once have I received a negative review.

In 1987, I assumed my present position, Fashion Club Director in the Remington Chicago store. Since that time, I have been praised for both my leadership and the results of my efforts. As illustrations, in 1991:

- Total store growth was 2 percent. Fashion Club growth was 16.4 percent.
- Store return rate was 18 percent. Fashion Club return rate was 8.8 percent.
- Every Fashion Club staff member's sales grew substantially in volume and dollars, while all selling costs for Fashion Club consultants were down for the year.
- The Chicago Fashion Club had a stronger client base—seventy-seven clients—than the Fashion Clubs in Seattle (sixteen), Miami (fifteen), and Washington (thirteen).

In the first five months of 1993, store growth was -2.7 percent. The Fashion Club growth was 17.1 percent. Bear in mind that this was achieved in the shadow of the dollar-value economic crisis; fully 26 percent of our sales are to Japanese tourists.

Following these achievements, and others, this year my new General Manager, Mr. Marvin Edwards, has given me an HR review calling for thirty-day review with disciplinary action. After fourteen years in Remington's employ with all positive performance reviews, and promotions, this year I have received, in effect, a thirty-day notice of termination.

Incidentally, if I understand the system breakdown correctly, as listed on the front page of the review, it appears Mr. Edwards, himself, may have broken Remington's own rules by calling for disciplinary action, including termination, even though my latest overall rating of "excellent" did not call for this.

Why, you may ask, am I to be terminated? The statistics, available for all to see, suggest promotion, not termination. I have read, discussed, and responded to my Performance Appraisal (a copy of which is enclosed for your review), but the evaluation of my performance flies directly in the face of my results, each and every year. To me, and to many others, it seems most probable I am being pushed out of my position in favor of a much younger woman, a close friend of Mr. Edwards, of great attractiveness but of little, if any, experience in Fashion Club matters.

I know that you have been a good friend of Mr. Edwards from your days together at Two-Brothers Stores. Mr. Edwards may be an experienced, competent, skilled manager, but my appeals to him, and to Remington Corporate Human Resources, have fallen on deaf ears. Mr. Edwards has now asked that I decide how I want to handle a storewide announcement explaining my "departure."

I am not at all inclined to "depart." Nonetheless, I do understand that there is finality to this decision. While I comprehend the finality of this decision, there is just no way I can possibly live with its ramifications.

Mr. Bigler, I just turned sixty-eight, am without spouse or wealth, and cannot accept as final the offer of nine weeks of severance. At the same time, I am not the type of person to fight or cause trouble, or to burn bridges that I know are important to me. Then again, I am not able to go without income, health insurance, or my other Remington Stores' benefits, especially pension contribution.

I ask you to consider my request that I be given severance and my other Remington benefits for a period of thirty-six months, so that I may be able to regain my financial footing. Health insurance is also paramount. A positive final reference would also be appreciated. Professional outplacement assistance would be helpful. Lastly, as my "departure" is most assuredly not my wish, I would expect that Remington Stores would not contest my unemployment-benefits application, should I make one.

I am a proud and self-sufficient person. I had no plans in my life but to continue with my Fashion Club success until retirement. I look to my friends, my church, and my support in the Chicago community for strength and personal sustenance, but I cannot do so for finances.

This termination is a big blow to me, in many ways. To my knowledge, you have the authority to make this situation "right." I do not ask for more than I need or deserve. Your considering this request for assistance is sincerely appreciated.

Very truly yours,
Jennifer Adams

[Sample Nonacceptance Letter B]

Ira P. Biencivega
17 Westerly Road
Bancroft, NJ 07242

January 16, 1994

Mr. James Schwalb
Co-Head, Investment Management
Western Banking
171 West 38th Street
New York, NY 10032

RE: SEVERANCE DISCUSSIONS

Dear Jim:

Following our recent talk about Western's termination of my

employment, I have carefully reviewed the details of the severance package presented. I have thought long and hard about my termination, discussed it extensively with my wife, and have come to accept its inevitability. I have also consulted with my accountant as well as an attorney who specializes in severance packages. The latter suggests I work out the basics with you, and that I reach him to finalize details after agreement is reached.

Everyone I have talked with agrees that I have to be comfortable with the package, and that, Jim, is why I write. There are two aspects of my life that make this situation so very much more difficult: the needs created by my health, especially my heart condition, and the needs of my family. Both weigh heavily on me; neither is very flexible.

I appreciate very sincerely the spirit of the overall package offered, but four certain elements are just not in keeping with my very real, urgent needs. As you can surely imagine, my utmost concern is how long I will remain unemployed, and what damage that delay and its stress may do to my finances, my health, and my insurance coverages. All of them are related.

A. Compensation

Severance: In the narrow sense of the term, the severance element of my package—two weeks for each year worked—seems short. Even middle-level management in the Chase/Chemical merger received, after their notice period, three weeks per year, while Managing Director level received four weeks per year, if not more. The just-announced four weeks per year from Wells Fargo (re: First Interstate) further recognizes the need for a material severance component in today's brutal employment market in financial services. This makes me question why I should deserve less than the increasingly standard four weeks per year of severance they and others are receiving, and I have real difficulty accepting less.

Notice/salary continuation: Each of these seems fair, at least at this time, though I'm certain that, as they come closer to being exhausted, the feeling of fairness will run thin. To address my very real concerns about the time it may take to achieve reemployment, I ask that Western permit combined notice, salary, and severance (with company benefits) to be paid to me as salary, and to run through December 1995 but to end as soon after June 30, 1995, as I am reemployed. This I would consider reasonable, and only fair, under the circumstances of my termination.

Continuation of the combined compensation as salary through at least June 30, 1995, is *absolutely critical* to me: it gets me to the ten-year service level, and therefore allows for possible retirement at age fifty-five, an extremely important option considering my health; it provides for the approximate amount of time someone at my level could expect to need to find a comparable position; it delays the activation date of the COBRA period.

B. Service Length and Calculations

In speaking to others who have gone through this before, I am told that the most common area of severance discussions these days is in pension "accommodations." Since I had planned to remain at Western and would have, except for this restructuring, I ask that, for pension calculation purposes, five years be added to my service length, especially in light of my very positive performance record and loyalty to the company. This would bring total service length to at least fifteen years, assuming I remain on the payroll until June 30, 1995. I also ask that five years be added to my age in calculations, making it the increasingly common "five plus five" plan many severed executives receive at other companies. This would be so very valuable to me, as it would get me to the "rule of seventy" level.

This second request is especially important to me, because at my age it is unlikely I'll have an opportunity to vest in any meaningful way in any other pension plan with a future employer. I believe this is (and has been) done under what is called "special situations," and I am hoping and expecting to qualify as one, too.

C. Insurance Coverages

With my serious heart condition and, more recently, back problems, and my pressing financial needs—two kids fast approaching college age—these are crucial. I would hope and expect that all coverages be continued and paid through the period of my combined compensation, that is, through December 1995, but as early as June 1995 if I am reemployed. Expiration of any one or more of life insurance, disability insurance, or COBRA-health coverage could be disastrous, as replacement without my being reemployed (indeed, even if I was reemployed) may prove impossible because of requalification requirements. Jim, the prospect of no insurance is daunting, to say the least. The prospect of no insurance and no work, given my situation, is frightening.

The necessary minimum coverage would be achieved by continuation of compensation through June 1995, as I have requested above. With COBRA starting no earlier than July 1995, I would then be covered in all events under our group policy for a thirty-six month period, which would be an acceptable—though still disconcerting—level of risk.

D. Outplacement

Along with the three basic concerns, above, I would request an extension of coverage to eighteen months, that is, through June 1995, to cover the possible gap in employment. Of course, upon reemployment I would discontinue the service.

Jim, you've always been fair and straightforward with me, and I thank you for that. I've always been a team player at Western, and am in a position of need that requires that I ask the company to go the extra yard for me. These requests are surely not beyond the company's resources, nor precedent setting. As you know, I preferred to remain a contributing member of the Group rather than be in my current position, but that is no longer possible.

I would like you to know that your commitment to consider these requests for me is highly appreciated.

Sincerely,

Ira P. Biencivega

cc: Mr. Martin Drazer
Chief Operating Officer—Investment Banking

Sample "Short-Form"
Severance Agreement, Waiver, and Release

Set forth below is an example of a "short-form" severance agreement used for the severance of a chief executive of a billion-dollar company. It was presented to my client and me on the very same day we received the long-form agreement that appears in the next section. This shorter agreement was prepared by the Human Resources department of a lending institution and is remarkable in its simplicity. You will note it is written in the form of two letters.

An agreement like this may suffice for the matter at hand, but it may also leave out especially important matters. Moreover, an agreement of this type requires us to "push uphill": instead of asking that objectionable material be deleted, we are faced with the greater burden of having to prepare new material and request its insertion. From an attorney's and negotiator's points of view, the former is far easier.

The names of the respective parties have been changed, as well as all information from which their identities could be determined.
October 11, 1991

Ms. Barbara Helberg
721 Fifth Avenue
New York, NY 10019

Dear Barbara,

Below I have outlined the agreement we have reached concerning your leaving the Company.

Effective October 11, you are no longer President/CEO of the Company. In addition, concurrently you are resigning your position on the Board of the Company. You will, however, continue to receive your regular pay through October 17. Within ten days following your concurrence with the conditions of this agreement, I will deliver to you a check for $95,000 less appropriate withholdings, reflecting your bonus for calendar year 1991. In addition I will arrange a separate payment for the four weeks of unused vacation from 1991.

Effective October 17 and for a period of nine months thereafter, we will ask you to serve as a consultant to the Company on issues of management concerns and future directions. For services rendered, in consulting fees, your compensation will be based on $225,000 per annum. Thereafter, if you have failed to secure other employment, you will be able to continue your role as an in-house consultant on a month-to-month basis (based on the same rate per annum) for up to a maximum of six additional months. We will treat you as an in-house consultant so that all of your current benefits, except vacation accrual, will stay in place. At the end of the twelve-month period, we will retain the option of providing you with an additional bonus for the consulting services you have provided. In addition, by virtue of your role as a consultant you will be able to maintain your holdings of Company restricted stock that you have not yet vested. Based on your decision to select an outplacement firm of your choice, the Company will pay the outplacement fee or offer to compensate you directly for the equivalent of a nine-month executive program valued at $18,000, less applicable withholdings.

You will receive a relocation allowance of $35,000 for geographical preference. In the event you will be held responsible for the remaining months of your apartment lease in New York, the Company will pay the monthly rent but will have full use of the apartment during that time. However, if instead, there is a lesser expense associated with forfeiting the lease, the Company will absorb the cost.

As we discussed, you currently have in your possession a laptop and printer that belong to the Company. If you are interested in retaining either or both, we can offset their costs against either the bonus or the accrued vacation payment.

I believe this reflects everything we have agreed to. By signing below, you acknowledge that you agree to the terms of this letter, that the moneys paid to you under this agreement exceed any payment or benefit that you otherwise would receive under any Company policy or plan, that this represents the full extent of the Company's obligations to you, that you have legal or otherwise, including but not limited to, claims under the Age Discrimination Employment Act of 1967, as amended, and that this agreement is governed by the laws of the State of New York.

I am also obliged under the law to inform you that you have twenty-one days from receipt of this letter to consider it before signing; that you may consult with an attorney before signing, although you are not required to do so; that after you have signed the agreement, you have seven days to revoke your decision by notifying me in writing; that the agreement will become effective on the eighth day after you have signed.

Please indicate your concurrence with these arrangements by signing below. Should you have any questions, please feel free to call me at extension 7599. Barbara, I wish you the best of luck in your future endeavors.

Sincerely,

Ronald Miller

Acknowledged: _____ Date: _____
                    Barbara Helberg

October 11, 1991

Ms. Barbara Helberg
721 Fifth Avenue
New York, NY 10019

Dear Barbara,

The purpose of this letter is to accompany the agreement we have reached concerning your resignation from the Company. In addition to the financial arrangements indicated in the other letter, we have arrived at the following understanding with regard to your restricted stock: you will have until March 13, 1992, to decide if you would like to take cash in lieu of shares (at the 10/13/91 share price) or if you would prefer to continue the vesting arrangement indicated in your grant letter through a continuing consulting type of relationship. This decision must be communicated to me in writing prior to November 13; if I do not hear from you, I will give instructions to cancel the shares and pay cash-in-lieu.

If you have any questions about this, please feel free to call me directly at extension 7599.

Best of luck,

Ronald Miller

Acknowledged: _____ Date: _____
                        Barbara Helberg

Sample "Long-Form"
Severance Agreement, Waiver, and Release

Set forth below is a sample severance agreement and release that was presented to my client and me for our review and comment. Of course, the names of the respective parties, as well as all information from which their identities could be determined, have been changed. Prepared by a large law firm, the document is well drafted and quite comprehensive, although it does not contain a noncompetition clause of any kind, as the facts and circumstances did not call for one.

The sample agreement is generally reasonable, as well, except for one provision—Paragraph 13—which was, to my mind and to the minds of other attorneys in my office, "from outer space." It is so over-reaching as to make the entire document of questionable worth. I negotiated strenuously to get it removed, without success. Its existence was attributable to circumstances that were unique. As with the famous tale of Dr. Seuss's "green cow," I've never seen one like it, and I hope never to again.

Separation Agreement and General Release

This **Separation Agreement** and **General Release** (the "Agreement") is made and entered into as of the Effective Date of this Agreement (as set forth in Paragraph 11 below), by and between **Robert Jones** ("Jones") and **Travel Company, Inc.** ("Travel"), on behalf of itself, its parents, subsidiaries, and affiliates including, without limitation, Tours Company, Inc., Hotels Company, Inc., and Cruises Company Inc. (collectively, the "Company").

FOR AND IN CONSIDERATION of the mutual promises and covenants herein contained and for good and valuable consideration, the sufficiency of which is hereby acknowledged, Jones and the Company (the "Parties") hereby agree as follows:

1. *Last Day of Employment/Termination of Prior Agreements and Under-standings.* Effective as of the close of business January 18, 1995, Jones resigns his employment and all positions he held with the Company. The Parties agree that any prior agreement and understanding between them, whether oral or written and of whatever nature, are hereby canceled, terminated, and super-seded by this Agreement and shall be of no further force or effect.

2. *Payments to Jones.* Travel, Inc. will pay or cause to be paid to Jones the amounts as set forth below, subject to all of the terms and conditions of this Agreement. These amounts, and each of them, shall be collectively and individually referred to as and shall constitute the "Separation Payments." Each amount shall be paid by check payable to the order of "Robert Jones" and mailed on the Payment Dates set forth below to Jones at the address listed in Paragraph 12 hereof.

   (a) *Biweekly Payments.* For the thirty-six-month period from January 19, 1995, through January 18, 1998 (the "Period of Salary Continuation"), Travel, Inc. will pay or cause to be paid to Jones equal biweekly payments based upon the annualized basis of $275,000.00 less applicable payroll with-holdings and deductions ("the Biweekly Salary Continuation Payments"). The Biweekly Salary Continuation Payments shall be paid commencing within ten (10) business days after the later of (i) the Effective Date of this Agreement or (ii) Jones's compliance with Paragraph 8(d) of this Agreement, and shall continue to be paid on the regular biweekly payday of the Company through the Period of Salary Continuation.

   (b) *Jones 1994 Bonus.* Travel, Inc. will pay or cause to be paid to Jones a onetime lump-sum payment in the amount of $50,000.00, less applicable payroll withholdings and deduc-tions, which shall constitute the entire bonus to Jones for 1994 ("Jones 1994 Bonus"). Jones's 1994 Bonus shall be paid within seven (7) business days after the later of (i) the Effective Date of this Agreement or (ii) Jones's compliance with Paragraph 8(d) of this Agreement.

   (c) *Payment of Employer Match for the Tours Company, Inc. Saving and Investment Plan.* Travel, Inc. will pay or cause to be paid to Jones a onetime lump-sum payment of $12,500.00, less applicable payroll withholdings and deductions, which rep-resents the equivalent of the total employer match for the

Tours Company Savings and Investment Plan had Jones
been a participant in the Plan during the Period of Salary
Continuation. This payment will be made within seven (7)
business days after the later of (i) the Effective Date of this
Agreement or (ii) Jones's compliance with Paragraph 8(d)
of this Agreement.

(d) *Payment of Accrued But Unused Vacation.* Travel, Inc. will pay
or cause to be paid to Jones the following onetime lump-
sum payments:

(i) A payment of 8,500.00, less applicable withholdings
and deductions, which represents payment of Jones's pre-
1995 accrued but unused vacation days.

(ii) A payment of $2,000.00, less applicable withholdings
and deductions, which represents payment for Jones's
accrued but unused 1994 vacation days.

(iii) Both payments shall be made within seven (7) business days after the later of (a) the Effective Date of this
Agreement or (b) Jones's compliance with Paragraph 8(d)
of this Agreement.

(e) *Reimbursement for Outplacement Services.* Travel, Inc. will pay
for the cost of outplacement counseling of Jones during
the Period of Salary Continuation, with the total amount of
this payment not to exceed $12,000.00. Such payment shall
be made within thirty (30) calendar days after receipt by
Travel of the relevant bill for these outplacement expenses.
The obligation to make such payment will commence
within seven (7) business days after the later of (i) the
Effective Date of this Agreement or (ii) Jones's compliance
with Paragraph 8(d) of this Agreement.

(f) *Payment on Account of Automobile.*

(i) Travel, Inc. will pay or cause to be paid to Jones a onetime lump-sum payment of $42,800.00 of (forty-two thou-
sand eight hundred U.S. dollars), which represents the
equivalent for the Period of Salary Continuation of the cost
of Jones's employee automobile benefit. Jones is free to
apply this payment to the lease or purchase of an automobile for his personal use or for any other purpose. Jones
hereby acknowledges and agrees that the Company is not
responsible for or obligated to make any further payment
of any kind in connection with Jones's automobile or
Jones's operation of any automobile and that Jones is solely
responsible for any such automobile.

(ii) Jones hereby warrants and represents that he has returned to the Company as of January 18, 1995, the Mercedes Benz (Serial number XRPX71BJR7Y32), which was the Company-leased automobile in his possession.

3. *Benefits to Jones.* Travel, Inc. will provide or cause to be provided to Jones the benefits set forth below (individually and collectively referred to as the "Benefits" or "Benefits"), subject to all of the terms and conditions of this Agreement:

(a) With respect to the Hotels Company Pension Plan, Jones will be given service credit for the Period of Salary Continuation. In addition, Jones will participate in the Hotels Company Supplemental Executive Retirement Plan and will receive additional service credit from the end of the Period of Salary Continuation until January 18, 2001. The Company reserves the right to cancel, withdraw, modify, and administer this Plan at its discretion, and nothing contained in this Agreement shall limit the exercise of that right or discretion.

(b) Effective January 18, 1995, Jones will no longer be eligible to make before-tax contributions to the Hotels Company Savings and Investment Plan.

(c) During the Period of Salary Continuation, Jones will be allowed to participate in, and will not be required to contribute toward, the cost of his coverage for medical, dental, and prescription drug plans pursuant to the Company Comprehensive Health Insurance Plan. In accordance with the terms, conditions, and procedures of the Company Comprehensive Health Insurance Plan, Jones may remain enrolled in an HMO until the conclusion of the Period of Salary Continuation. Upon termination of the Period of Salary Continuation, Jones will be allowed to participate in the Company Grandfathered Retiree Medical Plan. Jones will have a lifetime maximum of $1,000,000.00, less any medical benefits paid during Jones's active employment. Jones's benefits pursuant to the Company Comprehensive Health Insurance Plan and the Grandfathered Retiree Medical Plan of the Company are always subject to the terms and conditions of the Company Insurance Plan and the Grandfathered Retiree Medical Plan of the Company. The Company reserves the right to cancel, withdraw, modify, and administer these Plans at its discretion, and nothing contained in this Agreement shall limit the exercise of that right or discretion. The Parties agree that the continuation of Jones's medical coverage shall be in full and complete satisfaction of any and all obligations of the Company pursuant to the Consolidated Omnibus Budget Reconciliation Act of 1985.

(d) Jones will be allowed to participate in the Life Insurance, Accidental Death and Dismemberment Insurance, and Long Term Disability Plans of Hotels Company during the Period of Salary Continuation. Should Jones become entitled to benefits under the Long Term Disability Plan of Hotels Company during the Period of Salary Continuation, Jones shall assign such benefits to the Company until the Period of Salary Continuation terminates. The Company reserves the right to cancel, withdraw, modify, and administer these Plans at its discretion, and nothing contained in this Agreement shall limit the exercise of that right or discretion.

(e) Jones will retain stock options awarded to him prior to January 18, 1995, and will be allowed to exercise them in accordance with the terms and conditions of the Hotels Company 1992 United States Executive Share Option Scheme ("Scheme"). Set forth below is a schedule summarizing the dates by which Jones shall elect to exercise his unexercised Hotels Company stock option awards, subject to the terms and conditions of the Scheme. The Company, including without limitation Hotels Company, reserves the right to cancel, withdraw, modify, and administer this Scheme at its discretion, and nothing contained in this Agreement shall limit the exercise of that right or discretion.

Schedule of Jones's Unexercised Pearson Stock Options

Date of Grant	Number of Options Granted and Option Price		Type of Option	Last Date for Exercise
March 19, 1992	8,000	602p	ISO*	3 months from last day of employment (January 18, 1995)

Schedule of Jones's Unexercised Pearson Stock Options

Date of Grant	Number of Options Granted and Option Price		Type of Option	Last Date for Exercise
August 12, 1993	8,200	519p	ISO	3 months from last day of employment (January 18, 1996)
September 9, 1994	7,200	697p	ISO	3 months from last day of employment (January 18, 1997)

*Incentive Stock Option

(f) In the exercise of its discretion as reserved to the Company and referenced above in this Paragraph 3 and subject to all the terms and conditions of this Agreement, the Company is expected to apply factors, criteria, and/or considerations which it ordinarily would apply as to other senior level executives covered by the applicable plan, policies, or practices referenced above.

4. *Purpose of Payment.* The Company is providing and Jones is accepting the Separation Payments and the other good and valuable consideration provided for in this Agreement in full and complete satisfaction of all of Jones's Claims (as defined in Paragraph 6 hereof) against the Company, including but not limited to Hotels Company, its parents, subsidiaries, and affiliates, affiliated persons, partnerships, and corporations, including, without limitation, Cruises Company and Tour Company, Inc., successors and assigns, and all of their past and present directors, officers, consultants, agents, representatives, attorneys, shareholders, employees, employee benefit plans and plan fiduciaries, and pension plans and plan fiduciaries (collectively, the "Releasees"). Jones acknowledges (i) the sufficiency of the consideration for this Agreement generally and specifically for the release of any such Claims up to the Effective Date of this Agreement he may have ever had, may now have, or may hereafter assert against the Releases under the Age Discrimination in Employment Act of 1967, as amended by, inter alia, the Older Workers Benefit Protection Act of 1990, and (ii) that no other moneys, benefits, or consideration, except as expressly set forth in this Agreement, are due and

owing to him or on his behalf by the Company or any of the other Releasees. Jones and his counsel, if any, covenant and agree that neither Jones nor his counsel shall be entitled to recover attorneys' fees, cost, or disbursements for the Company in connection with the negotiation of this Agreement or otherwise. Neither Jones nor his counsel shall make any claim or commence any action or proceeding to recover attorneys' fees, cost, or disbursement. Nothing contained herein is intended to prevent enforcement of this Agreement.

5. *No Admissions.* This Agreement does not constitute an admission by any of the Releasees of any violation of any contract or of any statutory, constitutional, or common law of any federal, state, or local government of the United States or of any other country or political subdivision thereof, and the Releasees expressly deny any such liability. This Agreement may not be introduced in any proceeding by anyone for any purpose except to evidence its terms.

6. *Release by Jones.*

   (a) In consideration of this Agreement and the moneys and other good and valuable consideration provided to Jones pursuant to this Agreement, Jones hereby irrevocably and unconditionally releases, waives, and forever discharges the Company, including but not limited to Hotels Company and Tours Company, and each of the other Releasees from any and all actions, causes of action, claims, demands, damages, rights, remedies, and liabilities of whatsoever kind or character, in law or equity, suspected or unsuspected, past or present, that he has ever had, may now have, or may later assert against the Releasees or any of them (collectively, "Jones Claims"), including but not limited to, and whether or not arising out of or related to, Jones's employment by or the performance of any services to or on behalf of the Company or the termination of that employment and those services, from the beginning of time to the Effective Date hereof, including without limitation: (i) any Jones' Claims arising out of or related to any federal, state, and/or local labor or civil rights laws including, without limitation, the federal Civil Rights Acts of 1866, 1871, 1964, and 1991, the Age Discrimination in Employment Act of 1967, as amended by, inter alia, the Older Workers Benefit Protection Act of 1990, the Workers' Adjustment and Retraining Notification Act, the Employee Retirement

Income Security Act of 1974, the Consolidated Omnibus Budget Reconciliation Act of 1985, the Americans with Disabilities Act of 1990, the Fair Labor Standards Act of 1938, the New Jersey Law Against Discrimination, the New York State Labor Law, New York State Wage and Hour Laws, as each may have been amended from time to time, and (ii) any and all other Jones Claims arising out of or related to any contract, any federal, state, or local constitutions, statutes, rules, or regulations, under any common law right of any kind whatsoever, or under the laws of any country or political subdivision, including but not limited to the laws of the United States of America, and including, without limitation, any Jones Claims for any kind of tortious conduct (including but not limited to any claim of defamation or intentional or negligent infliction of emotional distress), breach of contract, copyright, promissory or equitable estoppel, breach of the Company's policies, rules, regulations, handbooks, or manuals, breach of express or implied covenants of good faith, wrongful discharge or dismissal, and failure to pay in whole or part any wages, salary, compensation, bonus, incentive compensation, commissions, overtime compensation, severance pay, attorney's fees, disability benefits, or benefits of any kind whatsoever. Expressly excluded from this release are Jones's rights, if any, with regard to vested benefits pursuant to the Company Pension Plan, the Company Savings and Investment Plan, or Jones's claim for New York Workers' Compensation (Claim No. 12367R) submitted to the Home Life Indemnity Co. Policy No. 24987, Claim No. P2453434333 arising out of his work-related injury on March 2, 1989.

(b) Execution of this Agreement by Jones operates as a complete bar and defense against any and all of the Jones Claims against the Company, including but not limited to the Company and/or the other Releasees. If Jones should hereafter make any of the Jones Claims in any action, claim, or proceeding against the Company or any of the Releasees, the Agreement may be raised as and shall constitute a complete bar to any such action, claim, or proceeding and the Company or the Releasees shall recover from Jones all cost incurred, including attorneys' fees, in defending against any such action, claim, or proceeding.

(c) Jones hereby warrants and represents that he has brought no complaint, claim, charge, action, or proceeding against any of the Releasees in any judicial, administrative, or any other forum. Jones warrants and represents that, to the fullest extent permitted by law, he will not lodge any formal or informal complaint in court, with any federal, state, or local agency or in any other forum, whether or not arising out of or related to Jones's employment by or the performance of any services to or on behalf of the Company or the termination of that employment and those services. Jones further warrants and represents that he has not in the past and will not in the future assign any of the Jones Claims to any person, corporation, or other entity.

(d) Nothing contained herein is intend to prevent either Jones or the Company from enforcing this Agreement.

7. *Warranty by Jones and Release by Company.*

(a) Jones expressly and unconditionally represents and warrants that, during and in connection with his employment by the Company, Jones: (i) has committed no violations of law; (ii) has not been involved in any matter as to which Jones did not act in good faith and/or in a manner he reasonably believed to be in or not opposed to the best interests of the Company; (iii) has been in full and complete compliance with the USA Conflict of Interest Policy, which is incorporated herein by reference and is an integral part of this representation and warranty; and (iv) has no information or involvement with respect to (1) any accounting irregularities concerning the collection, discounting, and accounting treatment of receivables or the accounting treatment of cooperative advertising and other credits (including without limitation the granting of discounts for the early payment of receivables, the failure to write off the discounted portion of receivables paid early, or the existence of cash payment or loan by any customer to the Company in advance of shipment to the payor), (2) the granting of discounts for the early payment of receivables, (3) any violations by the Company of the Consent Order and Judgment filed March 3, 1991, in the E.D.N.Y. action encaptioned American Travelers Association, et al. v. Travel Muffins Company, Inc., et. al. in 91 Civ. 4591 (JFK), (4) any violations by the Company of the Robinson Patman Act, or (5) any other violations of law relating to the Company. This representation and warranty is an essential and material term and condition of this Agreement.

(b) In consideration of this Agreement and the commitments by Jones contained herein, the Company hereby irrevocably and unconditionally releases, waives, and forever discharges Jones from any and all claims, actions, causes of action, demands, rights, damages, remedies, and liabilities of whatever kind or character, in law or equity, suspected or unsuspected, past or present, that it has ever had, may now have, or may assert later against Jones (hereinafter, "Company Claims") from the beginning of time to the Effective Date of this Agreement. Expressly excepted from this release are any Company Claims arising out of or in any way relating to any of the following: (i) any confidentiality agreement between Jones and the Company or any of the Releasees; (ii) violations of law by Jones; (iii) any matter as to which Jones did not act in good faith and/or in a manner he reasonably believed to be in or not opposed to the best interest of the Company; (iv) the Company Pension Plan, the Company Saving and Investment Plan; (v) violations by Jones of the Company Conflict of Interest Policy; or (vii) Jones's claim for New York Workers' Compensation (Claim No. 12348) submitted to the Home Life Indemnity Co. Policy No. 2368768 arising out of his work-related injury on June 12, 1996. As a further exception, limitation and condition of the Company's release of Jones herein, if the Company determines that Jones has violated any of the representations and warranties of Paragraph 7(a) hereof, in addition to and without limiting any other remedies the Company may have against Jones, the Company's release of Jones pursuant to this Paragraph shall be null and void and of no further force or effect.

(c) Execution of this Agreement by the Company operates as a complete bar and defense against any and all of the Company Claims against Jones, except those subject to the express exceptions, limitations, or conditions as set forth in Paragraph 7(b) hereof. If the Company should hereafter make any claims against Jones, which are not covered by the exceptions, limitations, or conditions as set forth in Paragraph 7(b) hereof, the Agreement may be raised as and shall constitute a complete bar to any such action, claim, or proceeding and Jones shall recover all cost from the Company, including attorneys' fees in defending against any such action, claim, or proceeding.

(d) Nothing contained herein is intended to prevent either Jones or the Company from enforcing this Agreement.

8. *Confidentiality.*

(a) Jones agrees that he will not, directly or indirectly, use or disclose, or permit or aid the disclosure, to any person, firm, entity, or corporation, of any privileged, confidential, or proprietary information arising out of or relating to the business, financial affairs, legal affairs, operational affairs, sales, customers, clients, suppliers, plans, proposals, financial condition, employees, employers, or shareholders of the Company or any of the other Releasees, including without limitation any aspect of these terms and conditions of his employment or the termination thereof (the "Confidential Information") with only the following exceptions:

(1) With the Company's express written consent; (2) in the ordinary course of Jones seeking the professional advice of his personal accountant, financial planner, medical doctor, mental health professional, or attorney (collectively and individually referred to as the "professional") and only to the extent necessary in seeking such advice and subject to and conditioned upon (i) Jones causing such professional to be bound by Jones's agreement as to confidentiality as set forth in this Paragraph 8 and (ii) Jones's representation and warranty that Jones shall be fully responsible and liable to the Company for any breach of confidentiality by any such professional which Jones's representation and warranty shall be deemed given to the Company by Jones in each instance that Jones gives any Confidential Information to any such professional; (3) in direct response to any subpoena initiated against or served upon Jones; or (4) in direct response to a formal request for information from the Equal Employment Opportunity Commission as part of an active investigation ("EEOC Request"). In the event disclosure is sought from Jones in direct response to any such subpoena or EEOC Request, Jones shall give the Company immediate written notice of such subpoena or EEOC request in order to afford the Company an opportunity to evaluate its legal rights and take such action as the Company considers to be appropriate to protect the interests of the Company. Jones

further agrees that he will not, directly or indirectly, use or disclose, or permit or aid the disclosure, to any person, firm, entity, or corporation, of any information arising out of or relating to the personal or private business or affairs of any of the individual Releasees, including but not limited to any personal or private information regarding any Company executives.

(b) The Parties agree that agreements between Jones and the Company relating to the confidentiality of information obtained by Jones during the course of his employment, if any, shall remain in full force and effect, and shall not limit, or be limited by any provision of this Agreement. Jones represents and warrants that he has not, directly or indirectly, used or disclosed to any person or entity any information described in or covered by Paragraph 8(a) above. By way of example, and without limitation, Jones represents and warrants that he has not, directly or indirectly, disclosed matters related to his employment to any individual or entity for the purpose of their use in any printed, audiovideo, or electronic media outlet, or for any other purpose.

(c) Jones and the Company agree that the existence of this Agreement and its terms and conditions shall remain confidential except to the extent that disclosure is expressly required by law or regulations of any governmental authority or to enforce this Agreement, or, as to the Company only, in connection with the conduct of business by the Company.

(d) Jones is obligated to surrender and acknowledges that he has surrendered or will surrender to the Company's counsel, Barry Dement, Esq., on or before the Effective Date, any and all papers, contracts, drafts, data, record, plans, proposals, photographs, tape recordings, video recordings, other electronic recordings, and other information, documents, or property, including any copies thereof, related to the Company or any of the Releasees in the possession of or under the control of Jones, including but not limited to any such items in the possession or under the control of his attorneys or any other agent or representative.

(e) Jones agrees that this Paragraph 8 and each of its provisions are respectively an essential and material term and condition of this Agreement.

(f) Jones acknowledges and agrees that monetary damages

would be both incalculable and an insufficient remedy for any breach or nonperformance by him or any of his representatives of any provision, representation, or warranty of this Paragraph 8, and that any such breach, continuing breach, or nonperformance would cause the Company irreparable harm. Accordingly, Jones agrees that in the event of any threatened, actual, or continuing breach of this Paragraph 8 or nonperformance of any representation or warranty by Jones, the Company shall be entitled, without the requirement of posting bond or other security, to equitable relief, including temporary, preliminary, and permanent injunctive relief and specific performance. Such remedy shall not be the exclusive remedy for any such breach or nonperformance but shall be in addition to all remedies available at law or equity to the Company.

9. *Cooperation.*

   (a) Jones hereby agrees without compensation to cooperate in the orderly transition of business affairs. Such cooperation shall be at reasonable times and includes, without limitation: (1) returning all files and other property relating to the business to the Company or its counsel; and (2) providing the Company with any information necessary to complete the transition. Jones shall not disparage the Company or any of the other Releasees.

   (b) At the request by or on behalf of the Company, and upon reasonable notice to Jones, Jones agrees without compensation to cooperate with the Company with respect to any potential litigation, investigation, legal proceedings, or dispute arising out of or in connection with the financial affairs and/or business matters of the Company (collectively, "such matters"), including providing the Company with full, complete, truthful, and accurate information, to the best of his knowledge, concerning such matters, testifying in regard to such matters and/or appearing in person with respect to such matters. Nothing required by this Paragraph 9(b) is intended to unreasonably limit or impede Jones's performance of any new job he may attain in the future. Commencing April 4, 1993, the Company will reimburse Jones for any reasonable out-of-pocket disbursements in excess of $100.00 which Jones incurs in long-distance travel to make himself available in person at the request of the Company pursuant to this Paragraph 9(b). Jones's cooperation required by this Agreement shall include, but shall not be limited to, the following:

(i) Jones will make himself available to be interviewed by representatives of the Company, the accountants for the Company, and attorneys for the Company;

(ii) Such interviews will commence at the earliest possible date and will continue from time to time as requested by the Company on reasonable notice to Jones;

(iii) Jones will give truthful answers to all questions on any subject relating to his employment by the Company, such as questions relating to the collection, discounting, and accounting treatment of receivables and accounting treatment of cooperative advertising and other credits (including without limitation the granting of discounts for the early payment of receivables, the failure to write off the discounted portion of receivables paid early, or the existence of cash payment or loan by any customer to the Company in advance of shipment to the payor);

(iv) Jones will make himself available, without subpoena and irrespective of whether he is beyond the reach of subpoenas issued in New York, and will give truthful answers to any questions asked; and

(v) In the event information known to him is sought by any governmental agency or department, Jones will provide such information truthfully and completely.

(c) Subject to and without limiting the provisions of Paragraph 8 hereof, this Paragraph shall not act to impede Jones from discussing legal matters personally relating to Jones with his lawyers and immediate family. If Jones discusses such legal matters with his lawyers or immediate family, he will advise each to honor the confidentiality provisions of Paragraph 8 of this Agreement.

(d) Jones agrees that this Paragraph 9 and each of its provisions are respectively an essential and material term and condition of this Agreement.

(e) Jones acknowledges and agrees that monetary damages would be both incalculable and an insufficient remedy for any breach or nonperformance of any provision, representation, or warranty of this Paragraph 9 by him or any of his representatives, and that any such breach, continuing breach, or nonperformance would cause the Company irreparable harm. Accordingly, Jones agrees that, in the event of any threatened, actual, or continuing breach of this Paragraph 9 or nonperformance of any representation or warranty by Jones, the Company shall be entitled, without the requirements of posting a bond or other security, to equitable relief, including temporary, preliminary, and permanent injunctive relief and specific performance. Such remedy shall not be the exclusive remedy for any such breach or nonperformance but shall be in addition to all other remedies available at law or equity to the Company.

10. *Miscellaneous Provisions.*

(a) Should any provision of this Agreement be held invalid, illegal, or unenforceable, it shall be deemed to be modified so that its purpose can lawfully be effectuated and the balance of this Agreement shall remain in full force and effect.

(b) This Agreement shall extend to, be binding upon, and inure to the benefit of the Parties and their respective successors, heirs, and assigns.

(c) This Agreement shall be governed by and construed in accordance with the laws of the State of New York. Jones and the Company, and each of them, hereby submit to the exclusive jurisdiction of the state and federal courts located in New York, New York, and further agree not to assert that any action brought in such jurisdiction has been brought in an inconvenient forum.

(d) This Agreement may be executed in any number of counterparts, each of which when so executed shall be deemed to be an original, and all of which when taken together shall constitute one and the same agreement.

(e) With the express exception of any confidentiality agreement between the Company and Jones, this is the entire Agreement between the Parties and supersedes any and all prior agreements, negotiations, discussions, or understandings between the Parties. No oral statement contrary to the terms of this Agreement exists. This Agreement shall be modified only in a writing signed by the Parties.

11. *Effective Date/Revocation.* Jones may revoke this Agreement in writing at any time during a period of seven (7) calendar days after the execution of this Agreement by both of the Parties (the "Revocation Period"). This Agreement shall become effective and enforceable automatically on the date of actual receipt by the Company's counsel, Barry Dement, Esq., of the Certificate of Nonrevocation of Separation Agreement and Mutual Release (the form of which is Exhibit A hereto) executed and

dated by Jones at least one day after expiration of the Revocation Period (the "Effective Date").

12. *Notices/Requests.* Any notice or request under this Agreement shall be in writing, and sent to the other party via the U.S. Mail Service, Federal Express, or other similar private express delivery service or via electronic facsimile (fax) transmission addressed as follows:

(a) If to Jones:

Jones
345 Pipers Road
Pound Ridge, NY 10876
Telephone: (914) 345-8730

with copy to:

Alan L. Sklover, Esq.
10 Rockefeller Plaza
New York, NY 10020
Telephone: (212) 757-5000
Fax: (212) 757-5002

(b) If to Company:

Company, Inc.
1200 Lexington Avenue
New York, NY 10018
Telephone: (212) 432-6791
Fax: (212) 457-4679

Attention: Debora Baaye, Esq.
General Counsel

with copy to:

Weel Getcha & Mangleya, LLP
4437 Park Avenue
New York, NY 10022
Telephone: (212) 873-0990
Fax: (212) 343-4444
Attention: Barry Dement, Esq.

13. *Remedies* Regardless of, in addition to, and without limiting any remedies described in Paragraph 8 and 9 hereof or any other rights or remedies the Company may otherwise have as against Jones, in the event the Company, in its discretion, has determined that Jones has breached, violated, failed, or refused to comply with any of the provisions, terms, or conditions of this Agreement or has violated any of the representations and warranties herein (the "Breach"), including without limitation the provisions of paragraphs 6, 7, 8, and 9, in its sole discretion the Company shall have the right to (i) terminate the making of any payments or providing of any Benefits to Jones under this agreement, (ii) recover any payments made to Jones under this Agreement, (iii) recover or cancel any of Jones Benefits provided under this Agreement, and (iv) recover against Jones damages (including reasonable attorneys' fees) accruing to the Company or any of the Releasees as a consequence of such Breach. In order to challenge the Company's exercise of its discretion pursuant to this Paragraph 13, Jones shall demonstrate in a court proceeding that the Company acted in bad faith or unreasonably in exercising its discretion. The prevailing Party in any such court proceeding shall be entitled to recover its reasonable expenses and costs, including attorneys' fees, incurred in that proceeding. Regardless of and in addition to any right to damages the Company may have, the Company shall have the right to injunctive relief to remedy any such Breach.

IN SIGNING THIS SEPARATION AGREEMENT AND MUTUAL RELEASE ("AGREEMENT"), JONES ACKNOWLEDGES THAT: (A) HE HAS READ AND UNDERSTANDS THIS AGREEMENT AND HE IS HEREBY ADVISED IN WRITING TO CONSULT WITH AN ATTORNEY PRIOR TO SIGNING THIS AGREEMENT, (B) HE HAS SIGNED THIS AGREEMENT VOLUNTARILY AND UNDERSTANDS THAT IT CONTAINS A FULL AND FINAL RELEASE OF ALL CLAIMS, AS SET FORTH IN PARAGRAPH 6, AGAINST THE RELEASEES AS OF THE EFFECTIVE DATE OF THIS AGREEMENT, (C) HE HAS BEEN OFFERED AT LEAST TWENTY-ONE (21) CALENDAR DAYS TO CONSIDER THE MATTER MEMORIALIZED IN THIS AGREEMENT, AND (D) THIS AGREEMENT IS NOT MADE IN CONNECTION WITH AN EXIT INCENTIVE OR OTHER EMPLOYMENT TERMINATION PROGRAM OFFERED TO A GROUP OR CLASS OF EMPLOYEES.

_____   _____, 1997
      Jones   Date of Execution by Jones

Company Inc.

By: _____   _____, 1997
                       Date of Execution by Company

Exhibit A

CERTIFICATE OF NONREVOCATION OF SEPARATION AGREEMENT AND MUTUAL RELEASE

I hereby certify and represent that seven (7) calendar days passed since the Parties signed the Separation Agreement and Mutual Release (the "Agreement"), to which this document is Exhibit A, and that I have NOT exercised my rights to revoke that Agreement pursuant to the Older Workers Benefit Protection Act of 1990. I understand that the Company, on behalf of itself and its parents, subsidiaries, and affiliates, in providing me with benefits under the Agreement, is relying on this Certificate, and that I can no longer revoke the Agreement.

_____   Date: _____
      Jones

IMPORTANT: This Certificate should be signed, dated, and returned to the Company's counsel, Barry Dement, Esq., no earlier than on the eight (8th) calendar day after the Agreement is executed by both of the Parties.

Sample Text of Agreed "Departure Statement"

[to be typed on company letterhead]

                             March XX, 19XX

To Whom It May Concern:

Jonathan Brewer served this Company and its shareholders with distinction from March 1988 through June 1996. During his tenure with this Company, he was several times promoted, from

Assistant Vice President to several positions, and was eventually named Chief Financial Officer in 1994.

Mr. Brewer's achievements with the Company in the areas of financial administration, cost reduction, and risk management were of considerable benefit to the Company. His introduction of new comparative techniques and software solutions were of special value, and these contributions will be to our fundamental and long-lasting advantage.

It is with deep regret that this Company accepts Mr. Brewer's decision to return to the field of independent consulting. But we have confidence that he will be successful in all of his future endeavors. We recommend his talents and services, without reservation.

Chief Executive
Officer

Sample Letter: Notice of Default

Andrew Spector
40 Walter Road
Amherst, NY 10709

May 9, 1998

BY FIRST CLASS MAIL
and   [NOTE: Delivery Mode Is
BY CERTIFIED MAIL   Almost Always in
RETURN RECEIPT REQUESTED   Agreement Text.]

Mr. Robert Epner
Quick-Seal Industries
109 Twelfth Street
Parker, UT 79234   [NOTE: Parties to Notify Are
                           Almost Always in
and   Agreement Text.]

Edgar Winter, Esq.
as Attorney for Quick-Seal Industries
Paskus and Case, Attorneys

741 Nonen Road
Salt Lake City, UT 79314

Re: Quick-Seal and Spector
Severance Agreement dated May 1, 1997
NOTICE OF DEFAULT

Dear Mr. Epner and Mr. Winter:

By this letter you are advised that Quick-Seal Industries is in default of its obligations to me under my Severance Agreement with that company dated May 1, 1997. To be more precise, Paragraph 19 of our Severance Agreement provides that Quick-Seal will pay to me, mailed to my home address written above, a check for $8,652.12 every month for twenty-four consecutive months, to arrive no later than the second day of each calendar month. Though today is the ninth day of this month, I have not yet received my check for this month.

This obligation is a "material" obligation. The payment of moneys under this agreement is a central obligation; it is not an insignificant one. This would make your default a material breach of the severance agreement, and entitle me to consider it null and void or to sue the company for the moneys due me, as well as for other related "damages," including among others, interest on the moneys owed and legal costs of enforcement and collection.

If I am mistaken in my belief that Quick-Seal has defaulted in its obligations to me, please let me know, in writing. If Quick-Seal has, indeed, defaulted, but the default is accidental and to be promptly corrected, or "cured," please also let me know in writing.

If you believe that Quick-Seal either has not defaulted or has not paid me with good reason, please also let me know, in writing.

If I do not hear from you within seven days of your receipt of this letter, I will have no choice but to initiate legal proceedings to protect all of my interests and rights. I sincerely hope that will not be necessary.

Very truly yours,

Andrew Spector

Index